D0999657

The Vision of PAUL TILLICH

The Vision of
PAUL TILLICH

CARL J. ARMBRUSTER, S.J.

SHEED AND WARD : NEW YORK

Library of Congress Catalog Card Number 67-13774

Manufactured in the United States of America

To my mother
and the memory of my father

Contents

Chronology   *xiii*
Abbreviations   *xv*

INTRODUCTION   *xvii*

Part I/Religion and Culture: The Structure

1/PAUL TILLICH: THE MAN AND THE
   THEOLOGIAN   5
Paul Tillich the Man   5
   Dimensions   6
   The Social Dimension   7
   The Historical Dimension   9
   The Intellectual Dimension   12
   The Personal Dimension   19
Paul Tillich the Theologian   21
   The Nature of Theology   21
   Ultimate Concern and the Theological Circle 23
   Sources, Medium, and Norm   26
   The Method of Correlation   30
   The Language of Theology   31
   Theology and Philosophy   34
Reflections and Appraisal   36

2/FAITH AND RELIGION: THE EXPERIENCE OF THE
   HOLY   47

Subjective Side of Faith   48
   Faith a Centered Act   48
   Passive Character of Faith   48
   Certainty of Faith   49
   Faith and the Unconditional   50
   Universality of Faith   52
   Faith and Atheism   53
Objective Side of Faith   55
   Content of Faith   55
   Doubt and Justification by Faith   56
   Courage and Absolute Faith   57
   Truth of Faith and the Protestant Principle   59
The Experience of the Holy   60
   Two Elements of the Holy   61
   Actual Holiness: the Ground and Abyss   62
   Moral Holiness: the Clean-Unclean   64
   Ambiguity of the Holy: the Demonic   65
Religion   67
   Not a Separate Function   68
   Two Senses of Religion   70
Revelation   72
   Relation of Faith, Religion, and Revelation   73
Reflections and Appraisal   74

3/FROM SECULAR TO THEONOMOUS CULTURE   82
Culture   82
   Definition   82
   Functions and Elements   84
   Style and the Theology of Culture   85
   Types of Culture   86
Autonomy   87
   The Secular   87
   Profanization of Religion   89
   Technology   90

Contents   ix

Heteronomy   91
    The Demonic   92
    Authority   94
Theonomy   97
    Spiritual Presence and Cultural Ambiguities   99
    Theonomous Interplay   101
    The Depth-Dimension   102
    The Holy and the Secular   104
The Dispute with Karl Barth   106
    The Dispute, 1923   107
    The Dispute, 1935   109
    Common Ground, but Different Paths 110
Reflections and Appraisal   112

Part II/Religion and Culture: The Content

4/BEING AND GOD   125
The Question of Being   126
    Ontological Concepts   127
    The Ontological Structure: Self and World 127
    The Ontological Elements   128
    The Ontological Characteristic: Finitude 131
    The Ontological Categories   134
    The Question of God   134
God as Being-Itself   136
    God as Phenomenon   136
    The Ground of Being   137
    The Living God   138
    The Personal God   139
Symbol and Analogy   140
God as Creator   144
    Originating Creativity   145
    Sustaining and Directing Creativity 146
The Supranatural and the Natural   147
    Supranaturalism   148
    Naturalism   149

    Beyond Naturalism and Supranaturalism   150
Reflections and Appraisal   151

5/EXISTENCE AND THE CHRIST   167
The Question of Existence   168
    Existence   168
    The Fall   170
    Estrangement and Sin   175
    The Quest for the New Being   177
The Reality of the Christ   180
    Historical Research and the Christ   181
    The New Being   183
    Christological Dogma   186
    The Cross and the Resurrection   188
    Salvation   191
Reflections and Appraisal   195

6/LIFE, THE SPIRIT, AND THE SPIRITUAL   208
  COMMUNITY
The Quest for Unambiguous Life   209
    Life   209
    Functions and Ambiguities of Life   210
    The Dimension of Spirit   211
    The Quest   211
The Spiritual Presence   212
The Spiritual Community   213
    Unambiguous, but Fragmentary   213
    New Being and the Spiritual Community   214
    Latent and Manifest Stages   215
    Religion and the Spiritual Community   217
The Churches   218
    The Paradox of the Churches   218
    The Individual and the Churches   219
    The Churches and Society   220
Protestantism   223
    Protestant Reality and Protestant Principle   223
    Grace   225

The Sacramental Element   228
Protestant Principle and Catholic Substance   230
Reflections and Appraisal   233

7/HISTORY AND THE KINGDOM OF GOD   243
The Notion of History   244
The Historical Dimension   244
Man and History   245
Historical Time   248
The Ambiguities of History   250
The Quest for the Kingdom of God   251
Interpretations of History   252
The Symbol "Kingdom of God"   254
The Kingdom of God within History   255
The Center of History   256
Kairos   257
The Kingdom and the Manifest Church   260
Eschatology: The Kingdom as the End of History   262
From the Temporal to the Eternal   263
Judgment: Exclusion of the Negative   264
Essentialization: Inclusion of the Positive   264
Immortality and Resurrection   267
Reflections and Appraisal   269

Conclusion/The Vision of Paul Tillich   282

Types of Visions: the Christ-Culture Relationship   282
Christ against Culture   284
The Christ of Culture   285
Christ above Culture   286
Christ and Culture in Paradox   287
Christ the Transformer of Culture   288
Tillich's Vision: Christ the Depth of Culture   289
A Vision of New Being   290
A Vision of Ultimate Concern   296
A Vision of Man   301

The Significance of Paul Tillich   304
   An Honest-to-God Theologian   304
   A Theologian of Synthesis   306

   Bibliography   311
   Index   321

Chronology of the Life of Paul Johannes Oskar Tillich

1886	August 20. Born at the village of Starzeddel, near Guben, in the province of Brandenburg, Germany.
1891	Moved to Schönfliess (Neumark). Elementary school.
1898	Began *Gymnasium* at Königsberg.
1900	Moved to Berlin. Attended *Gymnasium* there.
1904	Graduated from *Gymnasium*. Began at the University of Berlin.
1905	University of Tübingen.
1905–1907	University of Halle.
1911	Doctorate in Philosophy, University of Breslau.
1912	Licentiate in Theology, University of Halle. Ordained Lutheran minister.
1914–1918	Army chaplain.
1919–1924	*Privatdozent* of theology, University of Berlin.
1924–1925	Professor of Theology, University of Marburg.
1925–1929	Professor of Theology, University of Dresden and University of Leipzig.
1929–1933	Professor of Philosophy, University of Frankfurt.
1933	Emigrated to the United States.
1933–1955	Professor of Philosophical Theology, Union Theological Seminary and Columbia University.
1955–1962	University Professor, Harvard University.
1962–1965	Professor of Theology, University of Chicago.
1965	October 22. Died at the age of 79.

Abbreviations

(Editions listed are those used in this work; unless otherwise noted, the author is Paul Tillich.)

BR   — *Biblical Religion and the Search for Ultimate Reality,* Chicago: University of Chicago Press, 1955.

CB   — *The Courage to Be,* New Haven: Yale University Press, paperback, 1952.

CEWR   — *Christianity and the Encounter of the World Religions,* New York: Columbia University Press, 1963.

DF   — *Dynamics of Faith,* New York: Harper and Brothers, paperback, 1958 (first published 1957).

EN   — *The Eternal Now,* New York: Charles Scribner's Sons, 1963.

GW   — *Gesammelte Werke,* Renate Albrecht (ed.), Stuttgart: Evangelisches Verlagswerk.

        Band I, 1959   Band V, 1964
        Band II, 1962   Band VI, 1963
        Band IV, 1961   Band VII, 1962

IH   — *The Interpretation of History,* New York: Charles Scribner's Sons, 1936.

K and B   — Charles W. Kegley and Robert W. Bretall (eds.),
             The Theology of Paul Tillich, New York: Mac-
             millan, paperback, 1961 (first published 1952).
LPJ   — *Love, Power, and Justice,* New York: Oxford Uni-
             versity Press, paperback, 1960 (first published
             1954).
NB   — *The New Being,* New York: Charles Scribner's
             Sons, 1955.
O'M and W — Thomas A. O'Meara, O.P., and Celestin D. Weis-
             ser, O.P. (eds.), *Paul Tillich in Catholic
             Thought,* Dubuque, Iowa: Priory Press, 1964.
PE   — *The Protestant Era,* Chicago: University of Chi-
             cago Press, abridged edition, paperback, 1957
             (unabridged edition first published 1948).
RS   — *The Religious Situation,* New York: Meridian
             Books, paperback, 1956 (originally published
             in Berlin, 1926, as *Die Religiöse Lage der
             Gegenwart;* first translated in 1932).
SF   — *The Shaking of the Foundations,* New York:
             Charles Scribner's Sons, 1948.
ST   — *Systematic Theology,* Chicago: University of Chi-
             cago Press. Vol. I, 1951; Vol. II, 1957; Vol. III,
             1963.
TC   — *Theology of Culture,* New York: Oxford Univer-
             sity Press, 1959.

Introduction

To ANYONE who has been impressed by the Ravenna mosaics, the Sistine Chapel, or Rembrandt's portraits, Paul Tillich puts the following question: Is this experience cultural or religious?[1] A difficult choice indeed, but Tillich asserts that the answer is "both," that it is cultural in form and religious in substance. And the same must be said not only of art, but also of philosophy, science, morality, politics, social life—of all human activities, for finite, conditioned forms are the bearers of unconditioned meaning. This conviction has always animated Tillich's thought, as he himself confesses: "Through the experience of the substantially religious character of culture, I was led to the border of culture and religion, which I have never deserted."[2]

In fact, this close, reciprocal relationship between religion and culture has become one of the trademarks of his work. It is not by accident that a volume conveying the homage of world-renowned scholars bears the title *Religion and Culture: Essays in Honor of Paul Tillich*.[3] Although one risks inaccuracy in attempting to compress a vision within the narrow confines of a phrase, perhaps it can be said without exaggeration that Paul Tillich's thought on the relation of religion to culture is his most distinctive and most significant contribution.

But besides being a consuming interest and a distinguishing

characteristic, the problem of religion and culture serves also as a point of departure for penetrating his insights and as a point of reference for coordinating them. It provides a fixed horizon for plotting one's course through the enormous quantity and sometimes bewildering variety of his writings.[4] Nor is the choice of the theme of religion and culture a willful straight-jacketing of an otherwise unmanageable body of thought. For, as he himself states, "The problem of religion and culture has always been in the center of my interest. Most of my writing—including the two volumes of *Systematic Theology*—try to define the way in which Christianity is related to secular culture."[5]

A brief, preliminary description of the meaning of religion and culture is useful at this point, for Tillich understands them in a wider sense than one might expect. By "religion" he means two things. In the narrow or ordinary sense it refers to organized religions and their external trappings such as sacred books, creeds, rituals, priests, sacraments, and so forth. In the broader and more basic sense, religion is faith, the interior state of being grasped by an unconditioned, ultimate concern. Sometimes he intends both meanings under the term "religion"; at other times, only one, and this is made clear by the context or by an express designation.

"Culture" is used by Tillich in a very wide sense, echoing the German *Kultur* which encompasses all the productions of man's creative spirit (*Geist*). Hence, it includes not only literature, philosophy, and the fine arts, but also science, politics, economics, the patterns of social and individual life—in short, the achievements of man's spiritual life.

This introductory sketch of religion and culture would be misleading if it gave the impression that Tillich lays them beside each other as two separate blocks. On the contrary, he views them as interlocking or, better, interpenetrating, for "as the substance of culture is religion, so the form of religion is culture."[6] And he quite consistently follows out the consequences of this tight union. For instance, in the preface to his book on the religious situation of the present he declares that the book "must deal with the whole contemporary world, for there is nothing that is not in someway the expression of the religious situation."[7] Again, not only is culture grounded in religion, but "every religious act, not only in organized religion, but also in the most intimate movement of the soul, is culturally formed."[8]

The purpose of this study, then, is to explore in depth Tillich's understanding of the union between religion and culture. In Part I, after a prefatory inquiry into his theological method and background, the problem is discussed both from the side of religion and from the side of culture. Part II examines the theological cornerstones—God, Christ, the church, and eschatology—upon which rests the superstructure of the religio-cultural relationship. The conclusion attempts to disengage some basic insights which structure the whole of Tillich's system, and to convey the vision which accounts for his theological significance.

There are certain limitations in both the scope and viewpoint of our study. First of all, the area under discussion is theology, not philosophy, although a number of philosophical concepts come to the surface in the course of theological probing. The appearance of philosophical notions in a theological system is to be expected, but especially in Tillich's, for, as will be seen, the boundary which he establishes between philosophy and theology is fluid and often indistinct.

Within this theological scope our point of view is focused upon one type of approach, the analytical. That is to say, the principal effort is concentrated upon discovering what Tillich has to say about religion and culture, and then, since every analysis leads to a synthesis, drawing some conclusions. Other approaches are not totally excluded, but neither are they emphasized. For instance, the genetic development of Tillich's ideas is not stressed. It is safe to say that any evolution in his thought has not been by sudden mutations or even by significant shifts of opinion, but rather by a slow and careful refinement of the expression of his early insights.[9] Tillich himself, upon re-reading some of his earliest works, observes: ". . . much of what I believed to be a recent achievement is already explicitly or at least implicitly contained in them."[10] It is worth remarking that an external but nonetheless effective tool for retouching and polishing his ideas has been the English language, which he adopted after emigrating from Germany to the United States in 1933. He remarks, "The spirit of the English language has demanded the clarification of many ambiguities of my thought which were covered by the mystical vagueness of the classic philosophical German. . . ."[11] However, in certain instances we have reversed this process by returning to his German writings to get a fuller and, occasionally, sharper view of a particular doctrine.

Nor is our approach historical. The richness of Tillich's intellectual background will doubtless furnish material for innumerable dissertations that attempt to determine the influences he has undergone. While abstaining from a detailed search for his sources, we have at least outlined the historical context of his theologizing in order to give proper perspective to our analysis.

Attention must be called to the "systematic" character of Tillich's theology. This is not a mere catchword. It describes a distinctive way of thinking, as he himself confesses: "It always has been impossible for me to think theologically in any other than a systematic way. The smallest problem if taken seriously and radically, drove me to all other problems and to the anticipation of a whole in which they could find their solution."[12] A system is circular; it is a whole in which every part depends upon every other part. Thus he defines a system as "a totality made up of consistent, but not of deduced assertions."[13]

The problem, therefore, both for Tillich and his expositor, is one of presentation, for a "major difficulty of any systematic theology is that it presupposes all other parts in each of its parts."[14] The systematic concepts are so interlocked, so interdependent that an examination of one brick entails the dismantling of the whole house. As Tillich remarks, "A fragment is an implicit system; a system is an explicit fragment."[15] His ideas are so related to each other that the first cannot be properly understood until the last has been explained.[16] The only practical solution, therefore, is a graduated exposition in which each chapter is only a link in the chain. Since links necessarily overlap, a certain amount of repetition is unavoidable, but therein lies the strength of the system.

No exposition is entirely objective. We cannot claim to let Tillich speak for himself when the plain fact is that we speak for him. However, he always welcomed interpretations of his thought, because, as he tells us, ". . . interpretation can never be repetition. It must always be something new, created by the encounter of the text with the mind of the interpreter."[17] Exposing such a massive system as his necessitates a choice of what to include or omit, a decision about the emphasis to be given to the included parts, and an option to be taken when a need for clarification or organization of the material arises. Consequently, although the exposition strives to mirror Tillich's thought faithfully, it is not just a parroting of his sentences, but constitutes an implicit interpretation. More explicit interpretation is given in the reflections and appraisal which conclude each chapter.

In summary, we accompany Paul Tillich in his quest for the unity of religion and culture, that radiant point where the holy and the secular are fused. The scope is theological; the viewpoint, analytical; and the presentation, systematic. And we sincerely hope that the spirit and the results are ecumenical.

A special debt of gratitude is due to Rev. René Marlé, S.J., and Rev. Henri Bouillard, S.J., both of the *Institut Catholique de Paris*, for their wise counsel, generous help, and constant encouragement in the realization of this work.

Notes

1. IH, 49.
2. *Ibid.*
3. Walter Leibrecht (ed.) New York: Harper and Brothers, 1959. In a

special issue of *The Journal of Religion* commemorating Paul Tillich, Jerald C. Brauer sums up his significance as follows: "Whatever is formative of culture and illustrative of the outreach of the human spirit is of primary importance and concern to Tillich. . . . Perhaps the other side of Tillich that is so fascinating, intriguing, and informative to the modern intellectual is the religious concern he brings to everything he touches. He does not force the religious dimension into life; he exposes it at its depth in all of life." "Preface," *The Journal of Religion,* XLVI, January, 1966, No. 1, Part II, 89–90.

4. His collected works will number approximately eighteen volumes.

5. TC, v.

6. IH, 50.

7. RS, 25.

8. TC, 42.

9. See David H. Hopper, "Towards Understanding the Thought of Paul Tillich," *The Princeton Seminary Bulletin,* LV, April, 1962, 36–43. Hopper claims that Tillich's basic ideas can be found in his 1912 dissertation on Schelling. See also R. Allan Killen, *The Ontological Theology of Paul Tillich,* Kampen, Netherlands: J. H. Kok, 1956, 112.

10. PE, vii.

11. *Ibid.,* vi.

12. ST, I, vii.

13. *Ibid.,* 58–59. See also ST, II, 3–5 and ST, III, 3.

14. ST, I, 156.

15. *Ibid.,* 58.

16. Cf. James Luther Adams, *Paul Tillich's Philosophy of Culture, Science, and Religion,* New York: Harper & Row, 1965, 18. This work, originally submitted as a doctoral dissertation at the University of Chicago in 1945, is especially useful for the study of Tillich's writings up to that date.

17. "Reply to Gustave Weigel," O'M and W, 22.

The Vision of PAUL TILLICH

Part I

RELIGION AND CULTURE:
THE STRUCTURE

1 / Paul Tillich: The Man
and the Theologian

BEFORE PLUNGING into Paul Tillich's solution of the problem of religion and culture, we pause for some necessary biographical and methodological orientation. In this age of starting points and hermeneutics, it is quite obvious that the methodology more often than not *is* the solution in germ form. What is perhaps not quite so evident is that the solution of the thinker must be capable of exciting a sympathetic vibration in the personality of the man. Or more exactly, the thinker instinctively shies away from certain solutions and gravitates toward others simply because they strike or fail to strike a resonance in his temperament and background. Consequently, we shall first attempt to understand Paul Tillich the man and, secondly, the theologian and his method.

PAUL TILLICH THE MAN

Fortunately, Tillich has produced an abundance of autobiographical material which traces his intellectual development as well as his personal life.[1] The only problem, a minor one at that, is the selection of a literary device to organize and present this material. A straightforward chronological account has the merit of clearly preserving the historical progression, but it verges on the tedious. Tillich's own favorite image for describing his life is that of "the boundary." However, the image of the boundary requires very extensive treatment; he himself elaborates twelve boundary situations of his life. We prefer, therefore, the metaphor "dimension" for the presentation of Tillich the man. Besides being manageable, it too has the advantage of being one of his favorite and most distinctive images. It is introduced here somewhat at length, for it provides an insight into his manner of thinking and is thus more than a mere literary device.

Dimensions

Tillich maintains that the process of life can no longer be adequately described by the metaphor "level," and that the metaphor "dimension" must replace it.[2] The multiplicity of beings demands a principle of organization which in the past was the hierarchical principle with the concomitant image of levels. Besides social and political levels, life processes were described in terms of the body-soul levels, the organic-inorganic levels, the levels of religion and culture, and the levels of nature and supernature. Levels, however, are static, with no implications between them, and the only interaction is by interference, that is, control of one level by another, or revolt of one against the other. Since the Renaissance and the Reformation, however, these levels have been gradually broken down so that a new insight into the unity and compenetration of life demands a new metaphor.

"Dimension" is a geometric image which expresses unity within diversity. "Dimensions have this property that they meet in a point but do not interfere with each other. They do not lie next to one another, nor above one another, nor below one another. They lie in one another, and are united in the point where they meet."[3] Though all dimensions are present at any given point, one of them will predominate in the process of life. This dominant dimension is called a "realm" (*Bereich*), as for example, the inorganic and organic realms and the historical and spiritual realms. The simultaneous presence of all dimensions is explained by the distinction between the potential and the actual. Both are realities, for the potential has a power for being that has not yet been activated. Potential dimensions exist within actual ones. Since the actualization of potencies is a gradual, evolutionary process that extends in its totality over millions of years, some dimensions will prevail over others. But these successive realms do not constitute a pyramid of levels, for they lie within, not atop one another. One can say, therefore, that "in the atom is present the spiritual power that created Shakespeare's *Hamlet*, just as the movements of the atoms in Shakespeare's body participated in the spiritual acts that produced *Hamlet*."[4] Evidently, tensions and ambiguities exist in every life process, but these are not conflicts between levels. They are conflicts between forces that operate in every dimension.

We shall attempt to project the life of Paul Tillich in four dimensions: the social, historical, intellectual, and personal. No specifically religious dimension is constructed, for to do so would be to betray one of his cardinal principles: religion cannot be confined to a special realm; it permeates all dimensions, giving them depth. Furthermore, our interest is not so much biographical facts and details (confer Chronology) as the setting, the mood, the texture of experiences that have combined to shape him as an individual and a theologian.

The Social Dimension

"Social dimension" is used here in an arbitrary sense to denote relatively small communities of friends and associates. In Tillich's case they are the circles of family life, German university life, and American professorial life. He was born in 1886. He describes his home life in the Prussian province of Brandenburg as being influenced in two opposite ways. His mother was from the Rhineland of western Germany, and through her he experienced some of that region's zest for life, sensuous concreteness, flexibility, reasonableness, and democracy. The early death of his mother, however, resulted in the predominance of paternal influence. His

Prussian father, a Protestant pastor and superintendent (an office similar to that of bishop), incarnated the traits of eastern Germany: a melancholy, speculative bent, a heavy consciousness of duty and of guilt, a strong sense for authority and feudal traditions.[5]

The authoritarian position of his father as parent and church leader posed a serious problem for the brilliant young son who was developing into an independent thinker. The personal and religious authority of the father inextricably merged together so that every expression of autonomous thought on the part of the youthful Tillich became a religiously hazardous undertaking followed by unsettling feelings of guilt. But his father respected the autonomy of philosophy, and so it became an avenue of escape as the son took up philosophical positions different from his father's. So painful was this breaking of the bonds of a holy but nonetheless repressive authority that for the rest of his life Tillich rejected any semblance of a return to it.[6] The struggle against authoritarianism of every stripe permeates all his endeavors and is embodied in his emphasis upon the No of the Protestant protest. Karl Barth accused him of forever crusading against the "Grand Inquisitor."

Tillich pursued university studies at Berlin and Tübingen, but it was at the University of Halle that he became a leader of the Wingolf fraternity, an accomplishment which he rates "the proudest achievement of my life."[7] Life in a German university of the early 1900's tended to be very individualistic due to the lack of student dormitories, organizations, religious associations, and contact with professors. Thus the fraternities with their dueling and drinking filled a real need for companionship. Tillich's fraternity was extremely authoritarian in discipline, yet very liberal in creedal requirements and freedom of discussion. A controversy over whether belief in the Apostles' Creed should be a requisite for membership was settled in the negative. This dispute impressed upon Tillich that "if Christianity is a man's ultimate concern, he can still be a minister, though he may have many doubts."[8] However, he relates that the deepest impression Wingolf left upon him was a sense of Christian community in which "friendship, spiritual exchange on a very high level, intentional and unintentional education, joy of living, seriousness about the problems of communal life generally, and Christian communal life especially, could daily be experienced."[9]

Many years later Tillich had a similar experience, but in a totally different context: not in Germany, but in the United States; not in a university, but in a seminary; and not as a student, but as a professor. When he came to Union Theological Seminary in 1933, he found not only a refuge in exile, but also a tightly knit community of Christian life and scholarship. Professors and students, along with their families, met not only at academic and social gatherings, but also at religious services. Furthermore, the national and international makeup of the student body at Union Seminary, Columbia University, and Harvard University opened the door to the wider communities of American Protestantism and the religions of the world.[10]

The Historical Dimension

Two monumental events dominate the historical dimension of Paul Tillich's life: the shattering of nineteenth-century bourgeois civilization by World War I, and the rise of nazism with the ensuing World War II. Before 1914 he lived in a middle-class world that enjoyed a surface calm despite the rumblings of revolutionary impulses that presaged its spiritual disintegration. In the *Gymnasium* he received a humanistic education based on Greek and Latin, and afterwards he applied himself to the study of the great German philosophers. Even though he later on attacked nineteenth-century institutions, he retained a certain nostalgia for them, as he himself remarks: "I am one of those in my generation who, in spite of the radicalism with which they have criticized the nineteenth century, often feel a longing for its stability, its liberalism, its unbroken cultural traditions."[11]

With the outbreak of World War I, army chaplain Tillich, along with the rest of the world, was swept from the quiet backwaters of the nineteenth century into the raging turbulence of the twentieth. He remarks how before the war, "it still seemed possible then to sit in the center of the world and be able to understand everything."[12] But after a night attack in 1915 as he moved among the rows of the wounded and the dying, he discovered among the casualties his German classical philosophy and theology—the belief that man could master being by knowledge, that existence and essence are the same.

Upon his return from the war, history—or rather a theological interpretation of history—became the center of his interest. Certain historical realities led him in this direction: the chaotic condition of Germany and Europe, the end of the nineteenth-century bourgeois way of life, the split between Lutheranism and the proletariat, and the gap between Christianity and the hope of the revolutionary movements.[13] To translate his convictions into action, he helped to found the movement called "Religious Socialism." It was not a political party, although it demanded political action. It was not a religious organization, although it grounded its program in Christian principles. It sought to make religion socially effective, and to give socialism a religious depth. Tillich and his fellow Religious Socialists of the 1920's were buoyed up in their enthusiasm by the feeling that history was about to enter a period of *kairos*, a time when the holy would break through into human life in new and transforming ways. The expectancy of the *kairos*, heralded by the German socialist revolution of 1918, impelled him to work out a Protestant interpretation of history which constitutes his principal contribution to Religious Socialism.[14]

As the years wore on and the *kairos* did not materialize, the spiritual vacuum was filled by fascism, nazism, communism, and a host of other "isms" which formed a deep current of revolution. Tillich portrays Europe of the late 1930's as "the picture of a complete cultural distintegration," characterized by fear, uncertainty, loneliness, and the malaise of meaninglessness.[15] Demonic forces, such as National Socialism in Germany, responded to these desperate needs by offering security and certainty, by establishing the community of the *Reich,* and by providing powerful but pagan symbols of meaning. Long before 1933, Tillich openly objected to the nazi program which he termed "a brutal ideology of force."[16] Besides his constant opposition to it in his writings and speeches for the Religious Socialists, just before Hitler came to power in 1933 he published a lengthy tract, *Die sozialistische Entscheidung,* which indicted the nazi distortion of socialism.[17] Shortly after Hitler assumed the chancellorship, Tillich was dismissed from his professorial post at Frankfurt; he left Germany to take up residence in the United States.

The second World War did not bring the same brutal shock as the first, for Tillich interpreted it as part of a much vaster world revolution. In his opinion, the world is in process of becoming a *kosmos,* a unified, structured, historical whole in which all the parts interact with one another. But the forms of thought and action are still chaotically individualistic, and so "the world as a historical reality is being born in the labor pains of two wars." He describes this generative process as follows: "Following the breakdown of the natural or automatic harmony on which the system of life and thought during the eighteenth and nineteenth centuries was based, the attempt is now being made to produce a system of life and thought which is based on an intentional and planned unity."[18] But what shall be the spiritual center of this new world? Already religion has been largely replaced by political and social movements with their new myths of nation and social justice. Yet they have not proved equal to the task, and so, today, at the center of the world there is a vacuum which demonic forces struggle to fill. The vacuum is an absence of meaning: "The spiritual disintegration of our day consists in the loss of an ultimate meaning of life by the people of Western civilization."[19] Though both World Wars are part of the world revolution, there is this significant difference: World War I was followed by the ecstatic experience of belief in a proximate *kairos;* World War II was followed by pessimism and cynical realism.[20]

Whatever the explanation one attaches to the historical dimen-

sion of Paul Tillich's life, one thing is unmistakably clear. He and
the scholars of his generation differ from the generation of their
teachers in that the former have been thrust into history, forced to
face up to it realistically, and to interpret it theologically.[21]

The Intellectual Dimension

Tillich's intellectual background is vast and rich. To explore it
fully would be like taking inventory in a huge storehouse that has
been accumulating marked and unmarked items for over seventy
years. Fortunately, the owner of the storehouse can himself serve
as our guide, for he often makes reference to other authors either
as sources of, or as contrasts with, his own ideas. Nor are we primarily concerned with the objective accuracy of his estimate of
those sources, but rather with the use he makes of them. For instance, the fact that he judges Schelling to be the grandfather of
existentialism or that he considers Lutheranism to affirm the presence of the infinite in everything finite is more significant than
the objective truth or error of those statements.

But before picking our way through the specific "ists" and
"isms" of the intellectual realm, it is good to hear Tillich's own
description of the two intellectual atmospheres in which he has
labored, the German and the American.[22] He relates that at the re-
nowned theological faculties of Berlin, Tübingen, and Halle there
existed a consensus that identified the last four centuries of theology with the history of German theology. Consequently, "it was
our feeling that only in Germany was the problem of how to unite
Christianity and the modern mind taken absolutely seriously. All
this was a mixture of limitation, arrogance, and some elements of
truth."[23] Nor did German philosophy alter this conviction, for
fundamentally it shared the same attitude. Tillich explains how it
was felt that Germany, after 1800, succeeded to ancient Greece as
the center of philosophy. One trait in particular was supposed to
account for this superiority: "the attempt to reunite, in a great
synthesis, Christianity with the modern mind. It was in its heart

philosophy of religion, it was *Weltanschauung*, a vision of the world as a whole. And we despised every philosophy which was less than this."[24] Two events broke the grip of this intellectual provincialism on Tillich: the fact that the supposedly superior German culture could produce a Hitler; and secondly, his emigration to the quite different intellectual climate of the United States.

He characterizes American intellectual life by its intimate relating of theory to practice and by its wide-open horizons. Protestant theology in America cannot rest content with theorizing, but draws out practical conclusions; hence its special contribution in the field of social ethics. Mention has already been made of how its theological horizons have been kept broad, at least for Tillich in Union Theological Seminary, by the wide range of Protestant denominations and by contact with other religions. Despite the multiplicity of Protestant viewpoints, he feels there is a certain typically American unity of theological discussion, competition, and teamwork. In general, the American bent for practicality permits a widespread concrete realization of religious truth, while the European drive for ultimates insures its profundity. Tillich neatly sums up the contrast: "The European danger is a lack of horizontal actualization; the American danger is a lack of vertical depth."[25]

Turning now to more specific intellectual influences upon Tillich, we first consider the area of philosophy, and here the importance of Friedrich Wilhelm Joseph von Schelling is paramount. In recalling his youthful student days, Tillich relates: "Partly by chance of a bargain purchase, and partly by inner affinity I came under the influence of Schelling, whose collected works I read through several times with enthusiasm. . . ."[26] Moreover, his first two works—a doctoral thesis in philosophy and a licentiate dissertation in theology—deal with Schelling's philosophy of religion, and in other writings he calls attention to Schelling's strong, decisive impact upon his development.[27] Two recent studies have detailed the many areas in which this influence is perceptible, but, since discussions of Schelling's philosophy rapidly become lengthy

and terribly involved, we feel it sufficient for our purpose here to
indicate the general orientation of his two dissertations on Schelling.[28]

It has been pointed out that Schelling's chief concern was the
relationship between the infinite and the finite and that the complex evolution of his philosophizing can be explained as variations
on this basic theme.[29] Therefore, when Tillich schematizes Schelling's history of religion in presenting its suppositions, content, and
principles, the core of the discussion centers around God's relation
to the world and to man. Following upon the idealist principle that the absolute objectifies itself in nature and becomes conscious of itself through the reflection of man, nature is unconscious
but on the way to consciousness, and reaches it with the birth of
man. Human consciousness is that which realizes God; consequently, for Schelling all history is fundamentally the history of
religion. It is in history that man comes to a consciousness of God;
thus, even the cultural process is religious in its roots and can be
considered from the viewpoint of the history of religion.[30]

Schelling's basic problem of the infinite-finite relationship is
approached by Tillich in his second dissertation from the viewpoint of the religious experience of man. Tillich employs the
polarity of mysticism and sense of guilt (*Mystik und Schuldbewusstsein*) to focus Schelling's thought upon the problem of man's
union with and separation from God. He formulates the topic of
his study in the question: Did Schelling succeed in synthesizing
mysticism and guilt so that neither are destroyed? Mysticism
means the feeling of union with the absolute; it implies the principle of identity of absolute and individual spirit. Guilt means
the consciousness of opposition to God; it implies the experience
of conflict between the holy Lord and the sinful creature. Tillich's
detailed tracing out of this theme through the periods of Schelling's
development is not of immediate interest. What is significant,
however, is that Schelling's extremely close relationship of the infinite and the finite was the object of two intensive studies by the
young Tillich.[31]

In addition to Schelling, Tillich draws upon other important sources. He says that he began his philosophical schooling in German idealism and that he can never unlearn what he there acquired—if, by idealism, one means the identity of thought and being as the principle of truth.[32] It was through Dr. Fritz Medicus, then at the University of Halle, that he was formally introduced to German idealism by way of Fichte. Tillich admits his indebtedness to it for one of his basic positions: that between the human spirit and reality there exists a correspondence which is best expressed in the concept of meaning (*Sinn*). However, he rejects the idealists' claim that their system portrays reality as a whole. He prefers to view the system as the expression of a specific but limited encounter with reality.[33]

Tillich's study of marxism abetted his reaction to idealism. For the contradictions of existence as exemplified by the class struggle reveal idealism as an ideology, that is, a conceptual system that merely covers up the disruption in reality. He likes Marx's "economic materialism" which emphasizes that man lives in existence and not in essence, as the idealists would have him do.[34] In general, he describes his relation to marxism as dialectical, that is, combining a Yes and a No: "The Yes was based on the prophetic, humanistic, and realistic elements in Marx's passionate style and profound thought, the No on the calculating, materialistic, and resentful elements in Marx's analysis, polemics, and propaganda."[35]

Two other intellectual movements played an important role in Tillich's formation: existentialism and psychoanalysis, the latter understood in the sense of depth psychology. To elaborate upon them here is too large an undertaking, but Tillich provides a short cut in an article entitled "The Theological Significance of Existentialism and Psychoanalysis."[36] He relates depth psychology to existentialism as part to whole. Their common root is the protest against the philosophy of essence or consciousness which has dominated modern industrial society and endangered freedom, individuality, and creativity. Freud's discovery of the irrational, unconscious level of man helped enormously to combat this philosophy. Depth psychology and existentialism are both basically concerned with man's existential predicament—temporal, spatial, finite, and estranged—as opposed to man's essential nature. Looking at theology, Tillich finds there certain unmistakably existential themes: the original goodness of being and of man, the universal fall, and salvation as healing or making whole a disrupted world. Transposed into philosophical language, these themes are: essential goodness, existential estrangement, and the teleological nature of man which points to a unity beyond essence and existence. But while theology contributes its insights to the existentialist movement, existentialism returns the favor. It opens up a whole new psychological dimension in the immense religious literature of the past. It rediscovers sin as a state of separation instead of a series or moral acts. It lays bare the demonic structures that shape conscious decisions. It reinforces the meaning of grace as acceptance of the unacceptable—recall the manner in which an analyst handles his patient. And, finally, it raises the question of human existence which systematic theology must answer by the reinterpretation of religious symbols.

The extent to which Tillich is a true existentialist is extremely difficult to determine. As a fellow professor with Martin Heidegger at the University of Marburg in 1925, he met twentieth-century existentialism. His own comment best sums up his reaction: "It took years before I became fully aware of the impact of this encounter on my own thinking. I resisted, I tried to learn, I accepted the new way of thinking more than the answers it gave."[37]

Thus far we have been viewing the more properly philosophical dimension. But Tillich also clearly documents the theological influences in his life. As regards the Old Testament, for which he admits a certain preference, he singles out Wellhausen and Gunkel. In New Testament studies he acknowledges his indebtedness to the historical-critical work of Albert Schweitzer and Bultmann. Early in his career he took the position that "the foundation

of Christian belief is not the historical Jesus, but the biblical picture of Christ."[38]

Two of Tillich's contemporaries, Rudolf Otto and Karl Barth,
stand in a special relationship to him. Here we consider the points
of contact between Tillich and Otto, while reserving a discussion
of Barth for our third chapter. Tillich had read Otto's *Das Heilige*
while at the front in 1917. In it he found articulated his own experience of the holy as encountered in his Lutheran home, church,
and school. As he himself puts it,

When I first read Rudolf Otto's *Idea of the Holy*, I understood it immediately in the light of these early experiences, and took it into my
thinking as a constitutive element. It determined my method in the
philosophy of religion, wherein I started with the experiences of the
holy and advanced to the idea of God, and not the reverse way.[39]

The impact of Otto's work is evident in several ways. First of
all, Tillich admits that he has adopted Otto's method of beginning
with the experience of the holy and proceeding from it to the
notion of God. With such an approach, the existential experience
of the *mysterium tremendum et fascinans*—Tillich terms it "ultimate concern"—is destined to play a principal role. Secondly,
Tillich's notion of God as the abyss and ground of being is an
ontological explicitation of Otto's phenomenologically conceived
mysterium tremendum et fascinosum.[40] Thirdly, Tillich follows
Otto in liberating the holy from the dominance of the ethically
good. However, neither separates religion from morality. On the
contrary, Tillich maintains that "the relation of religion and morality is not an external one, but that the religious dimension, source,
and motivation are implicit in all morality, acknowledged or
not."[41] But he accepts Otto's insight that the holy is first experienced as a numinous reality and only secondly as a moral demand.[42]

Finally, Otto's influence is operative in Tillich's definition of
religion. The latter praises Otto's "splendidly developed phenom-

enology of religion" which broke down the "rationalistic and moralistic interpretation of religion" and recognized its "ecstatic, form-destroying character."[43] This means for Tillich that religion is no longer confined to institutions, cult, and doctrine—in a word, to the churches—but that religion is now the state of being ultimately concerned. Otto's distinction between the rational and non-rational factors in religion is echoed in Tillich's double definition of religion. There is religion in the narrow sense of institutionalized and formalized religion, and in the large sense of being grasped by an ultimate concern.

Among his professors, Martin Kähler exercised by far the most lasting influence upon him. Kähler's forte was the Protestant principle of justification through faith, which "rends every human claim in the face of God and every identification of God and man," and yet man is justified in the midst of his guilt and doubt.[44] In the light of this principle, the cross of Christ is seen as the embodiment of the divine Yes and No against the world, an interpretation which forms the core of Tillichian Christology and dogma. A union of this Protestant principle with the historico-critical biblical research then current led Tillich to reject nineteenth-century liberal dogmatic theology "which replaces the crucified Christ by the historical Jesus, and which dissolves the paradox of justification into moral categories."[45]

If behind Tillich one finds Kähler, then behind them both one senses the presence of a far more towering theological figure, Martin Luther. Tillich states unequivocally:

The substance of my religion is and remains Lutheran. It embodies the consciousness of the "corruption" of existence, the repudiation of every social Utopia, including the metaphysics of progress, the knowledge of the irrational demonic character of life, an appreciation of the mythical elements of religion, and a repudiation of Puritan legality in individual and social life.[46]

However, it would be inaccurate to label him a representative Lutheran theologian. Even though Luther's influence is diffused throughout his system, the system itself is original, and hence above facile classification.

A complete portrayal of his intellectual dimension would also include the ancient Greek philosophers, Nicholas of Cusa, Calvin, Jacob Böhme, Spinoza, Kant, Hegel, Schleiermacher, Kierkegaard, Nietzsche, Dilthey, Troeltsch, and Buber. Tillich has indeed read, digested, and incorporated into his own system an enormous range of thought. Many of his interpretations of these other philosophers and theologians are open to dispute, for he invariably approaches them from his own systematic viewpoint. However, that he cannot be closely identified with any of his predecessors and contemporaries testifies to his own originality and to the vigor with which he applies his dialectical Protestant principle. His own comment best describes his attitude: "As long as our thought remains autonomous, our relation to the great historical figures must be a Yes and a No. The undialectical No is as primitive and unproductive as the undialectical Yes."[47]

The Personal Dimension

The personal dimension of Tillich's life refers to personal likes and tastes which exercise a certain influence upon his theology, though perhaps indirectly. The ones considered here are his love of the sea, his preference for the city, and his interest in art. He relates that, from the age of eight, he spent several weeks, even months, at the seashore every year.[48] The meeting of sea and land meant for him a boundary-experience of the infinite and the finite. The sea with its never-resting, limitless expanse and depths became a symbol for the absolute, the ground and the abyss. Its dynamism would suddenly erupt in an ecstacy of storm and waves which aggressively broke over the land that quietly rested in its self-sufficient finitude. The sea provided an element of phantasy that Tillich considers essential to living thought.

His love for nature, however, goes hand-in-hand with a preference for the bustling life of the city.[49] He feels that the city is indispensable for developing the critical side of intellectual and artistic endeavor. Furthermore, in a large urban center one finds concentrated all the important political and social trends. To the realism of the city he attributes his escape from a romantic hostility against technology. And, strange to say, he finds the experience of the city analogous to the experience of the sea: "The impression of the big city was somehow similar to that of the sea: infinity, openness, unrestricted space! But beyond this it was the dynamic character of the life in Berlin that affected me. . . ."[50]

The discovery of art (in the sense of the visual arts, but especially painting) was for Tillich an event of far-reaching consequences.[51] Turning to it by way of reaction during the fearful, ugly, destructive years of World War I, he was later to produce numerous essays that touch on art. After the war he methodically studied the history of art, even taking a three-month hike through Italy with his wife, an art student, to discover the marvels of Italian medieval and Renaissance art and architecture. In his opinion, all the bookish church history in the world could never provide the kind of insights occasioned by the mosaics of the early Roman basilicas. His speculative reflection upon these artistic insights led to the discovery of two of his fundamental categories: form, which is culture, and content, which is religion in the broad sense. But Tillich was perhaps most deeply moved by the German expressionism of the early twentieth century. The disruptive, ecstatic power of its content brought him to a realization of the meaning of the "breakthrough," a key point in his doctrine of revelation and *kairos.* In a lecture "Art and Ultimate Reality," delivered at the Museum of Modern Art in New York, he shows the religious depth of art.[52] For ultimate reality is experienced and expressed directly in religious symbols and myths, but the artist, while intending nothing but good art, cannot help but indirectly express ultimate reality.

Besides being telescoped into the life of one man, these dimensions are linked together by other bonds of unity. In all of them one discerns the deep current of religious concern—in the search for Christian community, in the theological view of history, in the quest for a philosophy that is realistic and open to the transcendent, and in a sensitivity to the presence of the holy in nature and art. Every facet of Tillich's life is intensely religious. But in addition to the religious factor, his life is a unity because it unifies. It unifies in that it draws together the conflicting elements of an age in transition: authority and autonomy, theory and practice, nature and technology, idealism and existentialism, Christianity and marxism, world wars and world unity. Paul Tillich echoes this urgent cry of human hope and despair not only in his thought, but also in his experience. He is truly a man of his times.

PAUL TILLICH THE THEOLOGIAN

A theological methodology is never independent of the system which it constructs, as Tillich is at pains to point out.[53] Statements about what theology is and how to theologize are in themselves theological assertions derived from more remote and more fundamental theological positions. The presentation, therefore, of a theologian's method is inevitably incomplete and unsatisfying. Nevertheless, it is necessary and useful to present it in order to follow intelligently the theologian in his theologizing and to test his consistency. But only after the system is elaborated does the method become fully comprehensible.

Under the heading "Paul Tillich the Theologian" we consider his views on the nature of theology, the theological circle, the sources, medium, and norm of systematic theology, the method of correlation, theological language, and the relation of theology to philosophy.[54]

The Nature of Theology

Theology, as a function of the church, is the methodological interpretation of the Christian faith for the human situation. Thus it mediates between two poles, the eternal and the temporal.[55] The eternal pole is the Christian message, and one function of theology is to state its truth. The temporal pole is the human situation, and the other function of theology is to respond to its needs. The "situation" does not refer to the psychological or sociological condition of individuals or even of groups, as for instance, a feeling of uncertainty that demands an uncomplicated, unequivocal reassurance. Rather, it signifies "the totality of man's creative self-interpretation in a special period," that is, the sum of the artistic, scientific, philosophical, economic, political, and ethical forms in which men of a certain era express their understanding of life.

According to the emphasis laid upon the two poles, two different kinds of theology result. If one stresses "the unchangeable truth of the message (kerygma) over against the changing demands of the situation," the theology is "kerygmatic." Tillich praises Barth for producing just such a theology, one that preserves the Christian faith from the relativities of mundane exigencies. The drawback, however, is that kerygmatic theology hurls the message at the situation like a stone. It establishes no common ground with those in the situation, and so runs the risk of being irrelevant.

If, on the other hand, one first listens attentively to the questions implied in the temporal situation and then responds with the power of the eternal message, that theology is "apologetic." Apologetic theology is "answering theology." It bears no semblance to the discredited relic that has borne the name in the past. Apologetic theology, in Tillich's view, searches for the common ground between the message and the situation by listening to the questions that the situation poses before answering in terms of the message. The danger in such a procedure is that the word of the message may be distorted amid the clamor of the questions. But he unreservedly opts for an apologetic theology for two reasons, one a fact, the other a conviction. The fact is that for the last two hundred years the central problem of theology has been the adaptation of the Christian faith to the modern mind. His conviction is that such a synthesis is possible—and necessary—if Christianity is to avoid becoming a fossilized curiosity and if civilization is not to lose one of its most powerful stimulants.

Ultimate Concern and the Theological Circle

The theologian is a committed man, committed to the gospel message and committed to his task of interpreting it. He is a believing, self-surrendering, answering man.[56] Tillich explores the nature of this commitment by comparing the theologian to the philosopher of religion.[57] Both of them are committed in the sense that even their most scientific efforts are directed by a "mystical a priori"—"an immediate experience of something ultimate in value and being of which one can become intuitively aware." Examples of the mystical a priori are "being-itself" (the Scholastics), "universal substance" (Spinoza), "identity of spirit and nature" (Schelling), "absolute spirit" (Hegel), and "cosmic person" (Brightman). If, after scientific investigation, this a priori is discovered, it is only because it was present and operative from the very start. At this stage both theologian and philosopher are within a philosophical circle described by their mystical a priori, but there is no *petitio principii*, for spiritual things can be understood only in circular fashion. However, the theologian and the religious philosopher part company when the theologian steps inside the theological circle of commitment to the gospel message. The philosopher deals in the abstract, with universal concepts. The theologian works with a concrete message that claims historical uniqueness. The radius of the theological circle is shorter than that of the philosophical one.

Since it is necessary that the theologian place himself within the circle of Christian commitment, the problem arises: What is the touchstone for commitment? Who can be sure of his commitment, of his faith, his justification? Furthermore, Tillich's notion of faith includes doubt as an essential element. Therefore, he concludes that acceptance of the word of Christ as his ultimate concern is the only indication that a theologian is within the theological circle, that his presence there "depends on his being ultimately concerned with the Christian message even if he is sometimes inclined to attack and to reject it."[58]

At this point it is imperative to examine what Tillich means by "ultimate concern." This notion is absolutely fundamental to his theology, for, as will be seen in the next chapter, it defines not only the theologian, but also the concept of faith and religion. Ultimate concern cannot be explained easily or quickly; it will reappear in every chapter. Although a proper view of ultimate concern demands that it be viewed in a variety of contexts, what follows is a concise and, as far as possible, clear introduction to an important but difficult concept.

In a sermon entitled "Our Ultimate Concern," Tillich takes for his text the story of Martha and Mary, and he presents them as symbols of two views of life, of two kinds of concern. "Martha is concerned about many things, but all of them are finite, preliminary, transitory. Mary is concerned about one thing, which is infinite, ultimate, lasting." The concerns of Martha require attention, devotion, and passion, "but they do not demand infinite attention, unconditional devotion, ultimate passion." Our finite concerns about our work, our science, our money, and our nation will be taken from us by "the melancholy law of transitoriness." But if our concern is that of Mary, then "everything seems the same and yet everything is changed," for we are grasped by the one thing needed, by the infinite.[59]

Ultimate concern is the abstract formulation of the great commandment: "You shall love the Lord your God with all your heart, and with all your soul, and with all your might" (Deut. 6:5*). Concern not only means that one is related to or interested in something, but it also implies an existential element of anxious

* RSV: *The Holy Bible, Revised Standard Version,* New York: Nelson, 1953. Copyright 1946 and 1952 by the Division of Christian Education of the National Council of Churches of Christ in the U.S.A. and used by permission.

solicitude. Thus, man is concerned about many things—food and shelter, knowledge, art, social problems, politics—with varying degrees of urgency. But a concern becomes ultimate only when it demands total surrender and promises total fulfilment. Ultimate concern is unconditional, total, and infinite. Any concern less than this is a preliminary concern, for it is conditional, partial, and finite. The concern of Martha is preliminary; the concern of Mary, ultimate.[60]

Preliminary concern can be related to ultimate concern in three possible ways. First, by a "mutual indifference" ultimate concern can be placed beside preliminary concern so that the former loses its ultimacy. It fails to transcend; it becomes secularized. Secondly, preliminary concern can be "elevated to ultimacy," but in so doing it becomes demonic by usurping the place of the truly ultimate. Thirdly, preliminary concern can become a "vehicle of the ultimate concern without claiming ultimacy for itself." It points beyond itself; it is transparent to the holy.[61]

Extreme nationalism is one of Tillich's favorite examples of an ultimate concern—a demonic one to be sure, but all the more indicative of its unconditional character.[62] In the name of the god Nation, all other concerns are ruthlessly sacrificed and systematically subordinated. However, unconditional demand is balanced by unconditional fulfilment more or less vaguely expressed in such symbols as the greatness of the nation or the conquest of the world. Exclusion from the promised fulfilment is a threat which reinforces the demand.

The above example points to the ambiguous nature of ultimate concern. Ultimacy and holiness go together, for "the holy is the *quality* of that which concerns man ultimately. Only that which is holy can give man ultimate concern, and only that which gives man ultimate concern has the quality of holiness."[63] When this holy, ultimate concern is directed toward the infinite, the unconditioned, the truly ultimate, then it is divine. When directed toward the finite, the conditioned, the preliminary, then it is demonic and its holiness is idolatrous. But even in the latter case, "the holy which is demonic is still holy."[64] The ambiguity of ultimate concern lies in the fact that ultimacy consists of a demand for total surrender and a promise of total fulfilment, and even the demonic can demand sacrifice and offer promises.

Ultimate concern constitutes the basic credentials for admittance to the theological circle, but Tillich further refines the theologian's basic commitment by formulating two criteria for theological statements.[65] They are formal criteria, that is, abstracted from the content of the whole system. The first criterion states: *"The object of theology is what concerns us ultimately. Only those propositions are theological which deal with their object in so far as it can become a matter of ultimate concern for us."* This principle distinguishes theology from other sciences, for it rules out preliminary concerns. However, preliminary concerns may still fall within the radius of theology insofar as they are vehicles for ultimate concern. The second criterion handles the content of ultimate concern: *"Our ultimate concern is that which determines our being or not-being. Only those statements are theological which deal with their object in so far as it can become a matter of being or not-being for us."* In this statement, "being" does not refer to a man's life in time and space, but to "the whole of human reality, the structure, the meaning, and the aim of existence."

Sources, Medium, and Norm

Tillich makes a practical distinction between systematic and historical theology, though their mutual dependence is seen in the fact that the historical theologian operates from a systematic viewpoint, and the systematic theologian draws upon historical theology as his source in constructing theological explanations.[66] Historical theology provides three closely related blocks of source material: the Bible, church history, and the history of religion and culture. This threefold source may cause some Protestant and Catholic eyebrows to rise, but Tillich is quite emphatic when he says that "we must reject the assertion of neo-orthodox biblicism that the Bible is the *only* source." For the Bible can be understood only in the context of past religions and cultures, and it conveys a message to us only because the church experiences and participates in that message. Still, the Bible remains the basic theological source since it is the original document about the events of sacred history that led to the foundation of the Christian church. It is inspired in the sense that "the inspiration of the biblical writers is their receptive and creative response to potentially revelatory facts." Underlying Tillich's position on the Bible is his idea of revelation according to which no revelation takes place unless someone receives it.[67] Thus the act of reception is part of the revelatory event.

This stress on the receptive side of revelation allows room for church history and the history of religion and culture as theological sources in addition to the Bible.[68] The systematic theologian must consult ecclesiastical precedents even though he is not bound by them, for at least he is a member of the church that has received and continues to receive the biblical message. His affiliation with a particular denomination in one way narrows his appreciation of church history, but in another way it broadens it, for the concrete life of the church—its liturgy, hymns, sermons, and sacraments—can be savored only by joining the community of one denomination. The theologian must also employ the history of religion and culture, because his spiritual life, his thought patterns, his education, and the very language he speaks is conditioned by religious and cultural antecedents. But besides this somewhat indirect contact with religion and culture, the theologian also deals with them directly. He uses them for his modes of expression and for confirmation of his conclusions, he combats them when they oppose the Christian message, and, above all, he formulates from them the existential questions to which his theology is the answer.

What is the link between the theologian and his sources? Tillich's reply is that "experience is the medium through which the sources 'speak' to us, through which we can receive them."[69] For every theologian stands in an existential relation to truth in that he experiences, participates in, the religious power of his sources before he analyzes them. Experience, as the theological medium, is receptive, not productive. No new revelation is produced, and the unique event of Jesus as the Christ remains at the center of Christian theology. Subjectivity is excluded in the sense that experience is not a source. But subjectivity is active insofar as the theologian does not woodenly repeat his sources, but is seized by their power.

The negative purpose of experience as medium is quite clear: to exclude religious experience as a source of theology and thus to bolt the door against such disturbing possibilities as new, personal, or variable revelations.[70] However, the positive function of the medium is more complex.[71] Positively, experience as the medium of theology means participation in the reality of the revelatory events. The history of religion and of Christianity is an immense reservoir of religious experience, and in this sense it is content and, therefore, the source of theology. But experience as *event* is the medium. The event is a revelatory event, i.e., "the manifestation of the ultimate ground and meaning of human existence. . . . It is a matter of ultimate concern." The content can be had only if one participates in the event. The theologian must share in the revelatory character of his source, for "we can speak of it only if it has become revelation *for us,* if we have experienced it existentially." Tillich recognizes a point at which content and medium are identified: the awareness of the ultimate, of being-itself. But this experience of ultimate concern must be expressed in symbols, and this is the task of theology—to interpret the symbols of the revelatory event. Hence all theological statements must be inspired by the ultimacy of the mediating experience.

Sources and medium, however, are not enough—a theologian must be guided by a norm.[72] Theological norms grow unconsciously within the body of the church and slowly mature to meet its needs. They do not differ in substance, but only in their emphasis upon different facets of the content of the Christian message. Tillich illustrates this from history. In the early church the need to safeguard Christian doctrine led to the establishment of a formal or general norm, which was the authority of the hierarchy, and a material or concrete norm which was the creeds. Within the Catholic church the formal norm has swallowed up the material norm, so that Christian doctrine is simply what the hierarchy decrees it to be. At the time of the Reformation, Luther set up justification by faith as the material norm and took the Bible as the formal norm. Calvin kept the Bible, but substituted predestination for justification as the material norm. Liberal theology took the personal and social ideal of the synoptic Jesus for its norm.

Tillich advances his own norm with some hesitation, for a genuine norm is not the private opinion of a theologian, but the church's articulation of its encounter with the Christian message. He sums up today's needs in that "man experiences his present situation in terms of disruption, conflict, self-destruction, meaninglessness, and despair in all realms of life." Man seeks a reality to overcome the estrangement of existence, "a reality of reconciliation and reunion, of creativity, meaning, and hope."[73] Tillich calls this reality the "New Being," and it is manifest in Jesus as the Christ. Therefore, the material norm of his systematic theology is "the New Being in Jesus as the Christ as our ultimate concern."[74]

But what is the connection between the theological norm and the theological sources and medium?[75] The Bible is far too general, and a more concrete norm is required—for example, Luther's justification by faith. Hence, one can say that the norm is *derived* from the Bible and then governs the use of the Bible. The question of the canonicity of the biblical books clearly shows that the Bible is a source, not a norm. The norm results from an encounter between the church and the biblical message. Consequently, the norm is *produced* in church history, and every era consciously and unconsciously contributes to its formation. Because the church does not live in a vacuum, the norm is *conditioned* by the particular religio-cultural environment in which it is produced. The norm is also dependent upon the theological medium, for it is born in and nurtured by the collective experience of the church. But at the same time it is the criterion of this experience. In brief, the norm is derived from the Bible, produced in the church, conditioned by culture, and vivified by experience.

The Method of Correlation

The theologian in touch with his sources through the medium of experience and guided by his theological norm must still work methodically. Tillich calls his method the "method of correlation" and defines it as follows: "The method of correlation explains the contents of the Christian faith through existential questions and theological answers in mutual interdependence."[76] Revelation contains answers, but they are meaningful only if correlated with questions about the whole of human existence. And man can never get the ultimate answer to his own questions unless he seeks it in the revelatory events. The fact that man *is able* to ask the question of his existence reflects his essential unity with the infinite. The fact that he *must* ask it reflects his existential estrangement from it. Consequently, the procedure of the theologian is first to analyze the existential situation. He examines the cultural creations in which man expresses his interpretation of existence: philosophy, sociology, depth psychology, the novel, drama, poetry, and so forth. This analysis is fundamentally a philosophical task, and the theologian in performing it works as a philosopher, although he correlates the material with theological concepts. However, he operates autonomously, so that if he comes across something that does not correlate with the theological answer at hand, he will have to reshape the answer.

The second step is to demonstrate that the symbols of the Christian message really answer the questions. "These answers are contained in the revelatory events on which Christianity is based and are taken by systematic theology *from* the sources, *through* the medium, *under* the norm."[77] The mutual dependence of question and answer can be explained in terms of form and content. Theological answers derive their content from revelation; they take their form from the existential questions. For example, if existential analysis reveals the threat of non-being, then God must be called the power of being that overcomes this threat. If history is an incomprehensible puzzle, then the Kingdom of God must be termed the unity, meaning, and fulfilment of history. Christian symbols must always be open to, and in correlation with, the questions of existence.

Tillich brings the method of correlation into relief by contrasting it with other methods. The supranaturalistic method considers revelation as a strange bundle of truth that fell from heaven. It has nothing but answers, and from them it manufactures the questions. The naturalistic or humanistic method never gets beyond human existence. It extracts the answers from the questions themselves. Lastly, the dualistic method tries to construct a correlation, but fails. By such devices as natural revelation and the proofs for the existence of God it seeks to correlate natural answers with Christian answers, instead of questions with answers. If the proofs for God are taken as a question—as they are in the method of correlation—and not as an answer, then their use is justified.

Tillich admits that the method of correlation is not foolproof.[78] The answers may prejudice the questions, or the questions prejudice the answers. For theology, too, is ambiguous. Nor is the method of correlation new. "As a method, it is as old as theology." But what he has done is to explicitate the methodological implications of this perennial but ever relevant apologetic theology.

The Language of Theology

The language of theology consists of symbols and ontological terms. Though Tillich does not elaborate on them in his introduction to *Systematic Theology*, we include them here because they are the indispensable idiom of theological communication.

In a very strict sense, myth and symbol are not the language of theology, but of religion, i.e., of man's encounter with the holy.[79] The task of theology is to interpret the Christian symbols of this encounter in relation to the existential situation and in ontological terms. In brief, theology speaks ontologically about Christian symbols.[80] Symbols, therefore, necessarily enter into the theologian's vocabulary and method. We here present Tillich's general theory of religious symbolism, leaving to later chapters the treatment of individual symbols.

In an article, "The Nature of Religious Language," Tillich develops the idea of symbol in five steps.[81] The first step is to distinguish between symbols and signs, even though they have a common trait of pointing beyond themselves. But a sign—for example, the red light on the street corner—is an arbitrary convention that does not participate in the reality signified, while a symbol—for instance, the king of a country—does participate in the power and meaning of the reality symbolized. The second step is that symbols open up levels of reality that cannot be attained in any other way. And corresponding to levels of reality, levels of the soul are also opened up by symbols. A watercolor, a poem, or a symphony mediates something for which another mode of expression or even another painting or sonnet is utterly inadequate. Thus symbols are irreplaceable; new ones cannot be invented. They are born out of the "collective unconscious" which produces or at least accepts them. They die when they no longer respond to the "inner situation of the human group." The third step concerns religious symbols. The level of reality they open up is the depth dimension, the ground of all reality, being-itself or the ultimate power of being. In the soul they excite the experience of this ultimate reality, of the holy. But Tillich hastens to caution that although symbols participate in the holy, they are not identified with it. The constant danger of symbolism is demonization. The fourth step is to distinguish two levels within all religious

symbols. The transcendent level goes beyond the empirically encountered reality and includes the idea of God, his attributes, and
his acts. The immanent level is encountered within empirical
reality and includes incarnations and sacraments. The fifth and
last step considers the truth of religious symbols. Their truth is
their adequacy to the religious situation in which they exist. They
cannot be proven wrong or "killed" by historical and scientific
criticism, but they die when they no longer mediate the religious
experience of a community. Such was the case of the symbol of
the Blessed Virgin Mary which died among Protestants because
of their loss of the ascetic ideal of virginity and because of their
rejection of any mediator between God and man. But the external
criterion of all religious symbols which guards them from being
demonized is the cross of the Christ, for he who embodied the
divine presence sacrificed himself so as not to become an idol.

The theologian has in his hands the rich treasure of Christian
symbols. How is he to interpret them? The method of correlation
directs him to begin with an existential analysis of the religious
situation.[82] This analysis reveals that the questions asked are
ontological ones, questions of being and non-being, of ontological
anxiety, and of the ambiguities of life. Consequently, the answers
must also be in ontological terms if the Christian symbols are to
be relevant to the situation.

But there now arises the serious objection that ontology is alien
to the biblical message and that to use it is to betray the very
source of theology. In his little book *Biblical Religion and the
Search for Ultimate Reality* Tillich resolves this problem. On the
one hand, he characterizes biblical religion by its personalism, for,
in the Bible, God appears as a person in the I-Thou revelatory
encounter. Ontology, on the other hand, asks the question of
being-itself, describes the structure of being, and searches for
ultimate reality. The extremes of these definitions serve to highlight the conflict: a concrete person versus abstract being-itself.
One finds the same opposition in other concepts, for instance,
faith. Biblical faith is passionate, confident, and committed, while

ontology is detached, questioning, doubting. Tillich's solution is "to show that each of the biblical symbols drives inescapably to an ontological question and that the answers given by theology necessarily contain ontological elements."[83] There is a hidden but close correlation between biblical imagery and ontological concepts once one probes beneath the surface.

Theology and Philosophy

Before concluding the exposition of Tillich's method, one last point remains to be settled: the relationship between theology and philosophy. Several reasons force this issue to the foreground. The theological circle is drawn by ultimate concern about being, but the study of being has traditionally been the preserve of the philosopher. Moreover, the existential analysis performed by the theologian is basically philosophical. And, finally, theological answers must be couched in ontological terms. Philosophy and theology cannot pass like ships in the night, but Tillich does not underestimate the difficulty of bringing them together:

After at least two thousand years of thought dedicated to the solution of this problem, it is not easy to offer a new solution. Nevertheless, it must be attempted in every generation as long as theology exists, for the question of the relation of philosophy and theology is the question of the nature of theology itself.[84]

Theology has already been defined. He defines philosophy as "that cognitive endeavor in which the question of being is asked."[85] Or, "philosophy is the attempt to answer the most general questions about the nature of reality and human existence."[86] Or again, philosophy is "that cognitive approach to reality in which reality as such is the object."[87]

When Tillich compares philosophy with theology, he finds that they simultaneously diverge and converge.[88] They diverge in many ways. Although both ask the question of being, philosophy seeks to know the structure of being, while theology is concerned with being as it determines our being. The philosopher is detached in his research; the theologian is involved, committed. The philosophical source is the whole of reality, both subjective and objective *logos,* but the theological source is the *logos* contained in a particular event and received by the church. Although philosophy and theology both answer the question of being, the philosophical content is cosmological, descriptive of the universe, while the theological content is soteriological, healing the disruption of the cosmos. The philosopher's answer is abstract; the theologian's is concrete. To sum up: "religion deals existentially with the meaning of being; philosophy deals theoretically with the structure of being."[89]

The above divergencies, however, are balanced by a number of similarities which they share. Most important of all, they both have being as their common object.[90] They also converge in that every creative philosopher is motivated by a hidden ultimate concern and in that every theologian, in order to remain open to the ultimate, must be detached from the existential situation.[91] "The philosopher cannot avoid existential decisions, and the theologian cannot avoid ontological concepts."[92] In a word, theology is basically existential and philosophy is basically theoretical, but each participates to a certain extent in the characteristics of the other.

So far, the philosophy-theology relationship has been described. Can it be defined? Tillich's formulations of the relationship tend to be cloudy, for sometimes he stresses their identity, sometimes their distinction, and most of the time he is not concerned about harmonizing these statements scattered over the years in a variety of articles and books. Then, too, the problem itself is complex, for, although he distinguishes philosophy from theology, as he admits, "this distinction is not unambiguous."[93] He considers them as basically divergent, but partially convergent.[94] They are "not separated, and they are not identical, but they are correlated. . . ."[95] There is no necessary conflict between them, and if philosophers and theologians clash, it is because one or the other has left his proper domain. Nor is there any possible synthesis between them in the sense of a Christian philosophy, for they simply do not share a common basis.[96] Philosophy and theology in principle are essentially distinct, but in actual life they over-lap.[97] Their unity is emphasized when Tillich speaks of their "mutual immanence" as an actually, though fragmentarily, ful-filled eschatology. Their perfect, eschatological unity would be had when "the philosophical analysis of the structure of being-in-itself would be united with a theological expression of the meaning of being for us." But even then there is "a qualitative difference," for "unity does not exclude definitory distinction."[98] However, leaving behind these abstruse formulations, Tillich illustrates his practical attitude by the image of the boundary. He stands on the boundary between theology and philosophy; as a theologian he has sought to remain a philosopher, and as a philosopher he has sought to remain a theologian.[99] But a boundary not only divides; it is also the point of contact. In the last analysis, his tendency is to fuse rather than distinguish philosophy from theology, as the following quotation clearly indicates:

But the fact that metaphysics is directed towards being and its universal characteristics does not imply that it has no existential roots. It certainly has them, for the philosopher is a human being, and in every philosophical school human interests and passions are a driving force. No philosophy is without an ultimate concern in its background, whether this is acknowledged or denied. This makes the philosopher a theologian, always implicitly and sometimes explicitly.[100]

REFLECTIONS AND APPRAISAL

Tillich's theological method stands before us as an impressive piece of machinery: powerful in its simplicity, yet versatile in its subtle complexities. Innovations in design and the introduction of new accessories immediately catch the eye. Even the ordinary, substantial features take on a glint of novelty due to the over-all harmony of design and the vigor of conception which engineered it. The total impression is one of power and balance, shot through with a thrill of excitement about its expected performance.

Perhaps the most striking feature is the question-answer dialectic which constitutes the method of correlation. From Tillich's emphasis upon the question side of the dialectic it is obvious that he wants a theology which beats in rhythm with the pulse of modern life. His concern is that the Christian symbols speak to and be understood by man in his present existential situation. Tillich relies heavily upon philosophy to ensure the universality of the question, that is, its applicability to the majority of men. And to guarantee its profundity, to make certain that the question springs from the depth and not from the surface of existence, he employs ontology. Hence, he does not apologize when he uses the terms "metaphysics" and "ontology"; on the contrary, he exclaims emphatically, "One cannot escape ontology if one wants to know!"[101] This sets him apart from those philosophers who equate philosophy with some kind of logic or with epistemology, who are "always sharpening the knife of thought but never cutting," as he describes them.[102] Equally, his insistence on ontology removes him from those theologians who shun philosophy of any kind or who attempt to theologize in purely biblical categories. Ontology injects into his system a refreshing intellectual vigor and an antibody against narrowness. The result has been, as one commentator puts it, that "he has unquestionably made a great contribution to the revival of metaphysical thinking within Protestant circles in our day."[103]

This stress upon the philosophically formulated existential question is, without a doubt, one of the strong points of Tillich's theology. However, a considerable number of critics have voiced the fear that his philosophical question actually dominates his theological answer.[104] On the one hand, the objection testifies to his originality and modernity. Since the philosophical question represents man's here-and-now existential situation, it is novel, vibrant, demanding, and so tends to steal the spotlight from the theological symbols which have already been on the stage for several thousand years. But, on the other hand, the charge that the method of correlation distorts the gospel message by subordinating it to philosophy is indeed a serious one, for it threatens the very structure of the system. At this point we venture no opinion, but only introduce the problem in general terms; it must be pondered in the concrete context of specific philosophical questions and theological answers. For a serious objection has been raised, and it demands attention.

If we step around to view the other side of the method of correlation—the answering side—our gaze is arrested by several outstanding items. Perhaps the most attractive is Tillich's broad understanding of the sources of theology. Although he assigns the place of honor to the Bible, it is not the unique source. The theological source, adequately understood, includes the history of the church, of religion, and of culture, for these are the areas in which revelation is received and expressed. Both Protestants and Catholics alike can profit from this enrichment of the wellsprings of theology in order to avoid the impoverishment of a narrow biblicism or of a cramped clerical view of the history of salvation. It would be a superficial complaint to say that Tillich makes secular history a sacred source. He merely restores to theology its oft neglected historical perspective with an amplitude that surpasses the commonly accepted notion of tradition. Moreover, his realization of the historical and cultural perspective of revelation brings in its wake a sensitivity to religious aspirations outside his own milieu. For example, Tillich has managed to keep his theology open, at least a crack, to non-western cultures. This is manifest in his book *Christianity and the Encounter of the World Religions* and by the reception his work has received in Japan.[105]

Although his theory of method certainly incorporates the Bible, the further question arises as to what extent and how he uses it in his actual theologizing.[106] It is impossible to answer this question in this initial chapter, but it is useful to point it out early, for the matter can be settled only by observing the theologian at work. In a certain sense, the whole of Tillich's theology is exegesis, for he seeks to interpret the biblical symbols. Furthermore, he claims that, even if he does not employ biblical theology directly, "its influence is present in every part of the system."[107] True, he does not sprinkle his pages with biblical quotations, but such an omission does not necessarily mean that his thought is non-biblical. The real question is: How does he mesh the gears of exegesis and dogmatics? "Exegesis" is taken here not in the general sense of an interpretation of Christianity, but in the ordinary sense of detailed, critical studies of the text of the Bible. Not that Tillich, or any other systematic theologian, must necessarily perform exegesis himself. But the Bible is the main source of theology, and exegetes produce mountains of information about what it meant to people at the time its books were composed. How are the results of this exegesis to be related to dogmatics, or, to put it another way, what connection is there between the meaning of the Bible for the inhabitants of the biblical world and the meaning of the Bible for us today? The question touches upon the much discussed contemporary problem of theological hermeneutics and the development of dogma.[108] Tillich is not a participant in this current debate on hermeneutics; in fact, according to the following statement in a highly regarded recent book on the subject, he is rather peremptorily excluded from it: "Tillich is not directly considered since theologies as heavily dependent as his upon classical theological and philosophical categories are not acceptable to the new hermeneutic."[109] Be that as it may, the relation of exegesis to dogmatics is a problem for any theologian who seriously takes the Bible as his source, and hence it is legitimate and instructive to observe how he uses it, especially if the theologian is as eminent as Tillich.

Considering again the answering side of the method of correlation, one discerns there a note of urgency which can be accounted for by the prominent role assigned to ultimate concern. Ultimate concern about being and non-being is what makes a man a theologian. Moreover, his theologizing is measured against the theological norm which is "the New Being in Jesus as the Christ as our ultimate concern."[110] And, finally, the medium which links the theologian to his sources is the experience of being grasped by the ultimate concern manifested in the revelatory events. Although this buildup is more than enough to attract notice to ultimate concern, Tillich rivets attention upon it when, in discussing the credentials of the theologian, he states that "it depends on his being ultimately concerned with the Christian message even if he is sometimes inclined to attack and to reject it."[111] The same theme is enlarged upon in his sermon "The Theologian" in which the man who "is estranged from the Christian church and its foundation" and who doubts the gospel message is, nonetheless, a theologian if he asks the theological question, "the question of an ultimate concern and its manifestation in Jesus as the Christ."[112]

Ultimate concern appears to be not just an accessory gadget, but the mainspring of the system. Yet it is puzzling how ultimate concern can sometimes lead a theologian "to attack and to reject" the Christian message. The following chapter will delve into this difficult topic more deeply, but we wish to underline from the beginning its cardinal importance.

As we step back to look at the *ensemble* of Tillich's method of existential questions and theological answers, we are impressed by its energetic vitality, a vitality that springs from relevance. The apologetic nature of theology and the method of correlation engage him in an immediate contact with the spiritual problems of his day. Criticism has been voiced about the adequacy of the method, and there is, of course, room for disagreement about the precise nature of man's existential situation. But at least Tillich's method forces him to grapple with it. He cannot be accused of irrelevancy. For this reason one is encouraged in the expectation that his methodology will yield significant results for the relating of religion to culture.

Notes

1. Cf. "On the Boundary: An Autobiographical Sketch," introductory essay in IH; "Author's Introduction" in PE; "Autobiographical Reflections" in K and B; "The Conquest of Intellectual Provincialism: Europe and America" in TC; "Frontiers" in *The Future of Religions,* Jerald C. Brauer (ed.), New York: Harper & Row, 1966, 52–63.

2. *"Dimensionen, Schichten, und die Einheit des Seins,"* Vortrag im *Nordwestdeutschen Rundfunk,* March 26, 1959, found in GW, IV, 118–29. The same subject is treated in ST, III, 12–17.

3. GW, IV, 122.

4. *Ibid.,* 123.

5. IH, 4.

6. *Ibid.,* 22–24; "Autobiographical Reflections," K and B, 8.

7. Quoted in *Time,* March 16, 1959, 47.

8. *Ibid.*

9. "Autobiographical Reflections," K and B, 11–12.

10. *Ibid.,* 17–18; TC, 169–70; PE, vi.

11. "Autobiographical Reflections," K and B, 3.

12. Quoted in *Time,* March 16, 1959, 47.

13. PE, xiii.

14. His theory of history appeared piecemeal in a wide range of articles which for the most part can be found in IH, PE, and GW, VI. Its principles are systematically presented in ST, III.

15. PE, unabridged ed., 245–47.

16. IH, 201.

17. See GW, II, 219–365.

18. PE, unabridged ed., 239.

19. *Ibid.,* 262.

20. PE, xxv.

21. "Autobiographical Reflections," K and B, 21.

22. Cf. "The Conquest of Intellectual Provincialism: Europe and America," TC, 159–76.

23. *Ibid.,* 161.

24. *Ibid.,* 163.

25. *Ibid.,* 168.

26. IH, 31.

27. GW, I, 9; GW, IV, 133; "Reply to Gustave Weigel" in O'M and W, 23.

28. Cf. Daniel J. O'Hanlon, *The Influence of Schelling on the Thought of Paul Tillich,* Gregorian University: dissertation, 1957; Günter Friedrich Sommer, *The Significance of the Late Philosophy of Schelling for the Formation and Interpretation of the Thought of Paul Tillich,* Duke University: dissertation, 1960.

29. Frederick Copleston, *A History of Philosophy,* VII, London: Burns & Oates, 1963, 11, 99.

30. Paul Tillich, *Die religionsgeschichtliche Konstruktion in Schellings positiver Philosophie, ihre Voraussetzungen und Prinzipien* (Universität Breslau, Dissertation), Breslau: H. Fleischmann, 1910, 3, 43, 50–51.

31. Paul Tillich, *Mystik und Schuldbewusstsein in Schellings Philosophischer Entwicklung* (Universität Halle, Dissertation, 1912) in GW, I, 13–17.

32. IH, 60.

33. *Ibid.,* 61.

34. *Ibid.,* 64–65.

35. "Autobiographical Reflections," K and B, 13.

36. TC, 112–26. Peter Homans makes a fascinating attempt to relate psychology and religion by relating Freud to Tillich in terms of transference and transcendence. Cf. "Transference and Transcendence: Freud and Tillich on the Nature of Personal Relatedness," *The Journal of Religion,* XLVI, January, 1966, No. 1, Part II, 148–64. See also Tillich's "Rejoinder," *Ibid.,* 194–96.

37. "Autobiographical Reflections," K and B, 14.

38. IH, 34.

39. "Autobiographical Reflections," K and B, 6.

40. Cf. ST, I, 215–16; Paul Tillich, "Rechtfertigung und Zweifel," *Vorträge der Theologischen Konferenz zu Giessen,* N. 39, Giessen: Alfred Töpelmann, 1924, 28; Paul Tillich, "Die Kategorie des 'Heiligen' bei Rudolf Otto," *Theologische Blätter* (Leipzig), II, January, 1923, 11–12.

41. Paul Tillich, *Morality and Beyond,* New York: Harper and Row, 1963, 64.

42. See Paul Tillich, "Denker der Zeit: Der Religionsphilosoph Rudolf Otto," *Vossische Zeitung* (Berlin), No. 308, July 2, 1925.

43. RS, 215. See also GW, I, 375.

44. IH, 32, Cf. also PE, ix–x.

45. IH, 32.

46. *Ibid.,* 54 .

47. "Autobiographical Reflections," K and B, 13.

48. IH, 7–8.

49. *Ibid.,* 6–7.

50. "Autobiographical Reflections," K and B, 6–7.

51. IH, 15–17.

52. "Art and Ultimate Reality," *Cross Currents,* X, No. 1, 1960, 1–14.

53. ST, I, 8, 11, 34, 60.

54. Tillich's most complete and most recent exposition of his method is in ST, I, 3–68, although he treats it in other writings. Cf. "Uber die Idee einer Theologie der Kultur," *Philosophische Vorträge der Kant-Gesellschaft,* No. 24, Berlin: Reuther und Reichard, 1919, 28–52 (hereinafter referred to as "Theologie der Kultur"); *Das System der Wissenschaften nach Gegen-*

ständen und Methoden in GW, I, 271–77; IH, 30–41; "Philosophy and Theology" in PE, 83–93; "The Problem of Theological Method," *Journal of Religion*, XXVII, No. 1, January, 1947, 16–26, reprinted in *Four Existentialist Theologians*, Will Herberg (ed.), New York: Doubleday, paperback ed., 1958, 238–55; sermon "The Theologian" in SF, 118–129; "Reply to Interpretation and Criticism" in K and B, 329–49; and the whole of BR.

55. ST, I, 3–8.
56. See "The Theologian," SF, 126–27.
57. ST, I, 8–11.
58. *Ibid.*, 10.
59. NB, 152–60.
60. DF, 1–3; ST, I, 11–12; NB, 153–57.
61. ST, I, 13.
62. *Ibid.*; DF, 1–2.
63. ST, I, 215.
64. DF, 16.
65. ST, I, 11–15.
66. *Ibid.*, 29, 34–40.
67. Avery R. Dulles situates Tillich's use of Scripture within his system in an excellent article, "Paul Tillich and the Bible," *Theological Studies*, XVII, 1956, 345–67, reprinted in O'M and W, 109–32.
68. In *Systematic Theology* Tillich conspicuously avoids the term "tradition" in discussing the sources of theology. However, in an earlier article he freely employs it: "Positively, the Tradition shows the questions implied in the Christian message, the main possibilities of answers, and the points in which Christians have agreed and have disagreed. Negatively, the Tradition shows answers which have been characterized by the church as 'heretical.' He who takes the Tradition seriously must take heresies seriously. . . . This, of course, should not prevent anyone from following his theological conscience (as Luther did in Worms); but it should sharpen that conscience." "The Problem of Theological Method," in Herberg (ed.), *Four Existentialist Theologians*, 246.
69. ST, I, 40–46.
70. See "Reply" in K and B, 331.
71. Tillich barely touches on the positive purpose of the medium in ST, I, 40–46, but he expands on it considerably more in "The Problem of Theological Method," Herberg (ed.), *Four Existentialist Theologians*, 247–49.
72. ST, I, 47–52.
73. *Ibid.*, 49.
74. *Ibid.*, 50.
75. *Ibid.*, 50–52.
76. ST, I, 60. Cf. pp. 59–66 for the method of correlation. Also ST, II, 13–16.
77. ST, I, 64.

78. ST, II, 16.

79. GW, V, 231, 237. See also DF, 41–54. Tillich places myth in the basic category of symbol; it is a group of symbols arranged in a story which is, in turn, a symbol.

80. ST, I, 21; ST, II, 11–12. Robert P. Scharlemann's stimulating article describes Tillichian theological language as follows: "Religious assertions are symbolic (referring to the depth of being), ontological assertions are literal (referring to the structure of being), and theological assertions are literal descriptions of the correlation between the religious symbols and the ontological concepts." Thus, correlation speaks a "theontological language." "Tillich's Method of Correlation: Two Proposed Revisions," *The Journal of Religion*, XLVI, January, 1966, No. 1, Part II (special issue in honor of Paul Tillich), 93, 102. In the "Rejoinder" accompanying the article, Tillich accepts this formulation. *Ibid.*, 184.

81. TC, 53–67. GW, V, 187–244 has a whole section containing five essays on religious symbolism.

82. ST, I, 62–63. Cf. also Paul Tillich, "Existential Analyses and Religious Symbols" in *Contemporary Problems in Religion*, Harold A. Basilius (ed.), Detroit: Wayne University Press, 1956, 35–55, reprinted in *Four Existentialist Theologians*, Herberg (ed.), 277–91.

83. BR, vii. Cf. also ST, I, 21 and ST, II, 12.

84. PE, 83.

85. BR, 5. In his earlier works Tillich defines philosophy as "the science of the principles of meaning, i.e., of the functions and categories that impart meaning." GW, I, 232. To trace the evolution of this early definition into the later ones is too complex to be undertaken here, nor does it seem necessary.

86. DF, 90.

87. ST, I, 18.

88. Cf. PE, 83–93; ST, I, 18–28.

89. ST, I, 230.

90. LPJ, 107

91. ST, I, 24–26.

92. ST, II, 30–31.

93. "The Problem of Theological Method," *Four Existentialist Theologians*, Herberg (ed.), 240.

94. PE, 88.

95. *Ibid.*, xxii.

96. ST, I, 26–28.

97. DF, 91, 94. This particular statement is curious because it reverses the usual Tillichian principle of essential unity and existential separation.

98. "Reply," K and B, 336–37.

99. IH, 40–41.

100. Paul Tillich, "Relation of Metaphysics and Theology," *The Review of Metaphysics*, X, Sept., 1956, 59.

101. LPJ, 20. See also RS, 79–83. Throughout this work we employ the terms "ontology" and "metaphysics" as synonymous for the science of being as being. In one place Tillich distinguishes them, but the force of his distinction is not immediately apparent. He asks, "How is ontology distinguished from what has been called metaphysics? The answer is that ontology is the foundation of metaphysics, but not metaphysics itself. . . . Ontology is descriptive, not speculative. It tries to find out what the basic structures of being are. . . . It separates those elements of the real which are generic or particular from those elements which are constitutive for everything that is and therefore are universal. It leaves the former to the special sciences or to metaphysical constructions; it elaborates the latter through critical analysis." LPJ, 23.

102. PE, 89.

103. Dulles, "Paul Tillich and the Bible," O'M and W, 124.

104. Some bluntly charge that by trimming Christianity to fit the pattern of existentialism, Tillich subordinates theology to philosophy. See Killen, *The Ontological Theology of Paul Tillich*, 7–8, and George S. Hendry, "Review of Tillich's *Systematic Theology*, Vol. II," *Theology Today*, XV, April, 1958, 83. Avery Dulles observes: "But he does not sufficiently purify his philosophical categories in the light of the revealed message. Instead, he lets the exigencies of his philosophical system determine in advance what God's revelation can and cannot be. The biblical message is reduced to the dimensions of an all-too-human philosophy." "Paul Tillich and the Bible," O'M and W, 131. John C. Bennett says that Tillich "surrounds the Christian revelation with an ontology which seems . . . to dominate the revelation and to distort it." Cf. "A Protestant View of Authority in the Church," *Theology Digest*, XI, No. 4, 1963, 212. And even James Luther Adams, student and disciple of Tillich, admits there is room for doubt: "Yet one is frequently left wondering, Is this supposed to be Christian doctrine, or is this Tillichian philosophy, or has Tillich read his philosophy into the Christian terms?" Cf. *Paul Tillich's Philosophy of Culture, Science, and Religion*, 260. A recent, massive study of his apologetic theology finds many positive values in it, but concludes that he underplays the kerygmatic side of theology and overplays the ontological interpretation of revelation. Cf. Josef Schmitz, *Die apologetische Theologie Paul Tillichs*, Mainz: Matthias-Grünewald-Verlag, 1966, 271. Gordon D. Kaufman's statement sums up these objections: "There may well be a correlation and interdependence between philosophy and theology, but it is not the correlation of question and answer." Cf. "Can a Man Serve Two Masters?" *Theology Today*, XV, April, 1958, 64.

105. At least five of Tillich's books and several articles have been translated into Japanese, and he has established numerous contacts with Japanese intellectuals.

106. One author remarks: "If the Bible is the 'basic source,' why should it not be used more explicitly? Is not Tillich's failure to refer to it more often

likely to lead some of its readers to deny that at crucial points his theology is really based upon the Bible?" George F. Thomas, "The Method and Structure of Tillich's Theology," K and B, 95. See also Killen, *The Ontological Theology of Paul Tillich*, 117.

107. ST, III, 4.

108. See René Marlé, *Le Problème Théologique de l'Herméneutique,* Paris: Editions de l'Orante, 1963, and Herbert Vorgrimler (ed.), *Dogmatic Versus Biblical Theology,* London: Burns & Oates, 1964 (translation of *Exegese und Dogmatik,* Mainz: Matthias-Grünewald-Verlag, 1962).

109. John Dillenberger, "On Broadening the New Hermeneutic," in James M. Robinson and John B. Cobb, Jr. (eds.), *The New Hermeneutic,* Vol. II of *New Frontiers in Theology,* New York: Harper & Row, 1964, 147.

110. ST, I, 50.

111. *Ibid.,* 10.

112. SF, 121. Cf. also PE, x–xi.

2/Faith and Religion:
The Experience of the Holy

THE MOMENT or act in which one is grasped by the holy is described by Tillich "as in a thunderstorm at night, when the lightning throws a blinding clarity over all things, leaving them in complete darkness the next moment." Reality is seen as something new. "Its ground has become visible in an 'ecstatic' experience, called 'faith.' "[1] This chapter will examine first his concept of faith, and then of religion and revelation, since all three notions are offshoots from the same root, namely, ultimate concern as the experience of the holy. Our purpose is to get to the core of Tillich's understanding of religion and to appreciate its complexities and ramifications.

The first task is to discover what Tillich means by faith. Since ultimate concern was discussed at some length in the previous chapter, the introduction to his concept of faith has already been made, for he equates faith with ultimate concern: "Faith is a total and centered act of the personal self, the act of unconditional, infinite and ultimate concern."[2] Although the following exposition speaks of faith, at every step of the way it elucidates the meaning of ultimate concern, because they are one and the same thing.

At this point it is useful to introduce Tillich's distinction between the subjective and objective sides of faith. Since "somebody is concerned [subjective side] about something he considers of concern [objective side]," one can speak of the act of faith and the content of faith, the *fides qua creditur* and the *fides quae creditur*.[3] The precise understanding and validity of this distinction is taken up later. Here it merely serves as a handy device to block out the matter treated.

SUBJECTIVE SIDE OF FAITH

Under subjective faith will be discussed faith as a centered act, the passive character of faith, its certainty, faith and the unconditional, the universality of faith, and, finally, faith and atheism.

Faith a Centered Act

Faith is ultimate concern or "infinite passion," as Tillich sometimes puts it in recognition of Kierkegaard's insight.[4] Consequently, its all-consuming urgency requires that it be "an act of the total personality." Faith is not a special faculty nor is it a special function of man's being. Faith involves the whole person, and thus it is the integrating factor which gives unity and direction to all man's other concerns. "In the act of faith every nerve of man's body, every striving of man's soul, every function of man's spirit participates." An infinite passion is all-pervading, and no area of man's being can escape it: his body, for ultimate concern is passionate concern; his unconscious strivings, for they relate to the symbolic expression of faith; his conscious life, for faith concentrates man's activities upon the object of ultimate concern. Because faith is such a centered act, its identification with any one function leads to what Tillich calls the intellectualistic, voluntaristic, or emotionalistic distortion of faith.[5]

Passive Character of Faith

Since faith cannot spring from any of man's spiritual functions, but implies a power which unites and transcends all of them, Tillich lists as one of the primary notes of faith "its receptive character, its mere passivity in relation to the divine Spirit." This accords with "the basic theological truth that in relation to God everything is by God." Man's spiritual functions cannot attain the ultimate, although they tend toward it, "but the ultimate can grasp all of these functions and raise them beyond themselves by the creation of faith."[6] Although faith is in man, it is not from man.

The metaphor used by Tillich to intimate the passive character of faith is that of "being grasped." "Faith is the state of being grasped by an ultimate concern."[7] In contrast to this, "faith healing" is a psychological phenomenon of autosuggestion which "emphasizes an act of intensive concentration and self-determination."[8] Nothing could be farther from the receptive character of genuine religious faith, "the state of being grasped by the Spirit."

Certainty of Faith

Once a person has been grasped by the power of the ultimate, he possesses an absolute certainty of the fact which springs from an immediate awareness of it. In ecstasy, anxiety, and even in despair, he is as certain of the experience of the holy as he is of his own self. In fact, "it *is* the self in its self-transcending quality."[9] All this, of course, is on the subjective side of faith, for objectively there is always room for doubt about the content of faith.

In his sermon "Faith and Uncertainty" Tillich struggles to reconcile the assertive, confident nature of Luther's idea of faith with the low-pressure, sceptical attitude of the modern mind. The conflict is resolved by maintaining the subjective certainty of faith, while placing the source of this certitude outside the individual in accordance with the passive character of faith. "We may not grasp anything in the depth of our uncertainty, but that we are grasped by something ultimate, which keeps us in its grasp and from which we may strive in vain to escape, remains absolutely certain."[10]

Faith and the Unconditional

The power which grasps the individual in the experience of faith is the quality of the "unconditional," a term often used by Tillich in describing faith and ultimate concern. To explain faith as unconditional concern, the division between subjective and objective faith must be infringed upon to a certain extent. Unconditional or ultimate concern, subjectively, is a concern that demands total involvement, as pointed out in the section on faith as a centered act. However, the unconditional, absolute character of the demand stems from the unconditionality of the object of faith. Therefore, Tillich sometimes employs "unconditional" to refer to the subjective, absolute aspect of the concern of faith, while at other times the term refers to unconditioned meaning and being, i.e., God in the Tillichian sense. The context should be a sufficient guide to the intended use.

From the outset, a warning flag must be attached to the phrase "object of faith," for Tillich repeatedly insists that "the unconditioned" or the "unconditional" is not a being, but a quality:

The power grasping us in the state of faith is not a being beside others, not even the highest; it is not an object among objects, not even the greatest; but it is a quality of all beings and objects, the quality of pointing beyond themselves and their finite existence to the infinite, inexhaustible, and unapproachable depth of their being and meaning.[11]

Here, then, we are principally interested in that quality of things which unconditionally grips man's spirit. A fuller exposition of that toward which this quality points, the "depth of their being and meaning," is presented in our fourth chapter.

Tillich's use of the term "unconditional" becomes clearer if we recall his German origin. The German equivalent for unconditional is *unbedingt,* the connotation being that something is conditioned or limited by being made into a thing (*Ding*).[12] Thus, the unconditional (*das Unbedingte*) is not "thingish" at all, but rather "a quality which we experience in encountering reality."[13]

Before Tillich began to write in English, he elaborated his concepts of faith and religion in terms of *das Unbedingte*. The ordinary English rendering is "unconditioned" or "unconditional," but Tillich more often prefers "ultimate concern," not as a translation, but as an equivalent. Besides the fact that "ultimate concern" neatly ties in the subjective and objective aspects of faith, we hazard the opinion that he feels the English "unconditional" does not explicitly enough exclude "thingishness" as does the German *unbedingt*. Consequently, it will be enlightening to examine his presentation of faith in his earlier German works under the rubric of "the unconditional." That this is a sound procedure for probing more deeply into his basic ideas is indicated by the fact that the German translation for ultimate concern is *was uns unbedingt angeht* (what concerns us unconditionally).[14]

In his *Religionsphilosophie*, published in 1925, Tillich defines faith as "the tendency toward the unconditional" (*die Richtung auf das Unbedingte*).[15] Since faith is effective in all of man's spiritual functions, both theoretical and practical, it cannot be identified with any one of them. Faith comes to expression in these functions, and they, in turn, are rooted in faith.

Tendency toward the unconditional must be understood in connection with the concept of *Sinn*, which is best translated into English by "meaning" and into French by *sens*. Tillich institutes an analysis of *Sinn* and, since it is an unending circle to inquire about the meaning of meaning, he contents himself with presenting the elements of meaning as they appear in consciousness. They are three: (1) a complex of meaning (*Sinnzusammenhang*) in which stands every individual meaning; (2) the meaningfulness of this overall complex, i.e., an unconditioned meaning which is present in the whole and in individuals; (3) a demand (*Forderung*) upon every individual meaning to fulfill unconditional meaning.[16] In relation to the universal complex of meaning, individual meanings and relationships are called forms of meaning

(*Sinnformen*), and unconditioned meaning is called the content of meaning (*Sinngehalt*). In other words, the relation of unconditioned meaning to individual things must be understood as a polarity of form and content. This polarity stands in constant tension, for the unconditional never ceases to demand fulfilment in what would be an unconditioned form. However, unconditioned form is a contradictory notion impossible of realization, for the ground of meaning (*Sinngrund*) is also the abyss of meaning (*Sinnabgrund*) which transcends every form. The inexhaustibility of meaning (*Sinnunerschöpflichkeit*) would be rendered finite if it could be contained in a form. Nonetheless, each act of meaning must hearken to the demand that it strive to bring form and content to a unity of fulfilment.[17]

Two points are to be underscored in this theory of *Sinn*: the unconditional is meaning, and in the act of faith one tends toward it, but not as toward an object, since meaning is not an object or thing. One turns to a holy object in which the unconditional is symbolically expressed, but then faith passes beyond this object to the ground and abyss upon which it rests.[18]

Abstract and difficult though it be, Tillich's analysis of "faith in the unconditioned meaning of life" makes it a very human issue. For "unless some spark of that faith is present, there can be no spirit, for to live spiritually is to live in the presence of meaning, and without an ultimate meaning everything disappears into the abyss of meaninglessness."[19] Faith is unconditional, absolute, and ultimate, because without it man ceases to live as man.

Universality of Faith

If faith strikes a chord so deep in human nature, the question can be posed: Is faith universal? To answer it, Tillich distinguishes two definitions of faith: the formal and the material. "The formal definition is valid for every kind of faith in all religions and cultures. Faith, formally or generally defined, is the state of being grasped by that toward which self-transcendence aspires, the ultimate in being and meaning." This formal or universal definition of faith is particularized in the material definition of faith which is the Christian faith, "the state of being grasped by the New Being as it is manifest in Jesus as the Christ." Tillich is interested here in formal faith, for material faith broaches the questions of Christology and the uniqueness of Christianity, problems to be discussed later. Besides, whatever is said of formal faith applies to material faith, although the reverse is not true, because material faith contributes a specification not found in formal faith. It suffices for the present to say that Tillich reconciles the two definitions by holding that Christianity, as the particular (material) definition of faith, "expresses the fulfilment toward which all forms of faith are driven."[20]

The note of universality enters through the formal definition of faith, for "in this formal sense of faith as ultimate concern, every human being has faith."[21] Every human spirit drives toward the unconditional in the direction of self-transcendence. "He who is not able to perceive something ultimate, something infinitely significant, is not a man."[22] Faith is a universal "human potentiality" because the human heart is aware that it is ordered to the infinite, but is not yet in possession of it.[23] The seeds of faith are sown in the restlessness of man's spirit, his striving to transcend the stream of transitory, preliminary concerns in which he is submerged.

Thus, the state of being ultimately concerned is "a state which is universally human, whatever the content of the concern may be."[24] Of course, the content of ultimate concern can be demonically distorted so that faith becomes idolatrous faith, but it remains faith despite this ambiguity. "Our ultimate concern can destroy us as it can heal us, but we never can be without it."[25]

Faith and Atheism

If, as Tillich proposes, "God is the fundamental symbol for what concerns us ultimately," then the universality of faith seems to undercut the very possibility of atheism. For when a so-called atheist denies God, he does so in the name of another ultimate concern. In other words, "God can be denied only in the name of God," since, for Tillich, "ultimate" and "God" are interchangeable. Therefore, he concludes that the only logical type of atheism would be complete lack of ultimate concern, that is, total indifference to the meaning of one's existence, and he rates the possibility of such an attitude as very problematic.[26] Some people try to maintain a "cynical unconcern." But "the cynic is concerned, passionately concerned, about one thing, namely his unconcern."[27]

However, in several early works Tillich sets up a distinction between what could be called essential atheism and intentional atheism.[28] Essentially, *Form* cannot exist without *Gehalt* (content); the holy and the secular are essentially united. Consequently, essential atheism simply cannot exist, as explained above. However, the mind can consciously exclude any reference to the unconditional and remain at the level of conditioned forms. Such a decision would be intentional atheism, as exemplified in an attitude of cultural autonomy.

Yet Tillich never seems to urge this distinction, and, in effect, he denies the possibility of even intentional atheism, as when he strips Marx and Sartre of their atheistic badges and declares that they are humanists trying to respond to the question of existence "from hidden religious sources," and that their answers are "matters of ultimate concern or faith, although garbed in a secular gown."[29] In the final reckoning, faith as ultimate concern is so broad and so deep that "genuine atheism is not humanly possible," for "even the atheists stand in God—namely, that power out of which they live, the truth for which they grope, and the ultimate meaning of life in which they believe."[30]

In view of the radical universality of faith, Tillich postulates new categories for viewing history. The traditional view of world history as "the battlefield between faith and un-faith" must yield to a new view which sees faith versus faith, or, more precisely, faith versus idolatrous faith.[31] Once one can speak seriously of "secular faith," the implications for the relation of religion and culture are enormous.[32]

OBJECTIVE SIDE OF FAITH

Under this heading is considered the content of faith; doubt, risk, and anxiety; faith and courage; and the truth of faith and the Protestant principle.

Content of Faith

Although Tillich states that "there is no faith without a content toward which it is directed," as has been seen, the unconditional which is the object of ultimate concern is not an object in the sense of a thing or a being.[33] The name or symbol for that which concerns man ultimately is "God." But lest the usual theistic understanding of God obscure his meaning, Tillich hastens to explain that God does not first exist and then demand that man be ultimately concerned about him. Rather, whatever concerns man ultimately is god for him.[34]

Symbols are the language of faith, for ultimate concern must be expressed concretely and yet transcendently. The basic symbol of faith is God, but there can be others—for example, the divine attributes of power, justice, and love.[35] And if the word "God" no longer has meaning, Tillich exhorts us to "translate it, and speak of the depths of your life, of the source of your being, of your ultimate concern, of what you take seriously without any reservation . . . of the depth of history, of the ground and aim of our social life. . . ."[36] Perhaps one has to forget the word "God" altogether in order to comprehend what God is. The issue at stake is not the existence of God, but rather which symbol is most adequate to express the content of faith. In an argument with Einstein, Tillich defends the symbol "Personal God," but his final explanation of it reverts to the "ground and abyss of being and meaning."[37]

Doubt and Justification by Faith

The concreteness of the content of faith brings in its wake doubt, risk, and anxiety. Elementary psychology dictates a direct ratio between concreteness and concern; one can be far more concerned about a concrete object than an abstract one. But the more concretely the content of faith is expressed in a symbol, the greater is the possibility of error, for the element of absoluteness, of transcendence, may be edged out. A preliminary concern, so alluring in its concreteness, may become the content of faith. Nor do we enjoy any immediate awareness that the content to which faith has committed us is truly ultimate. Consequently, doubt is "an element which was always and will be always present in the act of faith."[38] This doubt is neither methodological doubt, which is a mode of scientific inquiry, nor sceptical doubt, which is really a cloak for concealed faith. It is existential doubt arising from the tension between the ultimacy of concern and the concreteness of content.

To complement the appearance of doubt, mention must be made also of risk and anxiety. While Tillich often speaks of doubt in regard to faith's incertitude, just as frequently he uses "risk" to include both objective doubt about the concrete content of faith and subjective commitment to it.[39] Risk is decision for the uncertain. Anxiety is a much broader concept, and, in fact, Tillich builds an ontology of anxiety. In this ontological sense, "anxiety is the existential awareness of nonbeing." Nonbeing can threaten in several different ways. The way it threatens man's spiritual life is by the "anxiety of meaninglessness," an anxiety "aroused by the loss of a spiritual center, of an answer, however symbolic and indirect, to the question of the meaning of existence."[40]

In his essay "Rechtfertigung und Zweifel," published in 1924, Tillich describes the condition of the doubter or sceptic (*der Zweifler*).[41] The doubter has lost God, truth, and the meaning of life, but he cannot rest in this loss, for he encounters the demand to find what he has lost. He is gripped by the relentless power of truth, and, since he cannot fulfill the law of truth, he falls into despair. He doubts about his salvation, except that in his case loss of salvation is not the divine sentence of condemnation, but the abyss of meaninglessness. Radical doubt is not an ethical problem of flight from God. It is the struggle for participation in the unconditioned meaning of life.

The justification of the doubter (*die Rechtfertigung des Zweiflers*) paradoxically is accomplished by faith. For faith is ultimate concern, not the acceptance of theological truths, even truths about God and Christ. It is legalism to insist upon adoption of creedal beliefs before God grants justification.[42] Tillich considers it to have been a major step in his theological development when he applied a radically conceived principle of justification by faith to the "religious-intellectual life." Not only the sinner, but the doubter, too, is saved by faith, by his ultimate concern. The more serious the doubt and the more despairing the doubter, the greater is his concern for the meaning of life. "This unconditional seriousness is the expression of the presence of the divine in the experience of utter separation from it."[43] Faith is found in the depths of doubt.

To put Tillich's idea of doubt in its proper context, attention is called to the fact that he intends to analyze the structure of faith, not describe an actual state of mind. Consequently, "doubt is not a permanent experience within the act of faith. But it is always present as an element in the structure of faith."[44] Similarly, extreme anxiety is not a common occurrence, "but the rare occasions in which it is present determine the interpretation of existence as a whole."[45]

Courage and Absolute Faith

Doubt, risk, and anxiety—inherent elements of faith—can be overcome only by another of its elements, courage. Courage, for Tillich, is an ontological concept, "the self-affirmation of being in spite of the fact of nonbeing."[46] Here we pass over its broader ontological aspects and consider it only in connection with faith. Faith is the experience of the holy; it is the state of being grasped by the power of being-itself. From this experience flows the power to assert oneself in the face of anxiety. Faith is participation in the object of faith, and yet is separation from it. In spite of separation, courage expresses participation in the power of being and meaning. This "in spite of" element is the courage that takes all doubt, risk, and anxiety into itself and overcomes them without removing them. Faith, then, is the basis of courage, and courage is the manifestation of faith.[47]

In the extreme situation of a person seized by radical doubt and confronted with the specter of universal meaninglessness, the question arises: Is there such a thing as the courage of despair? Tillich answers that such courage is entirely possible, for "the act of accepting meaninglessness is in itself a meaningful act."[48] The courage of despair enables one, even while in the grip of meaninglessness, to declare one's situation, and this declaration has meaning. In other words, if we understand Tillich correctly, there cannot be an infinite regression of negatives—in this case, negativity of meaning. At least, one has to admit, negation of meaning is meaningful, or meaninglessness will have lost all meaning.

The faith which feeds the courage of despair is called "absolute faith," for it can have no specific content. Its content is indefinable, "since everything defined is dissolved by doubt and meaninglessness." However, certain elements that constitute absolute faith can be discerned. There is an experience of the power of being in the face of nonbeing, an awareness of "a hidden meaning within the destruction of meaning." There is the dependence of nonbeing upon being, of meaninglessness upon meaning, of the negative upon the positive. And, lastly, there is the acceptance of the power to accept meaninglessness. Thus, absolute faith is "faith which has been deprived by doubt of any concrete content, which nevertheless is faith and the source of the most paradoxical manifestation of the courage to be."[49]

Tillich, however, cannot refrain from attempting to delineate the object of absolute faith. He claims that "it is without a *special* content, yet it is not without content. The content of absolute faith is the 'God above God.' " When people speak of God, they usually refer to the God of theism. Now theism can mean either a vague, unspecified affirmation of God, or a divine-human encounter of persons, or theological theism which makes God a being beside other beings. But the God of absolute faith is above and beyond the God of any theism, for the God above God is the power of being-itself. Consequently, the courage of despair stems from absolute faith as the experience of "the God who appears when God has disappeared in the anxiety of doubt."[50]

Truth of Faith and the Protestant Principle

The problem of the truth of faith presents itself from both the subjective and objective sides. Subjectively, faith is true "if it adequately expresses an ultimate concern," that is, if the symbols of faith are alive and speak to the heart with an urgency of concern that impels to action and reply. Tillich admits that this criterion is more a rule of thumb that works best for "obviously dead symbols" and is not so useful in judging contemporary ones. However, it is the objective truth of faith that interests us here. The content of faith is true if it is really and not just apparently ultimate. The great danger is demonization, elevation of the symbol to ultimacy, which results in idolatrous faith. Therefore, the criterion of faith is self-negation. The true symbol not only conveys the ultimate, but proclaims its own non-ultimacy. It pronounces a Yes and a No. For the Christian the Cross of the Christ is such a symbol. Tillich's name for this criterion—the No that follows immediately on the heels of the Yes—is "the Protestant principle."[51]

The Protestant principle pervades the whole of Tillich's theology, both systematically and chronologically. Chameleon-like, it changes its formula of expression against the background of di-

verse theological problems. Hence, a rapid rundown of its various
formulations is useful for identifying it. In succeeding chapters its
function will be pointed out whenever it is operative in a specific
question.

In addition to being the objective criterion of faith, the Protestant principle expresses man's infinite distance from God and
his dependence upon the divine initiative.[52] The Protestant principle is the prophetic protest against every form of self-absolutiz-
ing—for example, the demonic elevation of the churches, of the
Bible, and of the priesthood to absolute validity.[53] The Protestant
principle is "resistance to idolatry," that is, it stands for non-con-
formity in family, school, state, and church.[54] The Protestant principle protests the objectifying of grace (*die Vergegenständlichung
der Gnade*) and so smashes the barriers between the holy and the
secular.[55] For, by the Protestant principle, God is as near to the
lowest as he is to the highest, as close to the material as to
the spiritual.[56]

These manifold expressions of the Protestant principle can be
summarized in and derived from Tillich's basic doctrine that the
Protestant principle is "justification by grace through faith." He
rejects the traditional Protestant formula of "justification by faith"
on the grounds that it has been misunderstood to mean that the
human act of faith sets in motion God's justifying act. He insists
that faith itself is a gift of grace, that all justifying action is entirely on the part of God, and, consequently, that the more accurate formula is "justification by grace through faith."[57] The
Protestant principle ultimately rests upon "an experience of God's
majesty" that attributes absoluteness and holiness to him alone
and denies such dignity to all else.[58]

THE EXPERIENCE OF THE HOLY

Tillich concedes that his separation of the subjective from the
objective side of faith is not a real distinction, but a "theoretical
isolation."[59] The reason for this is the peculiar nature of faith.

Certainly faith intends something, is directed toward a content. Yet, this content can never be attained except in the act of faith. Faith is grace, and it is only in the active grasp of the ultimate that the believer can be ultimately concerned. In other words, the subject-object structure breaks down, or, rather, is transcended, as when, for example, St. Paul points out that prayer is the Spirit of God praying within us.

The subjective and objective sides of faith are rejoined in the experience of the holy where faith is born when one is grasped by an ultimate concern. In one of his lectures Tillich puts the matter very simply:

The ultimate for which we ask when we ask the question about the meaning of our life is manifest to us in an experience which I believe every human being has, namely, the experience of the Holy. Something is holy to everybody. This doesn't mean that you must evaluate the religions which you know and meet and encounter here and there. But it does mean that there is something in life for which you would give your life. And that means what you take with ultimate seriousness. . . . But in the moment in which something is your ultimate concern, you make it into your God. And that's what God first of all means, the object, the content of your ultimate concern.[60]

We shall now examine, in detail, the experience of the holy.

Two Elements of the Holy

Since Tillich tells us that "holiness is an experienced phenomenon,"[61] his sermon, entitled "The Experience of the Holy," is a good point of departure. The text is the sixth chapter of Isaiah, the vocation of the prophet, in which "his experience of God is an experience of the holiness of God."[62] The prophet does not describe God himself, but speaks of the throne, the seraphim, and the smoke. The mysteriousness of God veils him even when he reveals himself. The prophet feels his annihilation is near; so do the seraphim who echo his feelings with the cry of "Holy, Holy,

Holy." A twofold meaning is expressed in their cry: majesty and purity. The "terrifying and annihilating encounter" with the majesty of God shakes the foundations, masking, yet revealing him. The purity of God implies the moral perfection, the goodness, truth, and justice of God which compels the prophet to confess with his whole being that he is unclean.

This concrete example indicates the two elements which constitute Tillich's notion of the holy: "The experience of the holy as being, and the experience of the holy as what ought to be."[63] According to the emphasis given to each, there arises either a mystically or an ethically orientated religion, as in the case of Buddhism and the Judeo-Christian religion. However, neither of these elements is ever completely lacking in any genuine experience of the holy, for "the holy has a double relation to man, a relation of giving presence and commanding transcendence."[64]

Furthermore, even within the Christian religion, Tillich contrasts Catholicism with Protestantism on the basis of the two elements of the holy. He maintains that man experiences the holy as a gift and as a demand. This leads to the holiness of the "is" and the holiness of the "ought," a sacramental religion and an eschatological religion, one served by priests and one served by prophets; in short, Catholicism and Protestantism. Yet, even while contrasting the elements of the holy, Tillich emphasizes that both are present in each religion, but in different degrees.[65]

Actual Holiness: the Ground and Abyss

When we examine the holiness of the "is," namely, actual holiness, or the present reality of the holy, we find that Tillich describes it in Otto's terms as the *mysterium tremendum et fascinosum*, "the experience of 'the ultimate' in the double sense of that which is the abyss and that which is the ground of man's being."[66] The *mysterium fascinosum* is the positive side of the holy; it attracts because, as the ground of being, it implies the fulfilment and beatitude of the creature. The negative side is the *mysterium tremendum* which terrifies because, as the abyss of being, it implies an infinite, unbridgeable distance between the finite and the infinite. In the ecstatic experience of revelation one feels both "the elevating power of the divine presence" and its "annihilating power."[67]

This experience of the actual holiness of God is further described in one of Tillich's sermons, "The Escape from God."[68] He remarks that "a man who has never tried to flee God has never experienced the God who is really God." The gods of our own making, fashioned after the image of man, are easy to live with, but "man cannot stand the God who is really God." "Man tries to escape God, and hates him, because he cannot escape him. The protest against God, the will that there be no God, and the flight to atheism are all genuine elements of profound religion." Such is the shaking power of the *mysterium tremendum*. However, the *mysterium* is also *fascinosum*, for, as Tillich says:

The eyes of the Witness we cannot stand are also the eyes of One of infinite wisdom and supporting benevolence. The centre of being, in which our own centre is involved, is the source of the gracious beauty which we encounter again and again in the stars and mountains, in flowers and animals, in children and mature personalities.[69]

The holy can be viewed not only from a phenomenological point of view, but also from an ontological one. In some of his early writings Tillich relates the holy to transcendent meaning, to *Sinn*. Unconditioned meaning, since it contains the meaning of individuals and of the whole, is the ground of meaning (*Sinngrund*). It is also the abyss of meaning (*Sinnabgrund*) because it transcends every individual meaning and cannot be fully grasped in any act of meaning. Unconditioned meaning is the *tremendum et fascinosum*, the abyss and the ground of the meaning of things, not only in so far as they are (*Seins-Sinn*), but also in so far as they ought to be (*Sollens-Sinn*).[70] Against this ontological background Tillich can say, "The holy is not unperceptible, but it is not objective. The holy is contemplated not as an object (*nicht*

gegenständlich); it is contemplated as transcendent meaning." To
be sure, there exist holy objects, but to see them as holy is to
grasp through them the meaning of the unconditioned.[71]

In his later writings Tillich shifts the emphasis from the holy
as unconditioned meaning to the holy as being-itself or the power
of being.[72] These concepts will be treated in a later chapter. Here
we merely note that Tillich's phenomenology of the holy is rooted
in an ontology centered around unconditioned meaning and being-
itself.

Moral Holiness: the Clean-Unclean

Thus far only one element in the experience of the holy has
been considered, the element of present actuality. The other
element, moral demand, is best approached via the notion of the
"clean-unclean." Tillich is well aware that the primitive idea of
the holy did not distinguish the clean from the unclean, the divine
from the demonic.[73] This distinction marks a later development
which saw morality take its place in the holy under the guise of
the clean.

The example of the vocation of Isaiah illustrates a turning point
in the history of the holy, for it was only under the impact of
prophetic criticism that the unclean was separated from the holy
and received the meaning of immoral. Before that, "the unclean
designated something demonic, something which produced taboos
and numinous awe." Tillich sees in later Calvinism an extreme example of the expulsion of the unclean from the holy and the identification of the holy with the morally clean, so that "cleanliness
becomes holiness, ... the *tremendum* becomes fear of the law and
of judgment; the *fascinosum* becomes pride of self-control and
repression."[74] Tillich is concerned lest this prophetic emphasis
upon the holy as the clean (the morally good) undermine the holy
as present reality to the detriment of the notion of sacrament.[75]

Ambiguity of the Holy: the Demonic

The fact that the holy embraces both the clean and the unclean leads to what Tillich calls "the ambiguity of the holy." Ambiguity is a key Tillichian concept which appears on almost every page of the third volume of *Systematic Theology*. Ambiguity is a characteristic not of the structure of being, but of the process of life, according to which "positive and negative elements are mixed in such a way that a definite separation of the negative from the positive is impossible."[76] The positive elements are essential elements, and the negative ones are existential; however, they cannot be separated simply into good and evil, for "in all life processes an essential and an existential element, created goodness and estrangement, are merged in such a way that neither one nor the other is exclusively effective."[77] For example, one of the ambiguities of religion is that, on the one hand, it is self-transcendent—it points beyond itself to God; on the other hand, it is profanized—it becomes a finite institution, a sociological unit subject to the same laws that govern secular groups.

The source of ambiguity (*Zweideutigkeit*) is found in the very heart of the process of life. Life basically consists in a going-out (*das Über-sich-Hinausgehen*) and a return-to-self (*das Zu-sich-Zurückkehren*). Against this movement of life there is always a counter-movement, so that the life process of self-integration struggles against disintegration; self-creativity struggles against destruction; and self-transcendence struggles against profanization. This struggle of tendencies—one positive, one negative—is ambiguity.[78]

The holy is ambiguous because it embraces the clean (the positive) and the unclean (the negative), both of which produce "numinous awe." However, this ambiguity is merely an instance of the more radical ambiguity of the holy which embraces both the divine and the demonic.[79] The holy manifests itself in holy objects, "for without the finite bearer of the holy, the holy would remain unknowable."[80] These objects are not holy in themselves, but they become holy "only by negating themselves in pointing to the divine of which they are the medium." If their holiness is considered inherent, they become demonic. "They still are 'holy,' but their holiness is antidivine." These holy objects, whose function is to represent man's ultimate concern, usurp the place of the holy and establish themselves as his ultimate concern. "They are transformed into idols. Holiness provokes idolatry."[81] As an example of the demonic, Tillich cites the Roman empire which became "demonically possessed" in compelling men to worship itself.[82] Both the divine and the demonic appear in the concrete as ecstatic, overpowering, and awe-inspiring. But the demonic refuses to bow to the unconditioned, and, in fact, elevates itself to the same level.[83]

If the ambiguity of the divine-demonic loses its tension and the two elements are separated, the result is a religious dualism such as Manichaeism. "Religious dualism concentrates divine holiness in one realm and demonic holiness in another realm." Reality is then partitioned between the two realms, and what belongs to the demonic realm is essentially evil.[84] Tillich's concern, therefore, is to keep the divine and the demonic, the clean and the unclean, ambiguously united, as they are in the primitive notion of the holy. He never ceases to remind us that "the demonic's favored place is the holy."[85]

This analysis of the experience of the holy lays bare the roots of faith. The unconditionality of ultimate concern springs from an encounter with the *mysterium tremendum et fascinans*, the ground and abyss of being and meaning. The total demand of ultimate concern is explained by the stern "ought-to-be" of the holy, while ultimate concern's promise of total fulfilment arises from the majestic presence of the holy. The ambiguity of faith, the possibility of its deterioration into idolatrous faith, is accounted for by the ambiguity of the holy itself which is open to invasion by the demonic.

A systematic analysis inevitably dilutes the intensity of a religious experience. As a gesture to offset this loss, we conclude the exposition of faith with Tillich's poetic description of the moment of faith.[86] It is only in a concrete situation that "the ultimate power of being, the ground of reality" appears and reveals the infinite depth and meaning of the present moment. Yet, in the light of the ultimate the concrete present is shown in all its shallowness. Thus it affirms and negates; it is transparent for its ground which is also its abyss. The experience is like a blinding flash of lightning at night. Reality is seen as something new, for in the ecstasy of faith its ground is glimpsed. Nor do we remain as detached subjects staring at an object, for we are seized in the very center of our personality. "We are grasped, in the experience of faith, by the unapproachably holy which is the ground of our being and breaks into our existence and which judges us and heals us."

RELIGION

Tillich's notion of faith has been developed at length because, once it is understood, other key concepts, such as religion and revelation, are readily intelligible. If one simply stated that religion is ultimate concern, a turning toward the unconditional, and that it is not a special function of man's spirit but a centered act of his personality, that would be an adequate summation of what Tillich calls religion in the broad sense.[87] Here faith and religion are identical. The narrow sense of religion is the "churchy" sense—doctrine, rites, and all the appurtenances of an institution.

While the above paragraph sufficiently describes what Tillich means by religion, a somewhat deeper examination is called for. In his later writings he relies heavily on ultimate concern, but chronologically he evolved his basic insights more in terms of religion than faith; his early works center around the philosophy and history of religion. Furthermore, in both his early and later works certain crucial points of his doctrine are developed under the heading of religion.

Not a Separate Function

Tillich's insistence that religion cannot be identified with any of the functions of spirit (*Geist*) and that it cannot be placed beside them as a special function animated his thinking at a very early date, and he himself calls this insight "decisive."[88] This is quite clear in his work on Schelling.[89] Moreover, he clashes with other scholars on the point. Otto is criticized because he tends to make apprehension of the holy a special function.[90] Tillich rejects Hegel's assigning religion to the theoretical sphere, Kant's assigning it to the practical sphere, and Schleiermacher's assigning it to the emotional sphere.[91] Religion is an attitude of spirit (*ein Verhalten des Geistes*) which participates in all these spheres. Schleiermacher, especially, is taken to task for cutting off religion from the whole of the human personality and boxing it into the narrow confines of emotion.[92] Tillich's untiring defense and constant repetition of his position are a measure of the importance he attaches to it.

He elaborates the notion of spirit (*Geist*) in his treatise on the classification of sciences.[93] *Geist* depends upon two other concepts, thought (*Denken*) and being (*Sein*), which are in constant dynamic tension. *Geist* is neither pure thought nor pure being, but involves both. *Denken* and *Sein* are explained by Tillich as the essential components of the act of knowledge. The act or intention is *Denken,* and the object or thing intended is *Sein.* Thought, then, is the act which is directed toward being. When thought contemplates itself, it exists as being; it is spirit. For *Geist* is the form of thought-in-being (*Form des seienden Denkens*). Every being has something of thought in it, but the more thought it contains, the more reality it possesses. The most real of beings is the one in which thought as thought is realized, that is, a spirit-bearing totality (*eine geisttragende Gestalt*)—man.

Geist, or spirit, has many functions: logical, aesthetic, ethical, and social. But all of these spheres, theoretical and practical, are concerned with the fulfilment of meaning, for "every spiritual act

is an act of meaning (*Sinn*)." When *Geist* turns toward unconditioned meaning in whatever sphere, this is the act of religion.
Thus, in the sphere of knowledge, culture attends to conditioned
forms of being and their unity, while religion turns to unconditioned being as the ground and abyss of all. In the aesthetic
sphere, religion looks to the unconditioned content of meaning; in
the sphere of law, to the unconditioned personal as the ground of
every right; and, in the social sphere, to unconditioned love. In
brief, religion is the tendency of spirit toward the unconditional
in every sphere and so is not one spiritual function beside others.[94]

In the third volume of his *Systematic Theology*, one of his most
recent works, Tillich expresses the same ideas, but in a somewhat
different fashion. Here "spirit" is defined as "the actualization of
power and meaning in unity" and designates "the particularly
human dimension of life."[95] But to see the connection between
spirit and religion demands a brief sketch of the argument of the
third volume.

Life is the actualization of the potential; it is, therefore, an
ontological concept which describes the structure of reality. Life
actualizes itself in several dimensions or realms which, while distinct and often in conflict, yet compenetrate one another. These
dimensions are the inorganic, the organic, the psychological, the
spiritual, and the historical. In each of these dimensions life is
actualized in three basic functions: self-integration, self-creativity,
and self-transcendence. Within the dimension of spirit, the dimension proper to man, self-integration appears as morality; self-creativity, as culture; and self-transcendence, as religion. Thus Tillich
defines religion as "the self-transcendence of life under the dimension of spirit."[96] This amounts to the same as religion as the intention of *Geist* toward the unconditional. Occasionally he refers to
religion as a function of life or spirit along with the other functions, but this is more a manner of speaking, for he hastens to explain that essentially religion is a quality of the other functions
and not an independent one. This is so because of the peculiar
nature of the unconditional and of self-transcendence.

Tillich quite explicitly states the reason why religion cannot be restricted to any particular function or sphere. It follows immediately from the nature of the unconditioned, for "if religion is the state of being grasped by an ultimate concern, this state cannot be restricted to a special realm. The unconditional character of this concern implies that it refers to every moment of our life, to every space and every realm."[97] Since the unconditional has been treated earlier in this chapter, it suffices here to recall that subjective unconditionality, the total engagement of the person, is linked with objective unconditionality, the ground and abyss of being and meaning. Tillich's argument seems to say that, once in the grasp of such ultimates, man cannot limit his response to an isolated area. The scope of religion must be commensurate with its source, the ground of being and meaning. "Religion, like God, is omnipresent."[98]

From the viewpoint of self-transcendence, religion cannot serve one function beside others, "because, if it did, it would have to be itself transcended, and so on in endless repetition. Life cannot genuinely transcend itself in one of its own functions."[99] In other words, self-transcendence is not another horizontal line of actualization, but a "striving in the vertical direction toward ultimate and infinite being."[100] Religion cannot be confined to a particular area. It has no horizons; its only dimensions are the unlimited height and depth of being and meaning.

Two Senses of Religion

There is an obvious objection to Tillich's view of religion: Does not the *fact* of religion's separate existence prove that it is a separate realm? How account for the independent sphere of religion that has existed since the dawn of human history? Tillich's reply is based upon the principle of ambiguity. Self-transcendence of morality and culture is constantly endangered by the ambiguity of profanization.[101] To combat the secularizing forces, the power of religion concentrates in a special area, thus constructing the specifically religious sphere as a kind of fortress.

Ambiguity, however, is only the proximate, not the remote, answer to the objection. For one must ask: Why is there ambiguity? The ultimate answer lies in the nature of life itself, in the actualization of potentiality, in the transition from essence to existence. This matter is treated in our fifth chapter, and here we merely observe that, according to Tillich, the separate realm of religion witnesses to the fact that ours is a fallen world, i.e., in transition from essence to existence.[102]

To cope with the ambiguous character of religion—its essential all-pervading presence, and its existential confinement to a particular sphere—Tillich presents a twofold definition of religion.[103] Religion in the larger sense is the state of being ultimately concerned; it is "religion of the heart." Religion in the narrow sense is the expression of this concern in symbols of God and its formulation in dogma and cult; it is "public religion."[104] Religion as ultimate concern embraces but goes beyond religion in the narrow sense. The latter usually refers to institutional religion, and personal piety too, in so far as it is formalized. Strictly speaking, however, the axis of the distinction of the two senses of religion is not "concern/expression of concern," but rather "concern/concern expressed in theistic symbols." In other words, Tillich's quarrel is not with symbolic expression of ultimate concern as such, but with the historically evolved theistic symbols still so much in vogue. For even in the essential order the concern of religion must be symbolically expressed. But the tragedy of religion in the narrow sense is that its outmoded theistic symbols restrict it to a confined, perhaps irrelevant area. It is from this standpoint that he preaches against "the yoke of religion," a religion that has become a theoretical and practical burden because it is no longer rooted in the creative depth of ultimate concern.[105]

For a clear and succinct statement of Tillich's view of religion there is nothing better than the first chapter of his *Theology of Culture*.[106] In it he rejects as a starting point any theory which defines religion as "man's relation to divine beings." His own point of departure is "religion as an aspect of the human spirit," namely, "the dimension of depth in all of its functions." Thus, in the large sense, religion is ultimate concern; in the narrow sense, institutional religion. The latter exists "because of the tragic estrangement of man's spiritual life from its own ground and depth." The glory of religion, even of religion in the narrow sense, is that "it gives us the experience of the Holy." Its shame is that "it makes itself the ultimate and despises the secular realm."

But glorious or inglorious, genuine or distorted, religion cannot be avoided no matter how man twists or turns, for, as Tillich remarks:

It is less than human to live without asking the question, "What is the meaning of this life which is given to me?" And now this is what religion means. Religion means ultimate concern about the ultimate, unconditional seriousness about that which is ultimately serious, infinitely serious, namely, the question of the meaning of my life.[107]

REVELATION

At this point Tillich's notion of revelation can be conveniently introduced, at least in capsule fashion, for it is defined by reference to ultimate concern. "Revelation is the manifestation of what concerns us ultimately."[108] The same definition is found in his earlier scheme of thought where revelation is "the breakthrough of the unconditioned content of meaning through the form of meaning (*der Durchbruch des unbedingten Sinngehaltes durch die Sinnform*).[109]

Revelation, as faith, has two sides: the subjective and the objective.[110] Subjectively, someone is grasped by the mystery of being. This is the receiving side of revelation, for there is no revelation without someone to receive it. The subjective reception of revelation is the state of "ecstasy." Objectively, something occurs through which the mystery grasps the subject. This is the giving side of revelation; it is "miracle."

Ecstasy is not merely emotional feeling, nor is it the cognitive or ethical function. Ecstasy is the state in which reason stands outside itself, that is, transcends itself. The mind is thrown beyond itself by the "ontological shock" of the experience of nonbeing, of the abyss, as happens when the ultimate question is asked: Why is there something? Why not nothing? While the experience of the *mysterium tremendum,* the abyss, produces the ontological shock, it is the *mysterium fascinosum,* the ground of being, which overcomes it.

A miracle is a "sign-event" which astounds and shakes us, points to the mystery of being, and is received as a miracle in an ecstatic experience. Miracles, though presenting the mystery, do not destroy "the rational structure of reality" any more than ecstasy destroys "the rational structure of the mind." Hence Tillich denies that miracles can be explained by "supranatural interference in natural processes." The medium of revelation, the object which enters into the miraculous event, can be anything whatsoever—a person, a thing, or an event. For everything participates in the ground of being and meaning, and so is capable of conveying ultimate concern.

Relation of Faith, Religion, and Revelation

By now it should be quite obvious that ultimate concern lies at the bottom of Tillich's understanding of faith, religion, and revelation. The experience of the holy, of the unconditional, takes place in a state of ecstasy in which the human spirit is grasped by ultimate concern and transcends itself. This description applies equally to faith, religion, and revelation; they are substantially the same.[111] Though Tillich does not explicitly discuss their distinction, they seem to have some accidental differences or, at least, different points of emphasis. In *faith,* ultimate concern is considered more as it affects the individual in the center of his personality. The questions of doubt, risk, and courage here come to the fore. In *religion,* the symbolic expression of ultimate concern in myth and ritual and its embodiment in institutions receives more attention. For religion as ultimate concern drives toward expression, and it always includes within its scope religion in the narrow sense. In *revelation* the manifestation of ultimate concern in a correlation of event and ecstasy receives the stress. For the ground of being grasps us through beings.

These differences seem sufficiently marked and important enough to justify Tillich's use of three different terms. Whether faith, religion, and revelation are the most appropriate ones is another question, for a theologian's terminology must be understood according to the meaning he assigns to it, presuming that he stays within a certain recognizable area of discourse. The casual reader may be puzzled by Tillich's employment of traditional terms with not-so-traditional meanings. But the confusion should be dispelled once his definitions are grasped, especially the central concept of ultimate concern.

REFLECTIONS AND APPRAISAL

This exposition of faith and religion presents the first side of the religio-cultural relationship, but more as a blueprint than as a finished edifice. For we have sketched the origin and mechanics of faith in some detail, while the content has been indicated in rather general terms. From the blueprint, however, one can discern the over-all lines of the structure.

It is clear that Tillich's notion of faith is in harmony with the mood of the times. Roger Aubert, in the conclusion to his monumental history of the act of faith in Catholic theology, shows where the modern problem of faith lies:

It is the very idea of religion which creates difficulty nowadays. The modern mind resists the idea of the supernatural, even in the very large sense of a personal intervention of God in the world. It is at this level, the level of the very meaning of religion, that many men today find the problem of faith. . . . In these conditions, more than as a simple intellectual adhesion to dogmas, faith appears as an attitude of every religious man who takes a position in relation to the Absolute. It seems, moreover, to require for its foundations something other than rational arguments, and one can understand why so many recent authors appeal to a certain immediate experience in which to ground it.[112]

Whatever the final validity of Tillich's solution, by his explanation of faith as ultimate concern he has taken his stand in the middle of the terrain described by Aubert. If twentieth-century man resents divine intervention in the world, Tillich finds God already there. If modern man is skeptical of a personal God, Tillich confronts him with the ground and power of being. And if he is weary of rational arguments, Tillich invites him to open the depths of his being to the experience of the holy.

A good example of Tillich's sensitivity to contemporary religious problems is the allowance he makes for doubt. The merit of his approach to this pastoral problem is that he faces doubt squarely, making no effort to side-step it or to blunt it, for he is convinced that doubt itself is the disguised visage of faith.

Many Christians, as well as members of other religious groups, feel anxiety, guilt and despair about what they call "loss of faith." But serious doubt is confirmation of faith. It indicates the seriousness of the concern, its unconditional character.[113]

Although this straightforward doctrine could benefit from a few nuances,[114] it succeeds in stressing the positive side of doubt by uncovering the unextinguished faith that smolders beneath it.

Our primary aim in blueprinting Tillich's concept of religion is to see eventually how he relates it to culture. In view of this purpose, far-reaching consequences follow from his idea of religion in which "the relation to the gods is not a necessary element." With ultimate concern as the constitutive factor, religion can be extended to take in non-theistic and even "secular quasi-religions" in which "the ultimate concern is directed towards objects like nation, science, a particular form or stage of society or a highest ideal of humanity, which are then considered divine."[115] Thus the relation of religion to culture is erected upon a very broad basis indeed. Religion in the narrow sense cannot determine the limits of the relationship so long as one can say, as Tillich does, that "the most important religious movements are developing outside of religion."[116] The universality of the problematic flows from the relative simplicity of the operative factor: ultimate concern. For the old adage of logic is applicable here: the smaller the comprehension, the greater the extension. In this case, religion is wide in application because it is simple in constitution, being constituted by ultimate concern.

The simplicity of ultimate concern accounts for its easy adaptability and also for the difficulty in understanding it. Tillich uses phrases such as "total surrender," "unconditional concern," and "infinite passion" to describe it, but they too are hardly self-evident. One of the difficulties is that by his insistence upon faith as a centered act of the total personality, Tillich neglects to expound it in terms of intellect, will, and emotions, because he is afraid of being trapped into identifying it with one of these functions.[117] Thus he speaks of it only in its totality, but, as in the case of the simplicity of the atom, this can render it all but impenetrable.

Another obstacle to comprehending ultimate concern is that Tillich does not situate it within church history. He presents it in isolation and does not relate it to the accumulated insights of other theologians. On the contrary, he feels that the concept of faith has been twisted to such a degree that "there is hardly a word in the religious language, both theological and popular, which is subject to more misunderstandings, distortions, and questionable definitions than the word 'faith.' " Tempted to drop the term altogether, he contents himself with the effort "to reinterpret the word and remove the confusing and distorting connotations, some of which are the heritage of centuries."[118] On this point, it seems, the history of the church, one of the sources of theology, has run dry.

The only other way to bring ultimate concern into a better focus would be to specify it somehow from its object, but this Tillich steadfastly refuses to do: "Faith is the state of being ultimately concerned. The content matters infinitely for the life of the believer, but it does not matter for the formal definition of faith."[119] And one commentator hits off the normal response to that statement: "We thus face a strange paradox: what matters infinitely for the believer does not concern the nature of his faith. How can this be, if faith is ultimate concern?"[120]

These three aspects of Tillich's treatment of faith as ultimate concern—its indivisible totality, unrelatedness to traditional notions, and vagueness of content—do contribute to a certain bafflement about it. But there is another side to the coin: the intensity of faith which he conveys by stressing its totality, the freshness of his thought which does not mouth staid formulas, and the exhilarating sweep of the universality of faith. This last point, the universality of faith, raises a question about its content, but this question can be settled only after the main doctrines of Tillich's system have been presented, for the whole of his theology is an attempt to expose the meaning of Christian faith.

Tillich is aware of the intrinsic difficulty of explaining faith: "Faith is a concept—and a reality—which is difficult to grasp and to describe. . . . This cannot be otherwise, since faith is not a phenomenon beside others, but the central phenomenon in man's personal life, manifest and hidden at the same time."[121] Perhaps the title of his book, *Dynamics of Faith,* offers a clue to his approach. He seems to get at what faith is, its essence, by way of what it does, its dynamics. Consequently, in reply to our efforts to grasp ultimate concern, Tillich would probably say: "Let it grasp you. Faith is a primary notion, a primary reality; it cannot be properly defined, but only experienced."

Notes

1. PE, 78.
2. DF, 8. See also pp. 1 and 4.
3. ST, III, 130; DF, 9–10.
4. ST, I, 12, 154, 215; DF, 9. How indebted Tillich is to Kierkegaard for his notion of ultimate concern is an interesting question that would take us too far afield. It has been argued that Tillich's ultimate concern is a distortion of Kierkegaard's position. Cf. Kenneth Hamilton, *The System and the Gospel*, New York: Macmillan, 1963, 42–45. Whatever the case may be, "infinite passion" is useful as a descriptive term.
5. DF, 4, 105–107, 30–40; ST, III, 131–133.
6. *Ibid.*, 133. Cf. also GW, VII, 196–97.
7. ST, III, 130; DF, 99.
8. ST, III, 278, 279.
9. DF, 16–17, 102–103.
10. NB, 75–78.
11. PE, 163, 32.
12. See ST, I, 173.
13. PE, 32.
14. *Systematische Theologie*, I, Stuttgart: Evangelisches Verlagswerk, 1956, 19.
15. GW, I, 331. Cf. also GW, IV, 84 and Paul Tillich, "Kirche und Kultur," *Sammlung gemeinverständlicher Vorträge und Schriften aus dem Gebiet der Theologie und Religionsgeschichte*, No. 111, Tübingen: J. C. B. Mohr, 1924, 5–7 (translated as "Church and Culture," IH, 219–41).
16. GW, I, 318.
17. *Ibid.*, 319.
18. *Ibid.*, 331–332.
19. RS, 35.
20. ST, III, 130–131.
21. *Ibid.*, 130.
22. NB, 121.
23. DF, 9.
24. ST, II, 9.
25. DF, 16.
26. *Ibid.*, 45–46; SF, 57. In his sermon "What Is Truth?" Tillich says that indifference to the truth "is the way of the majority of the people today." Yet even here he holds that death and tragedy force the question to be asked. NB, 68–69.
27. NB, 158.
28. GW, I, 332; "Kirche und Kultur," 8. Tillich speaks in these passages of essential and intentional "un-faith" (*Unglaube*), but we have substituted the word "atheism" in order to focus on the significance of the argument. He

positively rejects the terms "belief" and "unbelief" as misleading, since belief means for him acceptance of knowledge which has a low degree of certitude. Even in his English writings he uses the rather awkward word "un-faith." Cf. ST, III, 130–131.

29. ST, II, 25–26. See also "Reply," K and B, 346–347.
30. SF, 127–128.
31. ST, III, 130–131.
32. DF, 69.
33. *Ibid.*, 10; ST, I, 12.
34. ST, I, 211.
35. DF, 45–47.
36. SF, 57, 59.
37. TC, 130–132.
38. DF, 16–22; ST, I, 211.
39. TC, 28; ST, II, 116.
40. CB, 35, 47
41. "Rechtfertigung und Zweifel," Giessen, 1924, 23–24.
42. PE, 202.
43. *Ibid.*, x–xi. See also IH, 34–35.
44. DF, 21.
45. CB, 57.
46. *Ibid.*, 155.
47. DF, 16–22, 99–105; CB, 172–173.
48. CB, 176.
49. *Ibid.*, 176–177.
50. *Ibid.*, 182–185, 190.
51. DF, 96–98; PE, 163.
52. TC, 68; ST, III, 224, 239.
53. ST, I, 37, 227; ST, III, 208; PE, 176.
54. EN, sermon 12: "Do Not Be Conformed," 135–44. The term "Protestant principle" does not appear in the text, but is clearly implied.
55. GW, VII, 50; PE, 174–175, 205.
56. ST, II, 147; ST, III, 210.
57. ST, III, 223–224.
58. PE, 226.
59. DF, 103, 10–12.
60. Paul Tillich, "God as Reality and Symbol," *Essays and Studies* (Tokyo) XI, March, 1961, 102.
61. ST, I, 215.
62. SF, 87–92.
63. CEWR, 58. See also pp. 59, 66–67; and DF, 56; TC, 182, 187.
64. Paul Tillich, "Jewish Influences on Contemporary Christian Theology," *Cross Currents*, II, No. 3, 1952, 40.
65. GW, VII, 124.
66. ST, I, 216.

67. *Ibid.*, 113. Cf. also GW, I, 337 and DF, 13.

68. SF, 38–51

69. *Ibid.*, 48.

70. "Kirche und Kultur," Tübingen, 1924, 5–7. Cf. also GW, I, 318–19, 335–37.

71. GW, VII, 41. Also GW, II, 86.

72. Cf. ST, I, 235–38; LPJ, 107–109; CB, 155 ff.

73. PE, 108.

74. ST, I, 217.

75. PE, 108–9.

76. ST, III, 32.

77. *Ibid.*, 107. See also pp. 44, 63, 98–100.

78. GW, IV, 126–29.

79. ST, I, 217–18.

80. GW, VII, 184.

81. ST, I, 216.

82. ST, III, 103 and PE, 168. The principle of ambiguity is applied even to the demonic. It is creative and destructive. The demonic Roman empire not only vested itself with divine holiness (the destructive side), but it also attained greatness and dignity in establishing order (the creative side). This is a good instance of how Tillich rings the changes on his concepts.

83. ST, I, 140; GW, I, 338–39; GW, II, 98.

84. ST, I, 224–25.

85. ST, III, 344. Cf. also DF, 16; PE, 108–9; GW, I, 339.

86. PE, 78.

87. ST, III, 96; GW, I, 329; TC, 5–8, 177; PE, 59; CEWR, 4–5; "Existentialist Aspects of Modern Art," in *Christianity and the Existentialists,* Carl Michalson (ed.), New York: Charles Scribner's Sons, 1956, 132–33; "Theologie der Kultur," 34–35.

88. GW, I, 350.

89. *Ibid.*, 101.

90. "Rechtfertigung und Zweifel," 28.

91. "Theologie der Kultur," 33–34.

92. TC, 23–24; ST, I, 15.

93. *Das System der Wissenschaften nach Gegenständen und Methoden,* Göttingen: Vandenhoeck und Ruprecht, 1923, in GW, I, 111–293. Cf. especially pages 117–120, 210–211.

94. GW, I, 318, 324–26, 329, 380; GW, V, 38.

95. ST, III, 21–22, 111.

96. *Ibid.*, 96.

97. TC, 41; GW, I, 329.

98. PE, xi–xii. See also CB, 156.

99. ST, III, 96.

100. *Ibid.*, 86. See also p. 31.

101. ST, III, 97.

102. PE, 59; TC, 8–9, 41–42; ST, II, 29.

103. His essay of 1919, "Theologie der Kultur," laid the foundations for the distinction of the two senses of religion (cf. especially pp. 34 and 49). Three years later he developed it fully in his article "Die Überwindung des Religionsbegriffs in der Religionsphilosophie" (cf. GW, I, 367–88).

104. TC, 7–9, 177; GW, VII, 133–34; CEWR, 3–5; "Existentialist Aspects of Modern Art," 132–33.

105. SF, 93–103.

106. TC, 3–9.

107. "God as Reality and Symbol," *Essays and Studies* (Tokyo), XI March, 1961, 101.

108. ST, I, 110.

109. GW, I, 353.

110. ST, I, 111–118.

111. In one place Tillich states, "It is equally wrong to identify religion with revelation, just as it is wrong to identify religion with the attempt at self-salvation. Religion, like all life, is ambiguous." ST, II, 80. The text clearly refers to the two senses of religion and it is religion in the narrow sense which cannot be identified with revelation.

112. Roger Aubert, *Le Problème de l'Acte de Foi*, 3rd ed., Louvain: E. Warny, 1958, 783–84.

113. DF, 22.

114. It seems that the identification of doubt with faith on the basis of a common ultimate concern is made somewhat too rapidly, for serious doubt differs from positive commitment as suspended animation differs from life. If doubt is an anguished state of faith, as Tillich holds, then, although painful, it is not ultimately dangerous. But doubt can lead to something worse, namely, destructive despair, as the suicide rate grimly testifies. Furthermore, despite his existential terminology, his explanation of doubt as meaninglessness sticks very close to the intellectual plane and lacks, for example, Guardini's delicate but hardheaded perception of the moral roots of doubt in a rebellious will. See Romano Guardini, "Faith and Doubt," in *Faith, Reason, and the Gospels*, John J. Heaney (ed.), Westminister, Md.: Newman Press, 1961, 30–32.

115. CEWR, 4–5.

116. RS, 157.

117. He states, "If one of the functions which constitute the totality of the personality is partly or completely identified with faith, the meaning of faith is distorted. Such interpretations are not altogether wrong because every function of the human mind participates in the act of faith. But the element of truth in them is embedded in a whole of error." DF, 30–31.

118. *Ibid.*, ix. See also BR, 52.

119. DF, 4.

120. George H. Tavard, *Paul Tillich and the Christian Message*, New York: Charles Scribner's Sons, 1962, 39.

121. DF, 126.

3/From Secular to Theonomous Culture

THE SECOND TERM of the religio-cultural relationship is culture. Our intent, however, is not merely to place it alongside religion like the counterbalance on a scale, but to illustrate the union between them. This juncture is achieved in theonomous culture, a culture in which religion is profoundly operative. Theonomy is Tillich's solution to the structural unity of religion and culture.

CULTURE

Tillich once stated that man has a "head" which is religion and a "body" which is cultural form.[1] The head has already been drawn. We shall finish the portrait by sketching the more important data about culture: its definition, functions and elements, cultural style, and cultural types.

Definition

After the universal extension of religion as ultimate concern, it is not surprising that Tillich also conceives culture in the broadest terms. Culture is in the realm of spirit (*Geist*). There it is the conditioned forms of meaning (*die bedingten Sinnformen*) while religion looks to unconditioned meaning. "Culture is the medium

82

of the unconditioned in the life of the spirit, just as things are the medium of the unconditioned in the world."[2] Tillich's passing references to cultural areas reveal the vast range of human activities which he groups under the term "culture": science, technology, art, philosophy, law, economics, politics, morality, personal and social life.[3] Consequently, his definition of culture must be elastic and comprehensive. Culture is "the self-creativity of life under the dimension of spirit."[4] Culture creates "a universe of meaning" as it actualizes the potentiality of the human spirit. Man, the microcosm, is "the point at which and the instrument through which a universe of meaning is actualized."[5] The macrocosm, the universe of being, is fulfilled as a universe of meaning at least in an anticipatory and fragmentary fashion through man's cultural creativity.

Tillich is cognizant that he employs "culture" in a very wide sense. The German *Kultur* refers primarily to the fulfilment of man and nature under the drive of the human spirit, while the French *culture* denotes the characteristics of an educated person who possesses good taste, critical sense, and sound judgment.[6] The English "culture" regularly takes on either meaning according to the context.[7] Tillich naturally uses it in the sense of the German *Kultur* whose English equivalent is perhaps more accurately "civilization."[8] H. Richard Niebuhr presents a concept of culture which echoes the definition of Tillich:

What we have in view when we deal with Christ and culture is that total process of human activity and that total result of such activity to which now the name *culture,* now the name *civilization,* is applied in common speech. Culture is the "artificial, secondary environment" which man superimposes on the natural. It comprises language, habits, ideas, beliefs, customs, social organization, inherited artifacts, technical processes, and values.[9]

In a word, culture is the spiritual creativity manifest in every area of human life and institutions.

Functions and Elements

The third volume of *Systematic Theology* contains a thorough presentation of culture as the self-creativity of life in the spiritual dimension.[10] Underlying self-creativity and growth is one of the structural polarities of being, the polarity of dynamics and form. Dynamics impels a formed reality to break out of its form, to go beyond itself, and to develop into a new reality. Form is the polar counterpart of dynamics. It makes the thing what it is, tends to keep it static, but then determines the new reality which emerges under the pressure of dynamics. The dynamics-form polarity is actualized in the life functions of growth (the non-spiritual dimension) and self-creativity (the spiritual dimension). However, the old form may stifle or the new form may not be reached, and so the whole creative process is subject to the ambiguity of destruction.

Tillich calls the receptive function of culture *theoria.* "Theoria is the act of looking at the encountered world in order to take something of it into the centered self as a meaningful, structured, whole."[11] As an example he cites language: "The word is the bearer of meaning; therefore, language is the first result of the self-creation of life under the dimension of spirit."[12] The instruments of *theoria* are cognitive concepts and aesthetic images, each of which mirrors a fragment of the universe of meaning. The true and the beautiful are received through *theoria* which prolongs the grasping function of the word.

But as man's spirit seizes reality, simultaneously he shapes it. Upon learning to speak, man fashioned tools. This primeval technical act is continued in the active function of culture termed by Tillich *praxis.* Technology controls the world of nature, but "*praxis* is the whole of cultural acts of centered personalities who as members of social groups act upon each other and themselves."[13] *Praxis* operates in the personal-communal area and seeks to procure individual and social good.

Every cultural creation, whether it results from *theoria* or *praxis*, comprises three elements: subject matter (*Inhalt*), form (*Form*), and substance (*Gehalt*).[14] The subject matter can be almost anything, but it is the form which is culturally decisive, in that form makes the creation what it is—an essay, a poem, or a law. Substance is described by Tillich as the soil out of which a cultural creation grows. Substance is the underlying power of meaning, the ultimate concern which inspires the creative spirit and imparts significance to the cultural production. "Subject matter is the accidental, substance is the essential, and form is the mediating element."[15]

Style and the Theology of Culture

When form is distinctively qualified by substance in a large number of cultural activities, the resulting pattern is what Tillich calls "style," a term borrowed from the world of art.[16] Style provides the key to a comparison of the cultures of different peoples and epochs, for cultural styles reflect the varied manner in which the human spirit encounters reality.

"He who can read the style of a culture can discover its ultimate concern, its religious substance."[17] This is precisely the goal of a theology of culture: to analyze cultural styles in order to "discover the ultimate concern in the ground of a philosophy, a political system, an artistic style, a set of ethical or social principles."[18] Systematic theology enunciates principles, but "it is the task of a constructive theology of culture to apply these principles to the concrete problems of our cultural existence."[19] In turn, by its analyses the theology of culture opens up to the systematic theologian one of the theological sources, the history of culture, just as the exegete makes the biblical source available.

Tillich has always shown keen interest in the theology of culture. His essay of 1919, "Über die Idee einer Theologie der Kultur," wrestles with the problem of how to link theology with culture so that a legitimate theology of culture emerges. His basic argument is that the middle term is spirit (*Geist*). Theology is the science of religion, and religion resides in *Geist*. *Geist* is also the domain of culture. Religion provides the substance (unconditioned meaning), while culture imparts form (conditioned form). Thus, the role of a theology of culture is sharply delimited. It cannot directly produce cultural creations, but it acts critically as a gauge to indicate the degree to which religious substance has been realized in cultural forms. More positively, it reveals the unity of a culture by working toward a cultural synthesis based on the transparency of form to substance.

Tillich himself has contributed to the theology of culture by numerous articles that attempt to decipher cultural style and thus uncover the ultimate concern which animates specific cultural creations. In addition to his many essays on socialism, marxism, political power, war aims, and depth-psychology, one can also instance occasional writings on technology, art, education, science, architecture, and even space exploration. A representative sampling is contained in his book *Theology of Culture*.[20]

Types of Culture

Since cultural styles result from a blend of form and substance, three general types of culture are possible.[21] These types never exist in the pure state, but they are very useful as principles for judging a culture, and as guidelines for the interpretation of history. If form is stressed at the expense of substance, Tillich calls the culture "autonomous." If substance dominates and overshadows form, the culture is "heteronomous." But if the two are harmoniously balanced, the culture is "theonomous." The etymology of autonomy, heteronomy, and theonomy indicates the presence of a predominating principle or law (*nomos*). In autonomy it is the principle of self-sufficient form; in heteronomy, a tyrannical and hence demonically distorted substance; and in theonomy, an equilibrium in which form is transparent to the ground of being, and religion is perfectly related to culture. We shall now examine this Tillichian triad—autonomy, heteronomy, and theonomy—which constitutes a sort of cultural dynamics.

AUTONOMY

Tillich defines autonomous culture as "the attempt to create the forms of personal and social life without any reference to something ultimate and unconditional, following only the demands of theoretical and practical rationality."[22] The law, the *nomos*, is reason itself as found in man who is the bearer of universal reason. Reason is structure. Subjectively, it is "the structure of the mind which enables it to grasp and shape reality." Objectively, it is "the structure of reality which the mind can grasp and according to which it can shape reality."[23] But reason has not only structure; it also has depth. The depth of reason precedes reason and transcends its structures in power and meaning. Metaphorically speaking, the depth of reason is truth-itself, beauty-itself, justice-itself, love-itself. Essentially, it should be manifest in the rational structures. However, under the conditions of existence, the polarity of structure and depth falls into conflict, with the result that reason "affirms and actualizes its structure without regarding its depth."[24] It is autonomous and independent, but, by the same token, superficial, shallow, and secular. "Autonomous culture is secularized in the degree to which it has lost its ultimate reference, its center of meaning, its spiritual substance."[25]

The Secular

Autonomy can be viewed under several aspects, the first of these being "the secular." The notion of the holy was developed in the previous chapter, and the secular is defined by reference to it. For the secular is the absence of holiness, of ultimacy. The holy is the realm of ultimate concern, of the unconditional, and of the infinite. The secular is the realm of preliminary concern, of the conditioned, and of the finite. Tillich points out that "secular," along with the German word *profan,* is a neutral term inasmuch as it does not imply the unclean, the morally bad. However, the English word "profane" connotes an attack on the holy, as when "profanity" stands for blasphemous language. Since the finite and preliminary is not necessarily hostile to the ultimate and, in fact, is open to it, he prefers the neutral term "secular" as the pole opposed to "holy."[26]

Since the secular, though positive in a limited sphere, is negative in its lack of ultimacy, an experience of it is more difficult to describe than the experience of the holy, just as blindness is harder to portray than vision. However, in a few of his sermons Tillich provides some insights into the experience of the secular. He observes that our period of history has decided for a secular world, and has dethroned a too powerful church. "Yet it excluded those deep things for which religion stands: the feeling for the inexhaustible mystery of life, the grip of an ultimate meaning of existence, and the invincible power of an unconditioned devotion."[27] Such is the defect of a secular world. In another sermon, entitled "In Thinking Be Mature," the secular mind is called an immature mind in that it lacks the wisdom born out of the shattering experience of the holy. The secular mind fails to go beyond itself, it stays on the banal surface of things, and it never asks the penetrating question of its own existence.[28]

Turning to the domain of history, Tillich characterizes nineteenth-century capitalist society as secular. For bourgeois society is impregnated with the spirit of self-sufficient finitude, so that its substance has been lost and its inner ardor has grown cold. "The spirit of a finitude which lives within itself" is the spirit of capitalist society.[29] Thus is produced an autonomous, secularized culture which "has lost its ultimate reference, its center of meaning, its spiritual substance."[30]

The secular, or profane, can also be understood by contrasting it with the demonic. The secular does not rise above itself; the demonic exalts itself to the stature of the divine. As Tillich puts it, "The demonic does not resist self-transcendence as does the profane, but it distorts self-transcendence."[31] With this distinction in mind, one can see how Tillich enlists the secular in the struggle against the demonic, how secularization (*Profanisierung*) brings about "de-demonizing" (*Entdämonisierung*). As examples of this process, he points to Greek philosophy which destroyed the Homeric gods, and the Enlightenment which did away with the devil. The weapon taken up by the secular against the demonic is rational form. Rational clarity leaves no room for the mystery of God and the fear of demons. The demons are banished and God is incorporated into an orderly world-system; neither can break into the world with the shaking power of the holy. Secularism favors the divine in that it upholds form against the negative, form-destroying power of the demonic. But it rejects the divine in that it denies transcendence, and so the price of "de-demonizing" is "de-divinizing" (*Entgöttlichung*). In either case, the characteristic of the secular is the rational.[32]

Profanization of Religion

Autonomy can also be considered as the result of an eviscerating process which Tillich describes as the profanization of religion by the secular. He prefers to call this process "profanization" rather than "secularization," because "the term 'profane' in its genuine meaning expresses exactly what we call 'resisting self-transcendence,' that is, remaining before the door of the temple, standing outside the holy. . . ."[33] Thus it is a more graphic expression, although equivalent to secularization.

The profanization of religion reduces it to a finite thing among other finite things. But religion should manifest the holy, should transcend itself, so that its elements—Holy Scripture, holy communities, acts, persons, and offices—should point beyond themselves, should be translucent to the holy. When this does not happen, the ambiguous character of religion asserts itself, and religion is profanized. Profanization occurs in two ways: the

institutional way and the reductive way. Religion is institutionalized when it becomes just another object—"a set of prescribed
activities to be performed, a set of stated doctrines to be accepted,
a social pressure group along with others, a political power with
all the implications of power politics."[34] It can also be profanized
by being reduced to culture and morality. This comes about when
"the veil of self-transcendence" is taken away from religion, and
one finds there cognitive insight and aesthetic expression, personality development, and principles of community.[35] Culture and
morality then have no need of religion, for it offers them nothing
that they do not already possess. In both processes of profanization, by either the institutional or the reductive way, the nature
of the secular appears as self-sufficiency which resists transcendence. Tillich warns that the Catholic Church runs the perennial
risk of profanization by superstitious devotions devoid of true
religious content, while Protestantism is always in danger of
reductive secularization.[36]

Technology

If autonomy is self-sufficiency, a word must be said about one
of the most powerful forces for man's independence—technology.
As one of the causes for the onslaught of secularization against
religion, Tillich points to technology:

The chief and always effective weapon for this attack is the invasion of
all religious groups by technology with its various waves of technical
revolution. Its effect was and is, first of all, a secularization which
destroys the old traditions, both of culture and religion. This is most
obvious in a country like Japan.[37]

He defines technology as "the formation of reality according to
a goal" (*Wirklichkeitsformung nach einem Zweck*). It produces
tools and machines which mold material to patterns determined
by man. As such, it serves man and is not in itself secular; in

fact, technology can and should be consecrated, as hand labor was in days gone by. However, it is the technical mentality that secularizes—the drive to subjugate reality by harnessing it as means to an end, the loss of reverence for nature, and the eventual reduction of man himself to a machine, a tool, a unit of labor.[38] What Tillich seems to be driving at is that technology fosters secularism by providing man with an instrument seemingly capable of achieving human self-sufficiency. Yet he also acknowledges the debt which our world owes to technology when he states, "In contrast to much of what has been said and much of what I myself have said against technology, I want to speak *for* the saving power of the technical control of nature." In technology he sees liberation from animal drudgery, conquest of the narrow confines of time and space, and protection from unnecessary pain and death. Technology undoubtedly possesses destructive possibilities. "Nevertheless, in the great feats of technical control we have a breakthrough of the eternal into the temporal."[39]

Autonomy has been considered from several viewpoints: the secular, the process of profanization, and technology. It can be summed up as a humanism that fails to transcend itself:

Humanism is the attitude which makes man the measure of his own spiritual life, in art and philosophy, in science and politics, in social relations and personal ethics. For humanism the divine is manifest in the human; the ultimate concern of man is man.[40]

An autonomous humanism stops at the door of the temple without crossing the threshold of the holy.

HETERONOMY

While autonomy insists that man is his own law, heteronomy, on the other hand, "asserts that man, being unable to act according to universal reason, must be subjected to a law, strange and

superior to him."[41] Substance, instead of warming cultural forms
with an inner glow, smothers them like an oversized garment.
Most frequently heteronomy originates in religion that has lost
God, that has degenerated into mere religion.[42] Tillich cites as
examples the late Middle Ages and Protestant orthodoxy. A
heteronomous culture "subjects the forms and laws of thinking
and acting to authoritative criteria of an ecclesiastical religion
or a political quasi-religion, even at the price of destroying the
structures of rationality."[43] Heteronomy is imposed by an institution or a personality which arrogates to itself "the claim to
speak in the name of the ground of being and therefore in an
unconditional and ultimate way."[44] Thus heteronomy is inevitably
demonic.

Like autonomy, heteronomy can be considered from several
angles. We shall first examine the salient characteristic of heteronomy—the demonic; secondly, the area into which it most
frequently infiltrates—authority.

The Demonic

Mention of the demonic has already been made in discussing
the experience of the holy, in order to put into clear relief the
ambiguity of the holy and of faith, for they embrace both the
divine and the demonic. Here we probe more deeply into the demonic, for it is one of Tillich's indispensable concepts, used
by him like a chisel to carve out his interpretation of culture,
religion, and history. He perfected it as early as 1926 in his essay
"Das Dämonische."[45]

Here his point of departure is primitive art: statues of gods,
fetishes, dance masks, and so on, which possess an artistic and
religious value often inaccessible to occidental consciousness.
Though these objects bear forms (men, animals, plants), we are
shocked by the manner in which they shatter form. Hands, feet,
teeth, eyes, sex organs are recognizable as such, but they also
burst through and distort their natural organic form. Yet we

cannot write off this impressive human production as devoid of cultural value. On the contrary, it demonstrates a truth which our form-ridden Western eyes overlook: "There is something positively contrary to form that is capable of fitting into an artistic form."[46] Call it lack of form, or contradiction of form, or the contrapositive. Tillich calls it "the demonic," "the actuality of that which is positively contrary to form."[47]

What primitive art reveals, the history of religions confirms by its "holy demonries"—phallic cults, ritual prostitution, laceration myths, cult of war gods, and so on. The most fearsome example from our own times is Dostoievsky's "Grand Inquisitor": "The religion which makes itself absolute and therefore must destroy the saint in whose name it is established—the demonic will to power of the sacred institution."[48] These examples contain the same tension as the creations of primitive art, i.e., the combination of a formative and a form-shattering element, of form-creation and form-destruction.[49] Therefore, the history of religions verifies the definition of the demonic: "the unity of form-creating and form-destroying strength."[50]

These artistic and religious manifestations of the demonic are rooted in a metaphysics. The destructiveness of form which marks the demonic is neither injected from without nor originates from within by weakness or deficiency. It arises from the depths of form itself, from the inexhaustibility of being. Being is the non-rational, non-demonstrable ground of all things. At the same time it is their abyss, for they can never exhaust it. This inexhaustibility of being, however, is not like a passive, peaceful reservoir, but an active, consuming fire which burns through the form in which it is confined. For "there dwells in everything the inner inexhaustibility of being, the will to realize in itself as an individual the active infinity of being, the impulse toward breaking through its own limited form, the longing to realize the abyss in itself."[51] The demonic is this surge of the abyss of being which tends to destroy form, but never quite succeeds, because "to come intó being means to come to form."[52] Moreover, the abyss of being is also the ground of being which is creative and conservative in a positive way. To sum up the ontology of the demonic: "Demonry is the form-destroying eruption of the creative basis of things."[53]

The phenomenon and the ontology of the demonic at first glance may seem far removed from heteronomy. A few more steps, however, and the fusion of the two becomes discernible. For instance, the demonic operates in the personality as the explosion of subconscious forces that splits the personality, with the result that it is "subjugated to a new power which is not a natural power"—the perfect definition of heteronomy.[54] On the social plane, demonry does not split the personality, but causes "the breaking of personality by the superindividual social structure"—a heteronomous imposition.[55] Demonry ends in heteronomy because of its abysmal, imperialistic drive to realize the unrealizable infinity of being in a finite reality. By the destruction of form it seeks to expand ever farther and thus encompass more being. Finally, it claims to have achieved the infinite in the finite, and this claim "is the root of all heteronomy and of all demonry. For the demonic is something finite, something limited, which puts on infinite, unlimited dignity."[56]

Authority

If heteronomy inevitably goes shipwreck on the rocks of the demonic, authority becomes a dangerous problem because "heteronomy is the authority claimed or exercised by a finite being in the name of the infinite."[57] Although the most sensitive point is the question of supreme authority, the problem touches authority of every stripe, since even lesser authorities have some link, however tenuous, with ultimate authority for their justification. In our first chapter, reference was made to Tillich's struggle to escape from the authoritarian atmosphere of his home life and training.[58] The scars from this battle never completely disappeared, as he himself confesses:

Most difficult to overcome was the impact of the authoritarian system on my personal life, especially on its religious and intellectual side. . . . It is this difficult and painful break-through to autonomy which has made me immune against any system of thought or life which demands the surrender of this autonomy.[59]

That Tillich's wariness of authority runs wide and deep is evidenced in utterances such as the following: "Submission to divine and secular authorities, i.e., heteronomy, was precisely what I, for my own self, had rejected; and to it I neither want to, nor can return."[60] He senses behind the mask of authority the demonic face of heteronomy, "subjection to a law which is not experienced as our own."[61]

The query, therefore, has been put to him: "Is there an authority which is not heteronomously distorted? Is there a theonomous authority?"[62] Tillich grants what he calls an "actual" authority based on a superiority of knowledge, ability, and experience, which is indispensable due to man's limitations and deficiencies. But he warns that it ambiguously degenerates into "established" authority attached to social positions, e.g., parents, kings, and priests, which trespasses upon the sacred domains of the personal self.[63] Thus his attitude is ambivalent. Keenly aware of the need for authority, an awareness intensified by the political chaos in Germany after World War I, he is even more sensitive to the ambiguity of authority and its constant need for a corrective.

Tillich tackles the problem of authority in several areas. In an essay written in 1931, "The Problem of Power," he seeks a formula for an effective but restrained political authority. His solution is the paradox of "power through the renunciation of power," a renunciation or moderation based not on weakness, but on the vitality of participation in the transcendent power beyond all finite power-structures.[64] In his book *Love, Power,* and *Justice,* subtitled "Ontological Analyses and Ethical Applications," the question of authority is obliquely treated in the discussion of

power as an ontological concept. Without unraveling here the
complexities of his argument, suffice it to say that Tillich insists
that the power of authority be directed toward fostering union,
but that this process of unification not be vitiated by an unjust
and meaningless conformity.

Tillich's sharpest and most satisfying treatment of authority is a
sermon that expounds the gospel scene (Lk 20:1–8) where the
chief priests, scribes, and elders ask Jesus by what authority he
teaches.[65] They know the source of their own authority: the chief
priests have their consecration in the line of Moses and Aaron, the
scribes rely upon their knowledge of the Scriptures, and the elders
call upon their wisdom and experience. All of them, including
Jesus, admit man's need for authority because we are so frail,
so dependent upon others, and "the acceptance of authority is the
acceptance of what is given by those who have more than we."[66]
The real question, then, is not authority as such, but the validity
of a particular authority. By pointing to John the Baptist, Jesus
asserts the possibility of "an authority guaranteed by its inner
power," not established by tradition, knowledge, or experience.
Throughout his career Jesus was in conflict with established
authorities. As a result, "there is something in the Christian message which is opposed to established authority. There is something in the Christian experience which revolts against subjection
to even the greatest and holiest experience of the past."[67] Beyond
pointing to the example of John the Baptist, Jesus gives no reply
about the source of his authority because he cannot. He cannot
single out any finite reality and attach to it or derive from it the
dignity of ultimate authority:

The place where God gives authority to a man cannot be circumscribed.
It cannot be legally defined. It cannot be put into the fences of doctrines and rituals. It is here, and you do not know where it comes
from. You cannot derive it. You must be grasped by it. You must participate in its power. This is the reason why the question of authority
never can get an ultimate answer.[68]

Authority is from God, but God is Spirit, the Spirit that blows where it wills and cannot be imprisoned in finite institutions. The God who is Spirit does not eliminate preliminary authorities from our lives—parental, social, political, and ecclesiastical—but he denies ultimacy to all of them. The only suitable symbol of authority is the Cross upon which Jesus witnessed, not to himself, but to "Him who is the ground and the negation of everything which is authority on earth and in heaven."[69]

Through Tillich's various solutions to the problem of authority which we have seen—power through renunciation of power, power inspired by love but tempered by justice, the acceptance of preliminary authorities but the denial of the possibility of localizing ultimate authority—through all of these solutions shines the Protestant principle, the paradoxical principle of simultaneous affirmation and negation. By the Protestant principle he accepts authority, but in the same breath criticizes it, for authority always leans toward heteronomy and thus presents a constant target for the prophetic protest against the demonic.

Heteronomy is a type of union of religion and culture, but a demonically distorted one. It fails to respect legitimately autonomous forms and imposes itself as an alien law. Thus heteronomy is more a subordination of culture to religion than an organic union of the two, for it is "the attempt of a religion to dominate autonomous cultural creativity from the outside. . . ."[70]

THEONOMY

The equilibrium between cultural substance and form is achieved in a theonomy which embraces the truth of autonomy and heteronomy while avoiding their errors. Theonomy rejects both a divine law imposed by outside authority and a self-sufficient reason divorced from its depth. It demands that man seek a superior law which is at the same time rooted in the divine ground of being that lies at the depth of reason. The result is a theonomous culture which "expresses in its creations an ultimate concern and a transcending meaning not as something strange but as its own spiritual ground."[71] Theonomous creations are "vessels of a spiritual content."[72] Tillich's oft-repeated epigrammatic statement of theonomy is: "Religion is the substance of culture, and culture the form of religion."[73]

Theonomy, autonomy, and heteronomy as cultural types constantly act and interact in dialectical fashion.[74] The shallowness of an autonomous, secularized culture creates a vacuum of despair, a "sacred void" which preludes the advent of a theonomous period in which empty cultural forms receive substance and depth. Theonomy, however, tends to degenerate into an oppressive heteronomy which, in turn, provokes an autonomous reaction, and so the cycle begins anew. For instance, Clement and Origen created a Christian theonomy which later came under the heteronomous influence of Athanasius and Augustine. The Middle Ages started as theonomy and ended in heteronomy. The Renaissance had theonomous qualities, but deteriorated into autonomy. The Reformation itself developed into the heteronomy of Protestant orthodoxy and then succumbed to the triumphant autonomy of the eighteenth and nineteenth centuries.[75] These examples illustrate that theonomy, though realizable, is ever fragile and incomplete. "Its victory is always fragmentary because of the existential estrangement underlying human history, and its defeat is always limited by the fact that human nature is essentially theonomous."[76]

A description of the general qualities of a theonomous culture serves to highlight the reciprocal influence of the three cultural types.[77] The first characteristic of theonomy is that "it communicates the experience of holiness, of something ultimate in being and meaning, in all its creations." This theonomous style appears "even in the most limited vehicles of meaning—a painted flower, a family habit, a technical tool, a form of social intercourse, the vision of a historical figure, an epistemological theory, a political document, and so on." The second characteristic is "the affirmation of the autonomous forms of the creative process." The moment theonomy fails to respect legitimate autonomy and the freedom of the human spirit, it becomes heteronomy. The third characteristic of a theonomous culture is "its permanent struggle against both an independent autonomy and an independent heteronomy." Only theonomy can prevent them from inflicting upon mankind either a meaningless or a destructive culture.

We shall now consider some of the various facets of theonomy.

Spiritual Presence and Cultural Ambiguities

One way to grasp the transforming power of theonomy is to see how cultural ambiguities are resolved under the impact of the "Spiritual Presence." It has already been explained how spirit (small "s") is "the actualization of power and meaning in unity" and is found only in man. But God can be symbolically described as "Spirit" (capital "S"), and his relation to man is metaphorically expressed in the statement that "the divine Spirit dwells and works in the human spirit." The former seizes the latter in an unconditioned and ultimate concern and, in a moment of ecstasy, drives the human spirit out of itself and into a state of self-transcendence. This "breaking-in" of the divine Spirit and the "going-out" of the human spirit is what Tillich calls "the Spiritual Presence."[78] It alone effects a theonomous culture.

Cultural ambiguity is the failure of a cultural creation to achieve the meaning it should achieve, although it is not entirely devoid of meaning. Tillich maintains that the basic ambiguity underlying all particular cultural ambiguities is the cleavage between subject and object.[79] In *theoria*, the receptive function of culture, "the subject tries to bridge the gap by receiving the object in words, concepts, and images, but never achieves this aim."[80] In *praxis*, the formative cultural function, the object is to be shaped according to the subject by technology and by personal and communal relationships, yet it manages to escape control. The split between subject and object can be healed only by the power of the Spiritual Presence which unites the two in a transcendence beyond subjectivity and objectivity, where the subject ceases to remain subject and the object ceases to remain object.

The fundamental subject-object ambiguity never appears as such, but always in a specific cultural form. Since obviously all possible cultural ambiguities cannot be discussed, we select the case of language to illustrate how the Spiritual Presence surmounts ambiguity to establish theonomy. Language seeks to unite subject with object by creating a universe of meaning, but "the inherent ambiguity of language is that, in transforming reality into meaning, it separates mind and reality."[81] For instance, there is the poverty of language in the midst of its own richness, in that, while grasping one facet of reality, it neglects innumerable others. Again, its universality is limited by the fact that it is tied to a particular linguistic structure. Furthermore, the definiteness of language is shot through with misleading indefiniteness. And, lastly, the communicative power of language can be so manipulated and perverted that it actually conceals instead of reveals. These ambiguities of language are ultimately explained by the ambiguous cleavage between subject and object which makes language possible and, at the same time, distorts it.

How does the Spiritual Presence attack and close the gap between subject and object in the matter of language? It does so insofar as "it witnesses, it expresses, it gives voice to what transcends the subject-object structure."[82] Under the influence of the Spirit the human word becomes the Word of God. This "Spirit-determined human word" is not bound to any particular religion or revelation. But whenever language becomes a bearer of the Spirit, it unites the speaker with that of which he speaks by reaching beyond the subject-object structure to the power of being and meaning in which they both are grounded. Consequently, the ambiguity of poverty and abundance is overcome in that "a few words become great words" when they convey the Spirit. The ambiguity of particularity and universality is conquered since the Spirit-bearing word, though particular, shares in the universality of the Spirit. Ambiguous indefiniteness yields, for "the word, determined by the Spiritual Presence, does not try to grasp an ever escaping object but expresses a union between the inexhaustible subject and the inexhaustible object. . . ."[83] Finally, the ambiguity of communication and anti-communication is overcome when the word, impregnated with the Spirit, penetrates to the center of both listener and speaker so that estrangement and, with it, the possibility of deception and distortion vanish. To sum up, the presence of the Spirit in human language is another Pentecost. The subject-object chasm is bridged, thus striking at the root of all linguistic ambiguities. The result is a theonomous cultural function.

Theonomous Interplay

Another illustration of theonomy is the interpenetration of morality, culture, and religion. At the risk of oversimplification, we briefly outline their three-way interplay.

Morality, "the constitution of the person as person in the encounter with other persons," looks to culture to provide it with concrete contents such as the ideal of personality and community. Morality receives from religion "the unconditional character of the moral imperative," and the ultimate moral aim, namely, reunion of the separated.[84] Tillich even calls his morality "theonomous ethics," for it is a matter of law, but not alien law (heteronomy) or superficial law (autonomy):

. . . the law given by God is man's essential nature, put against him as law. If man were not estranged from himself, if his essential nature were not distorted in his actual existence, no law would stand against him. The law is not strange to man. It is natural law. It represents his true nature from which he is estranged.[85]

Culture creates a universe of meaning, but the forms it produces are valid only if morality imparts to them the force of the moral imperative. Culture accepts from religion the substance or ground which alone affords the element of ultimacy.

Religion is the self-transcendence of life under the dimension of spirit, but this cannot occur without morality, i.e., "without the constitution of the moral self by the unconditional imperative." Furthermore, religion depends upon culture to provide the meaningful forms in which self-transcendence is expressed.[86]

Under the conditions of existence, religion, culture, and morality are ambiguously disrupted and tend to act independently of one another. However, their essential unity and interplay in the human spirit exemplify theonomy in yet another way.

The Depth-Dimension

Perhaps Tillich's most graphic expression of theonomy is the metaphor "depth." "Dimension" is one of his favorite images, and "depth" is the dimension he most frequently employs. The depth-dimension enters into the very definition of theonomy, for theonomy is "autonomous reason united with its own depth."[87] By means of depth he nuances the image of the union of religion and culture so that it does not appear as a crudely tied knot: "In spite of the theonomous union between religion and culture, these two do not lie on the same level. Religion is the depth-dimension of culture. . . ."[88]

The depth-dimension vividly describes the role of religion in theonomy. The abstract formulation is this: Religion is the substance of culture, and culture is the form of religion. More concretely, however, "Religion is ultimate concern. . . . As such it gives meaning, seriousness, and depth to all culture. . . ."[89] "It is always effective, giving inexhaustible depth to life and inexhaustible meaning to every cultural creation."[90] But Tillich is not merely painting intellectual pictures. He himself asks, "What does the metaphor *depth* mean? It means that the religious aspect points to that which is ultimate, infinite, unconditioned in man's spiritual life."[91]

He sums up the American religious revival of the 1950's as a search for the lost dimension, the religious dimension of depth.[92] For "man has lost the answer to the question of whence he comes, whither he goes, what he is doing, and what he should make of himself in the short span between birth and death."[93] This loss of the depth-dimension is reflected in the loss of symbols which traditionally convey it. The symbols of creation, original sin, the savior, salvation, and God have been interpreted on a horizontal level as reports about past events, as descriptions of things next to other things. Consequently, they have become meaningless. Rather, they must be interpreted vertically as expressions of the ground of being and meaning. The most religious currents—religious in the wide sense of ultimate concern—are found today in the modern novelists, poets, dramatists, painters, architects, and analytic and existential philosophers who penetrate to the lost dimension, who raise the ultimate question.

But what lies at the bottom of this murky dimension of depth? In his stirring sermon "The Depth of Existence" Tillich replies quite simply: "The name of this infinite and inexhaustible depth and ground of all being is *God*."[94] He deplores the aimless surface activity of our lives where we speed about like hit-and-run drivers, cruelly smashing ourselves and others. To avoid complete despair we must abandon this surface-life:

Let us rather plunge more deeply into the ground of our historical life, into the ultimate depth of history. The name of this infinite and inexhaustible ground of history is *God*. That is what the word means, and it is that to which the words *Kingdom of God* and *Divine Providence* point. And if these words do not have much meaning for you, translate them, and speak of the depth of history, of the ground and aim of our social life, and of what you take seriously without reservation in your moral and political activities.[95]

In fathoming the depths one achieves theonomy.

The Holy and the Secular

The theonomous union of religion and culture can be expressed in yet another way, by the relation of the holy to the secular. Tillich establishes three principles which govern this relationship: the principles of consecration, convergence, and essential union.

Consecration: The first is "the principle of the consecration of the secular."[96] By this, Tillich means "Nothing is essentially and inescapably secular. Everything has the dimension of depth, and in the moment in which the third dimension is actualized, holiness appears. Everything secular is potentially sacred, open to consecration."[97] Nor is the mediation of the churches, of religion in the narrow sense, necessary for this consecration. For the dimension of depth in the secular is religion—religion in the large sense of ultimate concern which cannot be restricted only to an ecclesiastical sphere. Once the autonomous, self-sufficient surface of the secular is broken through by an unconditioned concern, the holy reveals itself in the depths of the secular. In that moment, "the universe is God's sanctuary. Every work day is a day of the Lord, every supper a Lord's supper, every work the fulfillment of a divine task, every joy a joy in God. In all preliminary concerns, ultimate concern is present, consecrating them."[98] The concrete way in which consecration is effected is symbolism. When, under the influence of ultimate concern, a thing becomes a symbol of the holy, then to that degree it is sacred and participates in divine holiness. No object, no person, no activity is excluded from the possibility of symbolizing the holy, for everything in the world "rests on the ultimate ground of being."[99]

Convergence: The first principle, then, offers the possibility of finding the holy in the secular; the second principle, "the convergence of the holy and secular," maintains its necessity.[100] The secular resists self-transcendence, but this very resistance produces "the emptiness and meaninglessness which characterizes the finite when cut off from the infinite."[101] An exhausted secularism is driven to ask the question of a meaning and power of being beyond itself; it seeks the holy. On the other hand, the holy cannot manifest itself without the secular, "for it is through the finite alone that the infinite can express itself. It is through holy 'objects' that holiness must become actual."[102] Consequently, although they remain in tension, the poles of the holy-secular converge upon one another.

Essential Union: The third and last principle is that of "the essential belongingness of religion and culture to each other." In the existential, actual condition of mankind, the holy is separated from the secular, and this constitutes the state of sin. Essentially, however, they are united in that "religion is the substance of culture, and culture the form of religion."[103] Therefore, in the essential order the holy and the secular are not found as hostile or even divided spheres; rather, together they form a union in which the autonomy of the finite is not destroyed, while at the same time it achieves transcendence by revealing in its depths the presence of the infinite. The fact that in the existential order they confront each other from behind unyielding barriers is, for Tillich, tragic witness to the state of sin and separation in which man lives.[104]

Asked what the proof is for the fall of the world, I like to answer: religion itself, namely, a religious culture beside a secular culture, a temple beside a town hall, a Lord's supper beside a daily supper, prayer beside work, meditation beside research, *caritas* beside *eros*.[105]

This duality can never be fully overcome in history, but it should be prevented from widening into an unbridgeable chasm. The poles of the holy-secular can be at least fragmentarily united.

The above principles that relate the holy to the secular render intelligible the term "Protestant secularism" which Tillich employs occasionally for the following reasons:

The term "theonomy" may be objected to because its use by Catholics has created connotations of a clearly heteronomous character. Therefore, it may be wise to speak, in certain cases, of "Protestant secularism.". . .[106]

Theonomy "indicates that neither ecclesiastical heteronomy nor secular autonomy can have the last word in human culture."[107] For the shallow creations of an autonomous culture lack substance, and heteronomy rides roughshod over secular forms. But Tillich warns that theonomy is more than a needle which flickers between two extremes on the culture-gauge:

There is, however, . . . a difference between a culture which is theonomous, determined by direct and intentional expression of an ultimate concern, and a culture which oscillates between an empty autonomy and a suppressive heteronomy.[108]

Ultimate concern is the positive, life-giving taproot of theonomous culture.

THE DISPUTE WITH KARL BARTH

In the *Theologische Blätter* of 1923, Tillich engaged in an *Auseinandersetzung* with Karl Barth and Friederich Gogarten. Twelve years later he published an article entitled "What is Wrong with the 'Dialectic' Theology?" and in his *Systematic Theology* he differs with Barth on the nature and method of theology. The reason for inserting the Tillich-Barth dispute into the chapter on theonomous culture will become apparent as the discussion progresses, for its inclusion here demands some justification.

At this point we inject a reminder that the primary purpose of our study is to understand the mind of Paul Tillich. Consequently, what he *thinks* Barth says and *his reactions* to Barth are far more important than passing judgment on the accuracy of his analysis of Barthian theology. This latter task lies beyond our modest aim.[109]

The Dispute, 1923

In an article written in 1923, entitled "Kritisches und Positives Paradox," Tillich acknowledges the necessity and the power of Barth's protest.[110] However, the dialectic cannot go on forever. Ultimately it must be anchored in a positive position, in a Yes. We stand not only under judgment, but also under grace. Tillich accuses Barth and Gogarten of neglecting the positive (grace) which underlies the negative (judgment) in three areas: the relation of God and the world, God and Spirit, and God and history. Theology must always speak paradoxically in a Yes and a No, but if Barth's critical paradox only recognized its presuppositions, which are no longer judgment (*Krisis*) but creation and grace, it would correct itself and become a theology of positive paradox.

Barth's response, "Concerning the Paradox of the 'Positive Paradox,' " charges that Tillich belabors the obvious, that crisis theology, long aware of its positive root, does not build upon an infinitely regressing dialectic.[111] But it is in the relationship of God to nature, spirit, and history that Barth parts company with Tillich. Barth raises three objections: (1) the directness (*Direktheit*) with which Tillich relates God and the world is unparadoxical, as when, for example, the meaning at the depths (*Tiefen-Sinn*) becomes the depth of meaning (*Tiefsinn*) simply by being recognized as such; (2) his overconfident ease (*Leichtigkeit*) in manipulating the concepts of judgment and grace resembles more an exercise in logic than a theological treatment of mysteries; and (3) his readiness (*Freigebigkeit*) to cast the mantle of the positive paradox over everything results in a cheap universalism.

The tenor of Barth's answer is felt in passages like the following:

I reject . . . Tillich's grandiose generalizing, this setting up of relations between God and each and every thing in heaven and earth, this broad, universal sweep of faith and revelation . . . as if it were self-evident that everywhere, everywhere judgment and grace hold sway, that everything, simply everything *is* involved in the struggle and peace of the *positive paradox*. . . .[112]

Barth concludes by stating that he is still puzzled by Tillich's attack which he suspects is motivated by fear of the "Grand Inquisitor."

Tillich's reply seeks to clarify the stance (*Geisteslage*) from which he launches his criticism.[113] First of all, he admits that he is on the offensive against the Grand Inquisitor, for it is the nature of the Protestant principle to resist heteronomy, to protest justification by intellectual works even though they deal with the content of faith.[114] Some years later he retaliates by pinning the epithet on Barth himself: "The Grand Inquisitor is about to enter the Confessional Church and, strictly speaking, with a strong but tight-fitting armor of Barthian supranaturalism."[115]

Secondly, theology must communicate in terms meaningful to our age. One must speak of the unconditioned instead of God, of the Logos instead of Jesus Christ. In this way, traces of the divine Yes and No can be found in all cultures. If one prefers to call this a philosophy of culture, then our era requires of us *as* theologians *not to be* theologians, but philosophers of culture.

After this exposition of the *status quaestionis*, Tillich ends with two remarks to Barth. He fears that the Barthian dialectic has deteriorated into a very undialectical supranaturalism in pronouncing a simple No against the world. Furthermore, the reform theology in which Barth is grounded establishes a gulf between the secular and the holy which ends in profaning and emptying cultural life, and in reducing the religious life to fundamentalism (*Primitivisierung des religiösen Lebens*). Tillich calls for a new theonomy to supersede secular autonomy.

Gogarten's brief answer to Tillich summarizes their different points of departure. Gogarten claims that he and Barth seek an understanding of the world in Jesus Christ, whereas Tillich seeks an understanding of Jesus Christ in the world.[116]

The Dispute, 1935

Time passed, and the European scene rapidly changed, but Tillich's estimate of Barthian theology remained the same. In 1935, now an exile in the United States, he renews his charge that the so-called dialectic theology is not truly dialectic, but paradoxical.[117] "A dialectical theology is one in which Yes and No belong inseparably together." But Barth has separated them so that his theology is paradoxical, even supernatural, but certainly not dialectic. Barth's great contribution is that he "preserves the sovereign prerogative of God as expressed in the first commandment. God's sovereignty is not blended with any form of human existence and action." God is the "impossible possibility" who is beyond all human possibilities. But such statements, while paradoxical, do not involve a constantly interacting Yes and No. Rather, it is a reiterated No to creaturely possibilities: the world, the church, mysticism, the philosophy of religion, and cultural theology. The Barthian blast, consequently, demolishes liberal theology. For "in place of the sinner it [liberalism] substitutes the self-developing personality; in place of Christ, the self-developing religious man Jesus; in place of the word of God in Scripture, the self-developing religious consciousness of humanity."

As valuable as Barth's effort has been in proclaiming the paradox of the divine "impossible possibility" in the face of secularism and paganism, nevertheless he falls into a supernaturalism which cannot span the gap between the divine and the human. Tillich argues that "the *question* about the divine possibility is a human possibility." Furthermore, the question about the divine possibility could never have been asked unless the answer had not already been given in a preliminary and obscure fashion. In other words, "to be able to ask about God, man must already have experienced God as the goal of a possible question." If man cannot ask the question of God, then God's answer—revelation—falls on deaf ears. Revelation would then be injected into history as a foreign body. Barth's error of under-estimating the human possibility leads him into a supernatural theology. Hence, his understanding of man, nature, culture, history, and so forth, is incomplete, because it is too much under the power of the No. The mistake of liberal theology was in "identifying a continuity of humanly valuable activities with the realization of the Kingdom of God." Barth's mistake is in "the severance of human activities from both divine and demonic powers." Neither is truly dialectic.

Common Ground, but Different Paths

To find the decisive point of opposition between Tillich and Barth and to state it precisely is not an easy task, for even while matching blades they still share much common ground. They heartily concur in rejecting nineteenth-century liberal theology which reduced Christianity to humanism.[118] Tillich praises the purifying, prophetic power of Barthian theology:

This theology lets the judgment of the unconditionally transcendent God fall upon every attempt of culture and religion to claim value before him. In its conception the only relation which the world has to God is that the world stands in the divine negation, in the crisis, in the shaking of time by eternity.[119]

It also shakes liberal theology to its foundations, and on this score Tillich takes his stand with Barth.[120]

The point where Tillich and Barth part company has been described in a variety of terms. One commentator stresses Tillich's fear of a new orthodoxy that impelled him to break with Barth.[121] Another points out that Tillich maintains the openness of history to the transcendent, while, for Barth, judgment and grace bracket life without entering it.[122] Frequent mention is made of their differing notions of revelation: To what degree does it transcend culture and man's reception of it?[123] Finally, their theological starting points are said to be different: Barth begins with the word of God, while Tillich begins with the human experience of this word.[124]

While not denying the merit of these opinions, we prefer Tillich's notion of theonomous culture as the most sensitive center of disagreement between himself and Barth. This conclusion emerges from the progress of the debate just described. Undoubtedly their concepts of God, of revelation, and of theology are divergent. However, theonomy not only occasions a contrast of all these speculative points, but also separates the two men according to their natural bent and their theological reaction to historical crises—at least from Tillich's point of view. For Tillich instinctively gravitates toward a theonomy in which religion is the substance of culture and culture is the form of religion, but, to Barth, he could well appear as the liberal wolf in dialectical clothing. Nor is it any accident that the work that earned Barth a name in the theological world was his commentary on Romans with its prophetic protest, while, for Tillich, it was his essay on the theology of culture.

As we have seen, Tillich accuses Barth of neglecting the positive side of the Protestant protest. He complains that Barth puts the holy and the secular in a negative and not in a polar relationship.[125] The result is that for years Barth overlooked the "Gestalt of grace" latent in Protestantism.[126] Tillich further reproaches him for not applying the protest to his own theology, thus permitting it to harden into a neo-orthodoxy that has little sympathy for non-Christian religions.[127]

But the real bone in Tillich's throat is what he calls "the 'dialectic' indifference toward what is social."[128] He relates the irritation he experienced as professor at the University of Marburg:

During the three semesters of my teaching there I met the first radical effects of the neo-orthodox theology on theological students: cultural problems were excluded from theological thought; theologians, like Schleiermacher, Harnack, Troeltsch, Otto, were contemptuously

rejected; social and political ideas were banned from theological discussions. The contrast with the experiences in Berlin was overwhelm-
ing, at first depressing and then inciting: a new way had to be found.[129]

He always felt that Barth was neither then nor later the man to
blaze the trail because of his vacillation on the question of social
ethics.[130] It took the barbarity of the nazi regime to turn Barth
"from a theology of radical detachment from culture, religious as
well as secular, to an equally radical attachment to the fight against
a demonically distorted cultural system. Barth suddenly realized
that culture can never be indifferent toward the ultimate."[131]
These lines were written in 1946. Tillich attacked Barth in 1923
and 1935. Although, from 1938 on, Barth elaborated a theology of
political service, Tillich apparently has never forgiven him for
what he considers the paralysis of neo-orthodoxy *vis à vis* the
post-World War I political, social, and economic turmoil in Germany.[132]

If we have dwelt at length on this *Auseinandersetzung,* it is because Tillich's broadsides against Barth reveal much about his
own positions. Undoubtedly one could mount a good defense for
Barth, but the accent has been expressly laid upon Tillich's side,
the better to view his doctrine in the light of controversy.[133] Controversy brings out in relief not only the contours of his thought,
but also its verve and its emotional drive, all of which we find
most distinctively formulated in the idea of theonomous culture.

REFLECTIONS AND APPRAISAL

While theonomy is not a term or concept of strictly Tillichian
origin, his interpretation of it has made it a trademark of his
theology.[134] Theonomy (*Gottesgesetzlichkeit*) is arrived at by
way of autonomy (*Selbstgesetzlichkeit*) and heteronomy (*Frem-
desgesetzlichkeit*), which latter two were first worked out on a
large scale by Immanuel Kant in the field of ethics. Although the

notion of theonomy is occasionally employed today, the term itself has not been generally adopted.[135] Tillich's appropriaton of it
is natural and unforced, for theonomy is a logically smooth juncture of his concepts of culture and ultimate concern. In his view,
culture is form, and for content it must look elsewhere—in its
depths. But at the depths one discovers ultimate concern, the
power and the meaning which breathes a soul into the otherwise
dead body of culture. In theonomy the body is vigorous and
bursting with the energy of a truly ultimate concern. Religion and
culture are theonomously one.

Tillich's comprehensive treatment of culture—its nature, functions, elements, style, types, and ambiguities—is of value and
interest for philosophers, historians, sociologists, and anthropolo-
gists. However, it is of pressing importance for theologians, since
the notion of theonomous culture propels Christianity into the
midst of the world. Theonomy demands that religion permeate the
whole of society, even its hitherto considered profane areas. His
emphasis upon the tight unity of the holy and secular accounts
in large measure for the dynamic appeal of his theology. Without
a close bond between religion and culture, theology is left with
little to say to modern man in the majority of his consuming activities. Man today is not prepared to renounce the creations of
literature, art, politics, science, and technology as stumbling blocks
to the holy. On the contrary, if his attitude is at all religious, he
tends to view them as steppingstones which lead to a fuller and
profounder experience of the divine. Walter Leibrecht sums up
the import of theonomy as follows:

Tillich's call to theonomy is his greatest challenge to modern thought.
His is a vision of culture in which ultimate concern informs the whole
web of life and thought and for which the ultimate unity is an ever-
present horizon. With this idea of theonomy, Tillich overcomes the
easy deification of culture by liberal theology and yet makes religion
relevant to culture in a profound way. He bridges the gap which

Barth and the existentialists alike have been able to see but not to overcome. . . . Accordingly, Tillich has been successful, as perhaps no other modern writer, in showing the essential relatedness of each cultural expression to its religious ground. The Church has been powerfully called back out of its self-chosen ghetto, out of its disregard for culture, to do its task for the world.[136]

At the end of a brief essay entitled "Religion and Secular Culture," Tillich concludes:

I have not tried to present a well-balanced synthesis between religion and secular culture. I have tried to show their *one* theonomous root and the void which necessarily has followed their separation, and perhaps something of the longing of our time for a new theonomy, for an ultimate concern in all our concerns.[137]

The same can be said about this stage of our study. Although the framework of theonomy has been built up from both the side of religion and the side of culture, and a certain enthusiasm generated about its possibilities, many points are still unresolved. Further specification of its content is required.

This state of affairs is evidenced by the fact that questions can be posed which reveal an uncertainty about the direction in which theonomy leads. For instance, one might interpret it as eventually leading to total secularization,[138] since, once the depths of culture are fathomed, they are no longer deep, and the profundity of the secular may be merely a nicer term for what in reality may be the scaling-down of the holy to the secular level. In this case the divine transcendence is forfeited, and Christ does not break into history, but rather emerges from it as a kind of ideal. Because Tillich stands for a Protestantism which "denies in principle the cleavage between a sacred and a profane sphere," he himself recognizes "the danger of becoming exclusively secular."[139] On the other hand, one might conclude that theonomy results in a total "sacralization" of the world which entails the disappearance of the profane, for the more deeply one probes into the secular heart, and even the atheistic heart, the more one perceives there the throb of an ultimate concern, the life-force of faith. In this case the transparency of the secular to the holy reduces the former to the status of a ghost. And if the secular disappears, does not the divine breakthrough lose its dramatic, unlooked-for, grace-full quality? If everything is holy, there is nothing to be broken through. Moreover, salvation is assured, and the preaching of Christ's crucifixion and resurrection is no longer an urgent mission.

Leaving the categories of secularization and sacralization, one finds the same ambiguity in theonomy in regard to the church. In one sense theonomy renders the church unnecessary, even danger-ous, for the Spiritual Presence is active everywhere with no need for ecclesiastical channels, and the history of the church discloses the menace of heteronomy which lurks in it.[140] But in another sense the church is inevitable, for the presence of the Spirit draws men together into a holy community where their ultimate concern drives through to expression in symbols and cult.

Considering theonomy in yet another context, one might claim that it does not correspond to the hard facts of the human exist-ential situation, that a theonomous union of religion and culture has never existed, or, if it did, it was quickly eroded by man's proclivity to sin. In a word, history denies theonomy. And yet, eschatology demands it. For theonomy echoes the yearning cry of the human soul to find God in all things; it corresponds, not per-haps to man's achievement, but to his deepest religious instinct, to his most ardent hope.

These alternative interpretations of theonomy indicate that even a prolonged study of its structure—religion is the substance of culture, and culture is the form of religion—is insufficient to grasp the meaning Tillich intends for it. One must delve into its theological content, specifically the notion of God, the meaning of Jesus as the Christ, the nature of the church, and the question of history and eschatology.[141] Only when Tillich's position on these crucial doctrines is determined can one attempt a proper interpretation of theonomy. This investigation is the burden of Part II.

Notes

1. "Die Kategorie des 'Heiligen' bei Rudolf Otto," *Theologische Blätter*, II, January, 1923, 12.
2. GW, I, 329–30, 380.
3. "Kirche und Kultur," 21; GW, II, 27; PE, 57; ST, III, 250.
4. ST, III, 402–403. See also p. 57.
5. *Ibid.*, 84–85.
6. Cf. the article "Kultur" in *Lexikon für Theologie und Kirche*, Josef Höfer and Karl Rahner (eds.), VI, Freiburg (i.B.): Herder, 1961, 669, and André Lalande, *Vocabulaire Technique et Critique de la Philosophie*, ninth edition, Paris: Presses Universitaires de France, 1962, 199.
7. Cf. *Webster's Third New International Dictionary*, Philip B. Grove (ed.), unabridged, Springfield, Mass.: G. and C. Merriam Co., 1963, 552. "Culture" as an anthropological term meaning "the way of life of a society" was introduced in the late nineteenth century. Its use soon spread to other disciplines. See William Bridgwater and Seymour Kurtz, *The Columbia Encyclopedia*, third edition, New York: Columbia University Press, 1963, 521.
8. PE, 219.
9. H. Richard Niebuhr, *Christ and Culture*, New York: Harper and Row, paperback, 1956, 32.
10. ST, III, 50–86.
11. *Ibid.*, 62.
12. *Ibid.*, 68.
13. *Ibid.*, 65.
14. *Ibid.*, 60. Cf. also "Theologie der Kultur," 37–39.
15. *Ibid.*, 38.
16. ST, I, 40; ST, III, 60–61.
17. TC, 42–43.
18. ST, I, 39.
19. *Ibid.*, 149.
20. A complete list would be interminable, but the following are some rather unusual examples: "Masse und Geist," GW, II, 35–41 (where he analyzes the representation of the masses in the history of art); "Logos und Mythos der Technik," *Logos* (Tübingen), XVI, November, 1927, 356–65; "Art and Ultimate Reality," *Cross Currents*, X, 1960, 1–14; "Theology and Architecture," *Architectural Forum*, CIII, December, 1955, 131–136; "The Effects of Space Exploration on Man's Condition and Stature," *The Future of Religions*, Paul Tillich, copyrighted 1966 Mrs. Hannah Tillich, used by permission of Harper & Row, Publishers, Inc.

21. "Theologie der Kultur," 37, 39; PE, xii, 57.

22. PE, 57.

23. ST, I, 76–77.

24. *Ibid.,* 79–80, 83.

25. PE, 58.

26. ST, I, 218; ST, III, 87; DF, 63; GW, I, 335. In regard to the use of terms, Tillich's German origin should never be forgotten. The German word *heilig* expresses both the English "sacred" and "holy," and so he uses them interchangeably. He does the same with "secular" and "profane," which are translated by the German *profan,* despite his occasional and well-founded distinction between them, as above.

27. SF, 181.

28. EN, 159–60.

29. RS, 105. See also pp. 39, 47, 50, 111. Cf. also GW, VI, 36–7.

30. PE, 58.

31. ST, III, 102.

32. GW, VI, 62–64, 68.

33. ST, III, 87.

34. *Ibid.,* 99.

35. *Ibid.,* 100.

36. *Ibid.,* 379–80.

37. CEWR, 12.

38. GW, I, 177. See also GW, II, 107, 130; GW, IV, 79–80; ST, III, 258–60.

39. EN, 118–119.

40. DF, 62–63. See also ST, III, 85.

41. PE, 56.

42. GW, I, 386.

43. PE, 57.

44. ST, I, 84.

45. Found in GW, VI, 42–71. Translation in IH, 77–122.

46. IH, 79.

47. *Ibid.*

48. *Ibid.,* 80.

49. The demonic embraces these two elements. The Satanic, ontologically speaking, is the purely negative, destructive factor of the demonic. Mythologically speaking, Satan is the foremost of the demons. *Ibid.,* 80–81.

50. *Ibid.,* 81.

51. *Ibid.,* 84–85.

52. *Ibid.,* 84.

53. *Ibid.,* 85.

54. *Ibid.,* 88. Compare Tillich's definition of heteronomy as "subjection to a law which is not experienced as our own." "Afterword," O'M and W, 304.

55. IH, 92. Compare the following description: "Heteronomy imposes an

alien law, religious or secular, on man's mind. . . . It destroys the honesty
of truth and the dignity of the moral personality. It undermines creative
freedom and the humanity of man." PE, 46.

56. IH, 26.
57. ST, I, 148.
58. See "Autobiographical Reflections," K and B, 7–8, and IH, 22–24.
59. "Autobiographical Reflections," K and B, 8.
60. IH, 24.
61. "Afterword," O'M and W, 304.
62. Theodor Siegfried, "Tillich's Theology for the German Situation,"
K and B, 82.
63. ST, III, 82–83. See also LPJ, 89–90, where the same distinction is
made in terms of "authority in fact" (just authority) and "authority in principle" (unjust).
64. IH, 197–99. See also pp. 28–30.
65. "By What Authority?" NB, 79–91.
66. *Ibid.*, 84.
67. *Ibid.*, 87.
68. *Ibid.*, 88.
69. *Ibid.*, 91.
70. PE, xii.
71. *Ibid.*, 57.
72. *Ibid.*, xii.
73. *Ibid.*, 57.
74. Cf. ST, I, 148; ST, III, 250–52; GW, I, 330–31, 386–87; PE,
57–60.
75. ST I, 85–86.
76. ST, III, 250.
77. *Ibid.*, 250–52.
78. ST, III, 111–12. See also ST, I, 15, note 4.
79. ST, III, 72–73, 252–53.
80. *Ibid.*, 72.
81. *Ibid.*, 69.
82. *Ibid.*, 254.
83. *Ibid.*
84. *Ibid.*, 95.
85. LPJ, 76–77. See also Tillich's little book *Morality and Beyond,* New
York, 1963.
86. ST, III, 95.
87. ST, I, 85. Cf. pp. 79–81 for Tillich's elaboration of "the depth of
reason."
88. "Reply," K and B, 337.
89. PE, 59.
90. *Ibid.*, xii.
91. TC, 7.

92. GW, V, 43–50.

93. *Ibid.*, 43.

94. SF, 57.

95. *Ibid.*, 58–59.

96. ST, III, 247.

97. ST, I, 218.

98. TC, 41.

99. *Ibid.*, 59. Cf. also PE, 229–30 and ST, I, 218.

100. ST, III, 247.

101. *Ibid.*, 248.

102. ST, I, 218.

103. ST, III, 248.

104. ST, I, 218, GW, I, 329–30.

105. PE, 59.

106. *Ibid.*, 220.

107. *Ibid.*

108. "Reply," K and B, 347.

109. One would have to determine the stage in the development of Barth's thought at which Tillich attacks him, to weigh carefully their interpretations of the political and ecclesiastical scene in post-World War I Germany, and to examine thoroughly Barth's method and the main lines of his theology.

110. GW, VII, 216–25.

111. *Ibid.*, 226–39.

112. *Ibid.*, 234.

113. *Ibid.*, 240–43.

114. Cf. "Autobiographical Reflections," K and B, 8.

115. IH, 26.

116. GW, VII, 244–46.

117. Paul Tillich, "What Is Wrong with the 'Dialectic' Theology?" *The Journal of Religion*, XV, April, 1935, 127–45.

118. BR, 1; ST, I, 65.

119. RS, 217.

120. Tillich's criticism of liberal theology must not be exaggerated. He credits it with the following attainments: critical and historical research on the Bible, the involvement of Christianity with all of life and history, and a reconciliation of the Renaissance with the Reformation. On these counts he claims that Protestantism must always be in the liberal stream. PE, xxiii.

121. Walter M. Horton, "Tillich's Role in Contemporary Theology," K and B, 28.

122. Theodor Siegfried, "Tillich's Theology for the German Situation," *Ibid.*, 73.

123. David E. Roberts, "Tillich's Doctrine of Man," *Ibid.*, 112; Walter Leibrecht, "The Life and Mind of Paul Tillich," *Religion and Culture: Essays in Honor of Paul Tillich*, Walter W. Leibrecht (ed.), copyrighted 1959 Walter W. Leibrecht, used by permission of Harper & Brothers, Inc., now

Harper & Row, Publishers, Inc., 9, 17; John C. Bennett, "A Protestant View of Authority in the Church," *Theology Digest*, XI, 1963, 211–12.

124. Karl Hennig, "Paul Tillich: Leben und Werk," in *Der Spannungsbogen: Festgabe für Paul Tillich*, Karl Hennig (ed.), Stuttgart: Evangelisches Verlagswerk, 1961, 181.

125. IH, 220.

126. PE, 207.

127. CEWR, 44–45; ST, I, 4; ST, III, 285.

128. IH, 55.

129. "Autobiographical Reflections," K and B, 14.

130. TC, 166.

131. PE, 60–61.

132. Cf. Henri Bouillard, *Karl Barth*, III, Paris: Aubier, 1957, 261–83 for Barth's ethic of Christian political responsibility, especially pp. 262–63. Tillich's attitude appears in a statement by Walter A. Horton: "In discussion I have heard Tillich blame the influence of this Barthian supernaturalism for destroying all hope of an alliance between Protestantism and the labor movement, which might possibly have prevented the rise of Nazism." "Tillich's Role in Contemporary Theology," K and B, 31, note 15.

133. It seems possible to discern an ambivalence in Barth's stance toward man's cultural activity. For instances of the positive aspect, confer Bouillard, *Karl Barth*, I, 70, 243–45; II, 214–16; III, 261–83. For the negative aspect, *Ibid.*, I, 13, 22, 75–77, 154. For a combination of both, *Ibid.*, 67.

134. In 1931 Tillich contributed a brief article on *Theonomie* to the second edition of *Die Religion in Geschichte und Gegenwart*, Hermann Gunkel and Leopold Zscharnack (eds.), V, Tübingen: J. C. B. Mohr, 1128–29. But in the third edition of the same work, edited by Kurt Galling, one finds, under *Theonomie*, merely a reference to H. Blumenberg's article on *Autonomie* where, strangely enough, Tillich is not even mentioned.

135. Gerhardt Kuhlmann has taken *Theonomie* in a purely philosophical sense as "the meaning of life." He states: "Man's eternally new question about the meaning of life—that is the question about a theonomy of culture." Cf. Gerhardt Kuhlmann, *Brunstäd und Tillich: zum Problem einer Theonomie der Kultur*, Tübingen: J. C. B. Mohr, 1928, 3, 5. An interesting example of the heteronomy-autonomy-theonomy dialectic, but without the use of those terms, is found in François Roustang, *Une Initiation à la Vie Spirituelle*, Paris: Desclée de Brouwer, 1963, 17–39 (published in English as *Growth in the Spirit*, New York: Sheed and Ward, 1966). Man's encounter with God can be described as *Dieu est la loi* (heteronomy) or *Dieu est ma conscience* (autonomy). But both descriptions are incomplete and are only fulfilled in the encounter where *Dieu est esprit* (theonomy).

136. "The Life and Mind of Paul Tillich," *Religion and Culture*, Leibrecht (ed.), 17.

137. PE, 65.

138. Karl Heim calls attention to the peril of secularism inherent in Chris-

tianity: "In its mature form, however, secularism has grown only in the soil of the Christian culture of the West." The biblical view of God, man, and the world provides "the presuppositions from which secularism arises with a kind of neccessity." For, although God is transcendent to the world, creatures possess a certain autonomy over against him. Hence the biblical view gives man a choice: "the autonomy of the world or the absoluteness of God." Cf. "Christian Faith and the Growing Power of Secularism," *Religion and Culture,* Leibrecht (ed.), 183, 186–87.

139. PE, 229–30. See also IH, 220–21, and CEWR, 48.

140. Kuhlmann charges that Tillich's theory allows anyone access to the prophetic Spirit, the result being an "absolute individualism." Gerhardt Kuhlmann, *Brunstäd und Tillich: zum Problem einer Theonomie der Kultur,* Tübingen, 1928, 40–41.

141. Our choice of these particular doctrines coincides with those selected by Nels F. S. Ferré in his essay "Christian Presuppositions for a Creative Culture." He lists the Christ-event (including the church), a personal God, and life everlasting. Cf. *Religion and Culture,* Leibrecht (ed.), 79–87.

Part II

RELIGION AND CULTURE: THE CONTENT

4/Being and God

THE PRIMARY PURPOSE of Part II of this work is to flesh-out the structural contours of theonomy with theological content, so that its features become sharpened, its true character defined. At the same time, several secondary but worthy objectives are also attained.

First of all, the method of correlation is seen in action, the posing of existential questions followed by theological answers in the form of Christian symbols. Up to now the method of correlation has not been explicitly operative; rather, we have synthesized from many sources Tillich's understanding of the union of religion and culture. Correlation was not employed simply because Tillich himself does not formally use it in discussing these topics.

Secondly, the doctrinal content of Part II—God, the Christ, the church, history—corresponds to the major divisions of *Systematic Theology*, and so we gradually progress through Tillich's most important work, important because it systematically expresses a lifetime of theological endeavor.[1] Although his other works are freely used to complement and clarify *Systematic Theology*, nevertheless it remains the backbone of our exposition.

In short, Part II examines the central pillars of Tillich's system as they stand upon the foundation of the method of correlation. Obviously, it is neither possible nor desirable to duplicate his own thorough and lengthy elaborations, and a choice of material must be made. In making this choice, the effort has been made to strike a balance, that is, to expound his thought on a scale large enough to impart its savor and complexities, and yet on a scale small enough to convey its consistency and its relevance to the theonomous union of religion and culture.

In this chapter the existential question is the question of being, and the answer is God. Also treated is the problem of the natural-supranatural, and the problem of symbolism, or the way to speak about God. Thus we probe into the depth-dimension which underlies theonomous cultural forms, the holy which shines through the secular, the ground of being which alone can command the ultimacy of an ultimate concern.

THE QUESTION OF BEING

"God is the answer to the question implied in being."[2] With this statement Tillich assigns fundamental importance to the onto-logical question: What is being? He feels that, unfortunately, "we all are nominalists by birth. And as nominalists we are inclined to dissolve our world into things."[3] But the true ontological question "does not try to describe the nature of beings, either in their universal, generic qualities, or in their individual, historical mani-festation."[4] It simply asks: What does it mean to be? The pro-fundity and the seriousness of the question is realized only in "a 'metaphysical shock'—the shock of possible nonbeing."[5] The ques-tion, "Why is there something, why not nothing?" produces the shock by peering into the abyss of possible nothingness. But the answer to the question is always in terms of being, which permits it to be posed again and again in infinite regression. Furthermore, nonbeing cannot answer it, for nonbeing depends upon being. Therefore, we cannot go beyond being in order to explain being. Is ontology, then, condemned to mouth empty tautologies?

Ontological Concepts

Tillich defends the possibility of ontology on the basis of what he calls "ontological concepts" which are less universal than being, thus enabling us to get a grip on it, but more universal than any concept limited to a particular realm of beings.[6] Philosophers have labored for thousands of years to discover and organize ontological concepts and have assigned them a variety of names: principles, categories, ultimate notions, elements, structures, and so on. Before discussing them, it is essential to note that, for Tillich, "ontological concepts are a priori in the strict sense of the word. They determine the nature of experience. They are present whenever something is experienced."[7] This is not to say that they are known prior to experience nor that they constitute an immutable framework. But if an experience is had, it presupposes a structure. The experience changes only because its a priori structure changes. Consequently, "as long as there is experience in any definite sense of the word, there is a structure of experience which can be recognized within the process of experiencing and which can be elaborated critically."[8]

The experience that Tillich deals with here is the experience of being and nonbeing. Because these are such ultimate notions, he cannot spell out his ontological concepts with "definitional" precision, but only by "configurational" consistency, i.e., by describing their stable configuration in a variety of contexts.[9] Not only is the strict definition of ontological concepts impossible, but also their strict verification. "There is certainly not an experimental way, but there is an experiential way. . . . The only answer, but a sufficient answer, which can be given to the question of ontological verification is the appeal to intelligent recognition."[10]

The Ontological Structure: Self and World

The first ontological concept is that of the basic ontological structure, self and world.[11] The question of being supposes a subject who asks and an object about which he asks. This subject-object structure, in turn, reveals the self-world structure of being.

Man occupies the dominant position in ontology, for, although every being shares in the structure of being, only man is aware of it. Moreover, all levels of being are united in man and can be approached through him. Man experiences himself as a "self," as "being separated in some way from everything else, having everything else opposite one's self, being able to look at it and to act upon it. At the same time, however, this self is aware that it belongs to that at which it looks."[12] More precisely, man has an ego-self, since his self includes self-consciousness in addition to its subconscious and unconscious basis. By analogy, then, selfhood or self-centeredness is attributed to all beings, organic and inorganic. Man, the ego-self, has a world, a structural whole to which he belongs and which he perceives. The self of every being inferior to man has at least an environment to which it belongs, but which it cannot transcend.

Self and world stand in polar relation. "The self without a world is empty; the world without a self is dead."[13] The self-world polarity underlies the subject-object structure. It also explains *logos*. For objective reason is the structured whole of the world, and subjective reason is the structural centeredness of the self. The basic ontological structure is a polarity that cannot be derived, but only accepted. If one asks, "What precedes self and world?"—the answer must come from revelation, for reason stands at the brink of its limits.

The Ontological Elements

The second level of ontological concepts is that of the elements which constitute the basic ontological structure and are found in every being.[14] Like the structure, they, too, are polar and are meaningful only insofar as they refer to each other. There are three elements:

   (1) individuality—universality
   (2)   dynamics—form
   (3)   freedom—destiny

Before considering them separately, we draw attention to a common feature they share: their polar nature. Polarity is a mode of conception and development very characteristic of Tillich's thought. He defines it as follows: "A polar relation is a relation of interdependent elements, each of which is necessary for the other one and for the whole, although it is in tension with the opposite element."[15] Neither pole can stand by itself; it needs the other to complement it. But, at the same time, both poles clash as they expand at the expense of one another. Thus the poles limit and sustain each other. However, this ideal balance can be upset, for, "under the impact of finitude, polarity becomes tension," which is the tendency of unified elements to draw away from one another in opposite directions.[16] We now examine the three polarities which make up the three basic ontological elements.

Individualization and Participation: Individualization is implied in the self which, like a mathematical point, cannot be divided.[17] Though every being is analogously an individual, man is the totally centered self, completely individualized. He is a person. The individual self of every being participates in its environment, but man, the microcosm, participates in the whole universe by means of the rational structure of mind and reality. Finally, "when individualization reaches the perfect form which we call a 'person,' participation reaches the perfect form which we call 'communion'"—participation in another self who also is a person.[18]

Dynamics and Form: Being a self, being an individual, being something—this means having a form.[19] "The form which makes a thing what it is, is its content, its *essentia*, its definite power of being."[20] But a form must form something which Tillich calls "dynamics." Dynamics cannot be conceptualized but only symbolized, for it has no form, and yet it is not pure nothingness. "It is the *me on*, the potentiality of being, which is nonbeing in contrast to pure nonbeing"—for example, Bergson's *élan vital*, Nietzsche's will to power, and the unconscious of Freud.[21] In human experience dynamics appears as vitality, the power of life and growth.[22] Form appears as intentionality, the grasping and shaping of reality through universals and meaningful structures. To put it in still another way, self-transcendence (dynamics) is always in polar balance with self-conservation (form).

Freedom and Destiny: In describing the third ontological element, Tillich refuses to use the word "necessity."[23] For he rejects a polarity which pits mechanistic determinacy against indeterminate contingency, and which thus pictures freedom as a quality of a thing called the will. The freedom of a thing is contradictory. Only man is free, the total self, including even the cells and atoms of his body which share in the constitution of that individual, personal center. Furthermore, man experiences himself as a bearer of freedom, but within the larger structure to which he belongs. Consequently, Tillich prefers to speak of "destiny." Destiny is the world to which man pertains—his body, psychic drives, temperament, social community, material surroundings, conscious and unconscious past, and, above all, his former free decisions. "Destiny is not a strange power which determines what shall happen to me. It is myself as given, formed by nature, history, and myself. My destiny is the basis of my freedom, my freedom participates in shaping my destiny."[24] Within the bounds of destiny man experiences freedom as deliberation, decision, and responsibility. Obviously, the polarity freedom-destiny can be applied only analogously to beings inferior to man. In the subhuman realm it appears as the polarity of spontaneity and law.

The three ontological polarities have been viewed horizontally, with each polar element in balance with its opposite. If one were to split them vertically, the first side of these polarities—individuality, dynamics, and freedom—would express the self-relating power of being. The second side—universality, form, and destiny—expresses the belongingness of being, its participation in the universe of being. Thus the basic self-world structure is manifest within the ontological polarities.

The Ontological Characteristic: Finitude

Tillich's third ontological concept is that of finitude, and it is presented here somewhat at length because of its pertinence to our problem. At the very beginning of his ontological analysis he underlines its importance: ". . . the concept of finitude is the center of the following analysis, for it is the finitude of being which drives us to the question of God."[25]

The roots of finitude go as deep as the question of being and nonbeing raised by the ontological shock.[26] Man is terrified of nonbeing because his being does not secure him against it. His ability to question being, his separation from it, reveals that he shares in nonbeing. Tillich feels that the mystery of nonbeing can be handled only dialectically and that the ancient Greeks have given us the clue. The undialectical concept of being is *ouk on,* the nothingness referred to in the phrase *creatio ex nihilo.* It has no relation whatsoever to being; it is pure negation, and hence undialectical. *Me on,* on the other hand, is the dialectical concept of nonbeing. It is related to being in the sense of resistance to being, or perversion of being, or menace to being. It is dialectical. The problem of finitude, then, is the dialectical problem of nonbeing. For "being, limited by nonbeing, is finitude. Nonbeing appears as the 'not yet' of being and as the 'no more' of being."[27]

Dialectical nonbeing provides Tillich with material for a metaphorical description of being. "Being is the power of being! Power, however, presupposes, even in the metaphorical use of the word, something over which it proves its power. . . . That which is conquered by the power of being is nonbeing."[28] Being, therefore, is the "power of being which resists nonbeing." Nonbeing is not a stranger to being.[29] Metaphorically, it is "that quality of being by which everything that participates in being is negated. Nonbeing is the negation of being within being itself."[30] This is what is meant by finite being: being which contains nonbeing.

The next step is to relate the finite to the infinite. Human experience of the ontological structure and elements shows that "to be something is to be finite."[31] Yet the limitations of nonbeing are visible only against the backdrop of a potential infinity. For example, one realizes the finiteness of death only by imagining the possibility of something beyond death. Finitude is seen as finitude only if finite being transcends itself, steps out of itself in the direction of infinity. Infinity, then, "directs the mind to experience its own unlimited potentialities, but it does not establish the existence of an infinite being. . . . Infinity is a demand, not a thing."[32] Infinity negates the limitations of finitude; it negates nonbeing. But infinity is not being-itself. Tillich understands infinity in the sense of infinite self-transcendence, while "being-itself manifests itself to finite being in the infinite drive of the finite beyond itself."[33] Infinity is a manifestation of being-itself, but the two can never be identified, for being-itself precedes nonbeing and its negation by infinity.

The awareness of finitude produces an ontological anxiety, for finitude contains the threat of nonbeing. Fear is psychological and stems from a menacing object, but "anxiety is the self-awareness of the finite self as finite."[34] Anxiety is as all-pervasive as nonbeing. Since "anxiety is the existential awareness of nonbeing," it is perfectly natural to man.[35]

Finitude and anxiety appear also in the ontological elements.[36] A polarity supposes a balance, each pole limiting and supporting the other. But because of its finitude a polarity becomes tension, "the tendency of elements within a unity to draw away from one another," to disintegrate.[37] Thus, the polarity of individualization and participation becomes the tension of loneliness and collectivization. Dynamics and form become chaos and formalism. Freedom and destiny become arbitrariness and necessity. These tensions are threats to finite man, for if he loses one side of the polarity, he loses the other side. Once the polarity disintegrates, he is destroyed as a self. It must be insisted upon, however, that these finite tensions are only possibilities, tendencies, threats, if you will. But they do not necessarily lead to actual disintegration, just as every threat is not inevitably carried out.

Freedom is the pivot,[38] for it is only through freedom that the threat is carried out, that the finite tensions snap, that potential disruption is actualized. Freedom ushers in the basic distinction between essential being, threatened but integral, and existential being, real but distorted.

"Essence" is ambiguous in that it denotes a fact and connotes a value. It signifies the nature of a being, the universal, the logical ideal. But essence also pronounces judgment, for it is the undistorted state from which the being has fallen. Essence makes the being what it is and judges it.

"Existence" exhibits the same ambiguity of meaning, for it signifies not only actuality, standing out from potentiality, but also imperfection, the failure to measure up to essence. "Whatever exists, that is 'stands out' of mere potentiality, is more than it is in the state of mere potentiality and less than it could be in the power of its essential nature."[39]

Tillich describes Christianity's stance toward the relation of essence to existence as a middle-of-the-road position. Christian theology considers existence a positive fulfilment of creation, of essence. It also points out the split between essential created goodness and its existential distortion. The theologian cannot avoid this problem. "The distinction between essence and existence, which religiously speaking is the distinction between the created and the actual world, is the backbone of the whole body of theological thought."[40]

This discussion of finitude has ranged over a wide, difficult, and abstract terrain. We conclude with a few words from Tillich which sum it up with utmost simplicity:

If man is that being who asks the question of being, he has and has not the being for which he asks. He is separated from it while belong-

ing to it. Certainly we belong to being—its power is in us—otherwise
we would not be. But we are also separated from it; we do not possess
it fully. Our power of being is limited. We are a mixture of being and
nonbeing. This is precisely what is meant when we say that we are
finite.[41]

The Ontological Categories

The fourth ontological concept comprises the ontological categories of time, space, causality, and substance.[42] They are the
basic forms of thought and being through which the mind makes
contact with reality. Since they are forms of finitude, they express
a mixture of being and nonbeing, of positive and negative elements which Tillich prefers to discuss in terms of courage and
anxiety. Man's experience of time includes the anxiety of transitoriness and the courage of a self-affirming present. Space is not
only physical, but also social—a sphere of influence, a place in the
framework of value and meaning. The anxiety of insecurity arises
from the danger of losing one's place, only to be met by the
courage to carve out a niche for oneself. Causality brings forth
the anxiety of contingency, the awareness that one does not possess his own power of being. But courage is there too, for causality
affirms the reality of a being by pointing to its sources in the
power of being. Substance expresses the anxiety of change, of loss
of identity, along with the courage to affirm the finite by laboring
to produce cultural creations. Tillich spells out the significance
of the categories: "They express the union of being and nonbeing
in everything finite. They articulate the courage which accepts the
anxiety of nonbeing. The question of God is the question of the
possibility of this courage."[43]

The Question of God

The question of being leads to finitude which, in turn, leads to
the question of God.[44] Tillich conceives the arguments for the

existence of God as prolegomena which set up the possibility and necessity of the question of God.[45] But first he makes clear that "the existence of God" cannot be taken literally. God, the ground of being, is not found within the world of existing beings. Nor can existence be predicated of him, since it means an actual state of distorted being and of disruptive tensions. "God does not exist. He is being-itself beyond essence and existence. Therefore, to argue that God exists is to deny him."[46] Tillich also objects to the idea of an "argument" which searches for a conclusion from given data. To make the world the data and God the conclusion is to derive God from the world. Yet he esteems the arguments for God's existence as "expressions of the *question* of God which is implied in human finitude."[47]

The worth of the so-called ontological and moral arguments (Augustine, Anselm, Kant) lies in this, that they provide "a description of the way in which potential infinity is present in actual finitude."[48] Man has a prior awareness of God that enables him to ask about the infinite from which he is separated, about the source of his courage to face anxiety. The truth of the ontological and moral arguments is "the acknowledgment of the unconditional element in the structure of reason and reality."[49] They reveal an awareness of God which renders possible the question of God.

The cosmological and teleological arguments cannot prove the existence of a highest being, but they describe the threat of non-being, the ontological anxiety that drives man to ask the question of God. The cosmological argument is based on the categories of finitude. It seeks the "eternal now" in which time and space are affirmed and overcome, the "ground of being" in which cause and substance are rooted and conquered. The teleological argument asks for the ultimate meaning of the ontological polarities and tensions. But seeking is not finding, and to ask is not to receive. The cosmological and teleological arguments portray the inevitability and necessity of the question of God just as the ontological and moral arguments show its possibility.

The ontological analysis began with the question of being, and it ends with the question of God. How is he the answer to being?

GOD AS BEING-ITSELF

The most fundamental statement Tillich makes about God is that he is being-itself.[50] Negatively, this means that God is not *a* being, not even the highest being, alongside other beings. Positively, it means that God is the ground of being or the power of being. He is beyond essence and existence because as being-itself he does not participate in nonbeing and finitude. He does not exist; he is.

God as Phenomenon

Before presenting his theological answers, Tillich always prefaces them with a phenomenological description in order to clarify their meaning.[51] Only then does he take up their actuality. Since the phenomenological meaning of God has already been considered in our second chapter, under the heading of the experience of the holy, it suffices here merely to recall a few salient points.

"God" is the name for man's ultimate concern. However, this is not to say that there is first a supreme being who then obliges man to render the homage of ultimate concern. "It means that whatever concerns a man ultimately becomes god for him, and conversely, it means that man can be concerned ultimately only about that which is god for him."[52] Within ultimate concern there is a constant tension between fixation upon the concrete and the drive toward an ultimacy which tends to be universal and hence abstract. This tension between the concrete and abstract elements accounts for the fact that "the idea of God has a history," a history that ranges from every type of polytheism to the most stringent type of monotheism.[53]

Tillich places great stress upon an experienced phenomenology of the holy, for ". . . without an encounter with God in the center and the ground of our personal existence, God is an empty word."[54] The following description sums up the God who is the *mysterium tremendum et fascinosum* and, at the same time, introduces us to the God who is being-itself:

> But I speak of the God who is the creative ground of everything and in everything, who is always present, always creating and destroying, always experienced as nearer to ourselves than we ourselves are, always unapproachable, holy, fascinating, terrifying, the ground and meaning of everything that is. This is the living God, dynamic in himself, life as the ground of life. . . .[55]

The Ground of Being

Since being-itself is so abstract, Tillich refers to God in more concrete terms. The power of being has already been discussed. The ground of being is another term he frequently employs, and he has popularized it in one of his best sermons, "The Depth of Existence."[56] Obviously, the ground of being is closely connected with the depth-dimension. As a symbol, the ground of being "points to the mother-quality of giving birth, carrying, and embracing, and, at the same time, of calling back, resisting independence of the created, and swallowing it."[57]

"Ground," therefore, evokes the image of the earth, that upon which we stand, which underlies and sustains us. Everything that is rests upon being-itself as its ground, for, in order to be, a being must share in being-itself, must receive its being from the infinite source of being. Immediately one is tempted to conceive the ground of being as cause or substance.[58] Tillich, however, rejects a literal use of these categories. If God is called the cause of being, he is enmeshed in an endless but finite chain-reaction of causes and effects, for effects drag causes down to their own level. If God is termed the substance of being, it means that he is imprisoned in accidental beings, and they, in turn, forfeit their independence and freedom. But Tillich accepts a symbolic sense for cause and substance which is free from the finiteness of the literal sense and which relates beings to God without diminishing his infinity. Symbolically, God is *prima causa* and *ultima substantia* in the sense that "God is the cause of the entire series of causes and effects, he is the substance underlying the whole process of becoming."[59] As symbols, cause and substance amount to the same thing—the "underlying," the ground of being. Ground, therefore, "oscillates between cause and substance and transcends both of them."[60]

The notion of ground leads to the notion of abyss as naturally as the image "mountain" conjures up the image "valley." From the viewpoint of finite being, the ground of being as the source and power of being is creative, positive, and the *mysterium fascinosum*. But by its very inexhaustibility and the unlimited force of its power, the ground of being infinitely surpasses finite being. In this sense it is negative; it is the *tremendum*. For finite being is lost, swallowed up in the bottomless depths of the ground of being. The ground becomes the abyss.[61]

The Living God

The Bible confronts us with the living God. But does not God as being-itself or the ground of being seem dull, static, lifeless? Tillich criticizes the scholastic concept of *actus purus* on precisely this score.[62] He maintains, however, that his idea of God as being-itself is far removed from the stagnation of fixed identity.

"Life is the process in which potential being becomes actual being. It is the actualization of the structural elements of being in their unity and in their tension."[63] The elements of being here referred to are the ontological polarities: individualization-participation, dynamics-form, and freedom-destiny. Since in God there is no distinction and no transition between potentiality and actuality, life cannot be predicated of God in its proper meaning, but only symbolically.[64] The life-process is a constant movement of simultaneous separation and union of the polar elements. This process is rooted in the divine life, but the divine life is not subject to it and is consequently free of tension and the threat of dissolution.

The ontological elements are the only avenue of approach to the divine life.[65] For the categories describe God's relation to creatures, and the ontological structure of self-world implies separation, not interaction of the two poles. However, the first side of the polarities (individualization, dynamics, and freedom) represents the self. Man utilizes this subjective side in symbolizing the living God. "He sees the divine life as personal, dynamic, and free. He cannot see it in any other way, for God is man's ultimate concern, and therefore he stands in analogy to that which man himself is."[66] What Tillich seems to be getting at is that man can speak of the living God only in terms of life closest to himself, that is, his interior life of personality, dynamism, and freedom. And since the living God is also man's ultimate concern, he must reach into the deepest levels of his human self for symbols to convey it.

The Personal God

From among the many symbols of the divine discussed by Tillich we select that of "personal God" in order to illustrate in one stroke his theory of symbolism, the implications of God as being-itself, and one aspect of the living God.

He cites the fact that the religious encounter, the experience of the holy, demands an I-Thou relationship.[67] God cannot be an "It." Anything less than a personal God is incapable of arousing an ultimate concern in man. A sub-personal God is not God. "This is the reason that the symbol of the Personal God is indispensable for living religion."[68]

However, there are difficulties. Is not God as being-itself an impersonal God? Nothing seems more incompatible than the warmth of a person and the bleakness of being-itself. Moreover, if God is *a* person, is he not reduced to the status of *a* being alongside other beings? Due to these difficulties, particularly the latter, Tillich calls the personal God "a confusing symbol."[69]

His solution is the divine transcendence.[70] Calling God a person does not necessarily pull him down to the same level as other persons and beings, for the "absolute individual" is also the "absolute participant." The other polar element of participation guarantees that God remains being-itself who participates in all beings as their ground. Furthermore, God as being-itself means that "God is the ground of everything personal and that he carries within himself the ontological power of personality."[71] He is "the Personal-Itself, the ground and abyss of every person."[72] God is transpersonal in the sense that he includes the personal, but transcends it. Religiously speaking, man encounters the personal God. Theologically speaking, he encounters the ground of everything personal. But in either case the symbol of the personal God indicates "that our personal center is grasped by the manifestation of the inaccessible ground and abyss of being."[73]

SYMBOL AND ANALOGY

By now we have seen Tillich's basic understanding of the meaning of God. Before moving on to other symbols of the divine, it is profitable to investigate his theological epistemology in order to determine how he establishes their validity and their limits. His theory of symbolism was introduced in Chapter 1 in the section "The Language of Theology," but here we concentrate upon its ontological foundations.

"God must be approached cognitively through the structural elements of being-itself."[74] This follows if God is the ground and the structure of being.[75] The structural elements serve as symbols which are rooted in and point toward their ground. But before speaking symbolically of God, the theologian must make at least one nonsymbolic statement about him.[76] Otherwise there would be an infinite series of symbols pointing ever onward, for it is the nature of symbols not to rest in themselves, but to point. "The statement that God is being-itself is a nonsymbolic statement. It does not point beyond itself. It means what it says directly and properly. . . ." After this, "nothing else can be said about God as God which is not symbolic."[77]

Our ability to speak about God depends upon whether or not the finite can be used to assert something about the infinite. Tillich's answer is affirmative because the infinite is being-itself, and everything finite participates in it. "The *analogia entis* gives us our only justification of speaking at all about God."[78] Thus, by its participation in the ground of being, the meaning of the symbol is affirmed. Yet, at the same time, its proper meaning is negated, for the ground of being transcends its structural elements; the ground is also the abyss.

Religious symbols operate in two directions.[79] They bring the infinite down to the finite by concretizing it; and they elevate the finite by revealing its participation in the infinite. For example, if God is symbolized as "father" or "king," he is brought down to the level of human relationships. Yet simultaneously fatherhood and kingship are consecrated, for their theonomous depth, their holy character, is revealed.

There is abundant textual evidence that Tillich *grosso modo* equates symbolism and analogy.[80] The essentials for a commonplace idea of analogy are: (a) the existence of at least two realities, for nothing is analogous to itself, (b) their basic dissimilarity, and (c) at least a relative resemblance between them.[81] He certainly holds analogy in this general sense, for he uses finite reality in order to talk about infinite reality by both affirming and negating the former.

Before discussing the more difficult question of symbols of the divine, it is good to enlarge the problematic to make room for analogy on a less sublime level so that its general function as an instrument of knowledge and communication can be more readily grasped. For instance, Tillich makes man, the microcosm, the mirror of reality so that the structures of being found in him are found analogously in the subhuman realm.[82] Selfhood, inner awareness, freedom and destiny—all are verified analogously in subhuman beings. Furthermore, he employs the concepts of courage, love, power, and justice in order to describe analogously the characteristics of all beings and of being-itself.[83] The point we wish to make is that this use of analogy based on human experience seems to yield valid knowledge.

Moving up now to the relationship between man and God, one would expect that on the same principle, but with proper adjustments, man could get an analogous knowledge of God. But here Tillich shifts gears by introducing a distinction into the function of the *analogia entis*. Symbols are not a means of *knowing* God, but rather a way of *speaking* about him.[84] If one wishes to talk about God, finite material must be used, and this is justified by the fact that all finite beings participate in being-itself. However, Tillich cautions us not to interpret analogy as leading to a natural theology:

Without such an analogy nothing could be said about God. But the *analogia entis* is in no way able to create a natural theology. It is not a method of discovering truth about God; it is the form in which every knowledge of revelation must be expressed. In this sense *analogia entis*, like "religious symbol," points to the necessity of using material taken from finite reality in order to give content to the cognitive function in revelation.[85]

What this boils down to is that analogy or symbolism is the *expression* of an encounter with God.[86] Though the revelatory experience is far more than an intellectual communication—it is primarily a reunion with the ground of being—it contains a cognitive element conveyed by symbols which are qualified as channels of communication by their participation in being-itself.

One last question remains to be answered: Is ontological participation sufficient to explain the *de facto* symbols of the divine which are found in the Christian tradition? It seems not, for every creature participates in being-itself, and yet not everything is a religious symbol, although it has the potentiality to become one. What is the decisive ingredient of symbolism beyond ontological participation? Tillich's answer is experiential participation, for religious symbols convey the experience of the holy.

These symbols are not arbitrary interpretations of the concrete revelatory experiences. But they appear within this experience itself. They are not created intentionally, but they are born in the same dimension in which the revelatory experience takes place. In and through its symbols the religious encounter with reality opens up the dimension of reality in which ultimacy appears. There is no other way of expressing our encounter with the holy than in symbols.[87]

Man does not grasp God through symbols, but in the experience of faith one is grasped by an ultimate concern expressed in symbols. On the somewhat bewildering terrain of Tillichian symbolism we get our bearings from a familiar landmark: ultimate concern.[88] Every symbol descriptive of ultimate reality originates in an experience of ultimate concern and continues to live only insofar as it can introduce someone into the revelatory constellation by arousing a similar experience. Religious symbols participate in the power of being not merely ontologically, but experientially. They concretely convey the experience of ultimacy, of seizure by an ultimate concern. And lest this affirmation of the symbol open the door to the demonic, Tillich insists upon the negation of the symbol by the ultimate to which it points. He agrees with Weigel's observation about his penchant for the negative side of analogy: "I believe you are right when you say that my understanding of *analogia* is more negative-protesting than positive-affirming."[89]

The mechanism, then, of Tillich's religious symbolism is relatively simple: (1) Religious symbols participate in that which they symbolize, being-itself; (2) they participate by sharing in the ground of being, as do all finite beings; and (3) they participate by expressing the experience of ultimacy. This last element is decisive. One expresses the experience of the ground of being through the religious symbols which are formed in the crucible of the experience itself.

To summarize Tillich's symbolism and analogy, we propose the following four statements as our interpretation of a difficult topic which, unfortunately, he presents in a somewhat less than pellucid manner.

  (1) "God is being-itself" is the only nonsymbolic statement about God.
  (2) The religious experience of God is had through finite beings which participate in being-itself. The principle of analogy justifies this.
  (3) The expression of this experience is through religious symbols which participate in the experience itself.
  (4) Theology elaborates the meaning of religious symbols by using ontology. Analogy permits and even demands this procedure.

It is apparent that Tillich, while largely equating symbol and analogy, uses the principle of analogy for two purposes: to permit a religious encounter with God through finite beings and to justify the theological use of ontology. In a nutshell, theology speaks ontologically about religious symbols which express the encounter with God, our ultimate concern.[90]

GOD AS CREATOR

"The word 'creation' is one of the great symbol-words describing the relation of God to the universe."[91] For Tillich the doctrine of creation depicts a state; it does not relate an event that happened "once upon a time." Man asks the question of his finitude and of finitude in general, and creation answers it by pointing to "the situation of creatureliness and to its correlate, the divine creativity."[92] The divine creativity is the dynamic aspect of the divine life; it is beyond potentiality and actuality. Hence the question whether creation is a necessary or contingent act of God is meaningless. For nothing higher than God necessitates his creativity; neither does it happen to him as an accidental act. The divine life and the divine creativity are one. All three modes of time must be used to symbolize the infinite scope of the divine dynamism. Therefore, Tillich considers originating creativity (the past), sustaining creativity (the present), and directing creativity (the future).

Originating Creativity

The classical phrase to express the Christian doctrine of creation is *creatio ex nihilo.* Tillich sees in it the exclusion of the pagan idea of *me on,* of the "given" which resists the divine creativity.[93] Though *ouk on,* absolute nothingness, suffices to explain *nihilo,* the *ex* demands something more positive to describe the origin of the creature. The solution lies in the dialectic of being and nonbeing. *Ex nihilo* indicates the "heritage of nonbeing" which is the lot of every creature. Yet the creature *is*; it participates in the power of being which holds nonbeing in check. "Being a creature includes both the heritage of nonbeing (anxiety) and the heritage of being (courage)."[94] Two important consequences flow from this interpretation. First of all, creation is essentially good, for it is not the offspring of *me on,* of some semi-divine power that opposes being-itself. The way to the incarnation lies open, for finitude essentially is not in conflict with God. Secondly, the element of nonbeing in creatureliness provides the potentiality for tragic disruption within finitude itself. Eschatology is forbidden to do violence to the finite by eliminating the possibility of conflict, by locating salvation in an unreal world above our finite, tragic world.

Thus far, creation has been considered within the order proper to it, the essential order. But man as the creature that exercises freedom brings us to the boundary line of the existential order of tragedy and dissolution.[95] God as the creator is beyond the distinction of essence and existence. He does not depend upon essences or divine ideas which govern his creativity. His creative vision simultaneously embraces both the essence of a creature and each moment of its existence. But created being does not lie buried within the divine life. It exists in the universe of reality, and its existence is different from its essence. Man provides the clearest insight into creaturely existence because only he possesses finite freedom. Man, and analogously the rest of reality, is not only grounded in the creative ground of being, but he is also outside it inasmuch as he "stands upon" himself when he exercises his freedom. He can only actualize his essence, be a real man, by positing free acts which inevitably clash with his essential nature. "Fully developed creatureliness is fallen creatureliness."[96] At this pivotal point of freedom the doctrine of creation (the essential order) and the doctrine of the fall (the existential order) merge and become indistinguishable. Tillich sums up his position as follows:

Being a creature means both to be rooted in the creative ground of the divine life and to actualize one's self through freedom. Creation is fulfilled in the creaturely self-realization which simultaneously is freedom and destiny. But it is fulfilled through separation from the creative ground through a break between existence and essence. Creaturely freedom is the point at which creation and fall coincide.[97]

Since the end of creation is the beginning of the fall, further discussion of this knotty but crucial point is reserved for the following chapter on existence.

Sustaining and Directing Creativity

By "sustaining creativity" Tillich means the theological notion of "preservation of the world."[98] Creaturehood implies a twofold resistance: resistance against nonbeing, and resistance against the ground of being by actualized freedom. God as the creative power of being-itself imparts the power of resistance in both cases. His sustaining creativity preserves the structure of reality.

The question arises whether God is immanent or transcendent

to the world, and the usual answer is that he is both. But the real problem is the meaning of these spatial symbols "in" and "above" in ontological terms. The divine immanence is explained in that God is the permanent creative ground of the world, and his transcendence is accounted for by the abyss that divides the finite from the infinite. Although he accepts this explanation, Tillich is not quite satisfied with it in regard to God's transcendence. For the abyss is the obverse of the ground; the finite is infinitely overshadowed by the infinite upon which it totally depends—and one is right back at immanence again. Religious experience demands a less ambiguous transcendence which is better explained in terms of freedom. The otherness of the wholly other is not merely its infinity, but the freedom of a Thou which conflicts with my freedom. Therefore, Tillich prefers to say that "the divine transcendence is the possible conflict and the possible reconciliation of infinite and finite freedom."[99] This kind of transcendence corresponds more accurately to the demands of the religious encounter.

"Providence" is the more traditional name for "directing creativity."[100] He does not like the expression "the purpose of creation" because it tends to imply that God created in order to gain something. From the creature's viewpoint, the goal of creation is the creature itself, the actualization of its potentialities. In regard to God, the end of creation is simply the exercise of the divine creativity. In neither case does creation have a purpose beyond itself. Thus, Tillich likes to speak of "the *telos* of creativity—the inner aim of fulfilling in actuality what is beyond potentiality and actuality in the divine life."[101] God's providence, then, is an inner quality present in every set of circumstances which drives or lures the creature to its fulfilment.

THE SUPRANATURAL AND THE NATURAL

Finitude finds its answer in creaturehood and the divine creativity. But for centuries theologians discussed God's relation to the world in terms of the natural and the supranatural; Tillich's criticism of their approach is revealing. Because of his preference for thinking in dimensions instead of layers, it is no surprise that he objects to the natural-supranatural scheme.[102] But he does more than object. His whole system is a concerted campaign to slay the theological dragon called "the supranatural."[103] He considers the concept of the supranatural and its application to such specific problems as inspiration, miracles, and ethics simply intolerable. It is a "metaphysical devaluation of the natural"; it is static, without dynamism.[104] It is "docetic-monophysitic," "sorcery," and leads to "superstitious consequences."[105] He maintains that his idea of God is not transcendent in a supranatural sense, that is to say,

if "transcendent" means the establishment of a "world" behind the world, if "incarnation" means the descent of a divine being from a heavenly place and its metamorphosis into a human being, if "immortality" is understood as the continuation of temporal existence after death, if the latent church within cultures and religions is denied, if a dramatic end-catastrophe some time in the future is affirmed. All this is a supranaturalism against which my theology stands.[106]

To criticism springing from traditional supranaturalism, Tillich has but one answer: No![107]

Supranaturalism

Tillich's belligerent attitude to supranaturalism has deep roots. The first work he published after the two theses on Schelling was an essay on the supranatural, *Der Begriff des Übernatürlichen*, which appeared in 1915.[108] His principal sources are German theologians of the late eighteenth and early nineteenth centuries: the Tübingen School of Gottlob Christian Storr, the brothers Carl Christian Flatt and Johann Friedrich Flatt, Karl Friedrich Süsskind, and Friedrich Steudal—who expounded their supranatural viewpoint in the *Magazin für christliche Dogmatik und Moral*—

along with Franz Volkmar Reinhard, Johann August Tittman, Karl Friedrich Stäudlin, Heinrich Plank, and Heinrich Gottlieb Tzschirner. Their concept of the supranatural is dialectic; it is arrived at by opposition to the natural.[109] Whatever cannot be derived from the law of nature is supranatural. The basis of definition is the natural, and the essential element is the *supra*. Thus the dialectic of the supranatural involves two movements. The first denies the natural. The second, the *supra*, duplicates the natural by affirming it on a higher level. From this basic position the supranaturalistic theologians develop their concept of God, his aseity and transcendence. They link him to the world by causality, yet confine him to the realm that is above nature, i.e., the supranatural order.

Tillich never ceased to reiterate his reproach of the supranaturalistic view of God that makes him a being above the world.[110] And he charges that the rest of supranaturalistic theology marches to the same beat. Its method treats the Christian message as a package of supranatural truth that fell into the natural world.[111] Miracles are the effects of supranatural tinkering with natural laws.[112] Creation is a supranatural act that began time and nature, and eschatology is a cataclysm that ushers in an idealized reduplication of natural life.[113] In a word, Tillich characterizes supranaturalism as dualistic, "in the sense of a theology that imagines a supranatural world beside or above the natural one, a world in which the unconditional finds a local habitation, thus making God a transcendent object. . . ."[114] By this standard he feels justified in speaking of "the supranaturalism of the Roman Catholic system, the dualism of nature and grace. . . ."[115]

Naturalism

He does not intend, however, that his rebuttal of supranaturalism be construed as an endorsement of pantheistic naturalism.[116] Supranaturalism fails by degrading God into an object alongside finite objects; it denies that he is the ground of being.

On the other hand, naturalism defaults by identifying the finite and the infinite; it denies that God is the abyss.

Pantheism, according to Tillich, is often misinterpreted to mean that God is the totality of natural objects—an absurd doctrine never held by anyone.[117] The real meaning of pantheism, he observes, is that God is the universal essence or substance, and he is swift to disown this teaching. For pantheism is bondage. It incarcerates God in finite beings and, at the same time, shackles their freedom. He has been accused of veering toward pantheism because he claims that a correct concept of God as *ipsum esse* contains a "pantheistic element," i.e., the ground of being.[118] His answer is that, as being-itself, God transcends the polarities of individuality-universality, of freedom-destiny. He transcends essence and existence.[119]

Beyond Naturalism and Supranaturalism

Tillich takes his stand not between supranaturalism and naturalism, but beyond them. He wants a truly transcendent God, but one whose transcendence leaves a palpable imprint on finite beings. His solution is the "self-transcendence" of being, which means "that, within itself, the finite world points beyond itself."[120] Finitude searches for the ground of its being only to discover that it is peering into the abyss of infinity. Discarding traditional terms which place God "above" or "in" the world, we can speak of God who stands for the world and against the world. Man's finite freedom is the clue, for his freedom dramatizes that the creature is independent of the divine ground (God stands against the world), and his finiteness shows his dependence upon the power of being (God stands for the world). In terms of theological method, the notion of self-transcendence demands the method of correlation. In terms of immediate religious experience, self-transcendence is the encounter with the holy.

REFLECTIONS AND APPRAISAL

One really does not know where to begin, for Tillich's views on being, God, and symbolism stimulate a mixture of enthusiastic approval, frowning objection, and puzzled uncertainty, as the rather abundant literature on these subjects demonstrates. Certainly it is impossible to treat the whole range of intriguing philosophical and theological points which he raises. Consequently, hewing to the line of our purpose, we limit ourselves to comment on those areas which immediately and most intimately affect the relation of religion and culture.

First of all, is Tillich's theonomy, in which God is being-itself and the ground of being, some kind of pantheism? The charge has been made that he dilutes the divine transcendence and thus falls into pantheism, principally by doing away with a personal God.[121] Other commentators judge that he not only escapes pantheism, but is, in fact, a champion of the transcendent deity.[122]

Tillich is perhaps more keenly conscious of the pitfall of pantheism than his accusers, and he has taken steps, successfully it seems, to avoid it. He repeatedly insists that God is not only the ground of being, but also the abyss of being which infinitely surpasses finite beings and thus prevents him from being identified with them. But is it possible that, although God is not identified with finite beings, they are identified with him? Against this possibility Tillich erects the bulwark of freedom by which man has the power to contradict even the ground of being. Finally, Tillich's God is beyond potentiality and actuality, beyond essence and existence, a doctrine which, although not entirely limpid to the understanding, is hardly pantheistic immanence. His massive effort to find a meaningful union between religion and culture cannot be lightly dismissed by labeling it pantheism.

The theonomous union of religion and culture can be achieved only by grace, by being grasped in the ultimate concern which is faith. Consequently, a far more serious problem is the personal encounter demanded by an ultimate concern. Is Tillich's God so transcendent that a personal encounter, and hence ultimate concern, is rendered impossible? The problem is further aggravated by his contention that, theologically speaking, God is not a person, although, as we have seen, he concedes the necessity of the symbol of the personal God for the religious encounter. He puts it as follows:

The problem would not be so serious if it were not for the situation of prayer. The ego-thou relation is essential for it. Therefore, God is not less than we. As the ground of everything personal, he is also personal in relation to a person. . . . But God also transcends the personal. . . . The reason is that God as Spirit means that he is not-personally present to not-personal life, personal to personal life, and supra-personal to all life.[123]

Many critics conclude that God as being-itself leaves no room for a personal God in any sense, despite Tillich's protestations to the contrary. One author claims that Tillich suffers from ontological schizophrenia, being pulled in two opposite directions, toward the personal God of the Bible and toward the impersonal God of ontology.[124] Guy Hammond's careful analysis of Tillich's concept of the personal God concludes that "Tillich's ontology does not preserve the ultimacy of a personal divine-human encounter. On the other hand, his position does provide a strong basis for the ontological ultimacy of the personal, that is, the view that the power of personal existence is rooted in being-itself."[125]

To all these critics Tillich retorts that he does preserve the ultimacy of a personal encounter between God and man. The proof is the simple fact of ultimate concern. No one can be ultimately concerned about something less than a person, but, at the same time, God is more than a person because he is the ground and abyss of everything personal.

Perhaps the reason why his doctrine has not been more readily accepted is that Tillich's explanation is not quite explicit enough, for he fails to bring out clearly how an encounter with more than a person is still a personal encounter. It is like trying to sell white cloth to a customer who wants multicolored cloth by telling him that white includes all the colors and they can all be derived from it. A more positive and more conciliatory approach would have been for Tillich to say that God is a person, but he is also more than a person, instead of saying that God is not a person, but he is not less than one. Although Tillich could do so without sacrificing any principles,[126] he hesitates to refer to God as a person, despite his admission that the religious experience demands a personal encounter. Behind this refusal is Tillich's view that to designate God a person is to make him a being next to other beings—and, with that step, one plunges over the precipice into theism and supranaturalism. However, what his critics fear is that if God as being-itself is not a person, then he is an impersonal, unintelligent, undirected, and non-directive force analogous to electricity or nuclear energy, but not the living God of the Bible.

It is our opinion that, as is clearly evident from his book *Biblical Religion and the Search for Ultimate Reality,* Tillich needs, wants, and has the basis for a personal God. However, his aversion to what he feels is supranaturalistic theism restrains him from unreservedly endorsing a personal God—to the confusion and consternation of those who have a greater dread of an impersonal, non-personal, or supra-personal God.

Tillich's doctrine of God has undoubtedly been shaped to a considerable extent by his antipathy to the supernatural. One of his remarkable gifts is that of assimilation, the genius to seize upon and incorporate the merits of even an opposing theological system or philosophical analysis, but this talent fails him when confronted with the theology of the supernatural. His examination of the shadowy eighteenth- and nineteenth-century German theologians, whom he considers its representatives, apparently was a traumatic experience. At the mention of the supernatural, he reacts violently and negatively. This is regrettable because the idea of the supernatural which he rejects—a "split-level" theology of miraculous, divine tinkering with the world from above and from outside—does not correspond to the more profound notion of the supernatural as participation in the divine life. In this latter sense, the theology of the supernatural which is manifest in and elevates nature resembles Tillich's own theology of the New Being which appears in and overcomes existence.

Consequently, it is unfortunate and somewhat inconsistent that Tillich cannot attribute a more honorable place to the natural-supernatural scheme which has a venerable and still vital theological history and deserves credit for its contribution to the unending effort to understand the ever mysterious relation of God to his creatures.[127] Furthermore, he does not seem aware of Roman Catholic attempts to reinterpret the supernatural and to clarify some of the misconceptions about it. The names of Rondet, de Lubac, and Karl Rahner immediately come to mind.[128] Rahner, for example, in his article "Natur und Gnade," criticizes the standard (i.e., post-Tridentine, neo-scholastic) view of the supernatural because of its tendency to fall into a kind of "extrinsicity" by making nature and grace two superimposed but impenetrable layers.[129] Here he and Tillich can be said to be in broad agreement. However, Rahner then delves into the history of theology, especially St. Thomas, to show other aspects of the supernatural which serve as correctives to the standard view. For instance, the sense in which grace is not completely beyond man's conscious life, uncreated grace as quasi-formal causal communication of God himself, the Scotists' idea of the close connection between creation and the incarnation, the possibility of supernatural acts by the unjustified, the *de facto* situation that the state of pure nature does not exist, but that there is only nature in a supernatural order, a more positive notion of *potentia obedientialis*—all these theological data are orchestrated by Rahner into a concept of the supernatural which is rich with tradition and contemporary in its appeal.

However, it must be admitted that Tillich does not rest in a merely negative and barren denunciation of the natural-supernatural framework; he does develop a positive doctrine of God as the ground and power of being, a God whose sustaining and vitalizing activity constantly touches every corner of the universe and penetrates to the deepest level of every creature, its very being. With this positive conception he replaces the divinity of the supranaturalists and deists, a God so remote from the world that he is irrelevant once his creative push has set the wheels of time in motion.

In this sense, Tillich parallels the thrust of the thought of Bonhoeffer who rejects a theology that places God at the farthest fringe of our universe as the last, desperate answer when the natural sources of knowledge have run dry.[130] The danger is that, as man's circle of knowledge widens, God recedes farther and farther from the center of his life. For example, is it not true that, in the minds of most people, evolution dispenses with, or greatly diminishes, God's role in the creation of man? A theology for an adult world places God at the hub of human activity as the wellspring of man's strength, love, accomplishments, and hopes, instead of establishing him as an oracle that sends answers from the darkness beyond the frontier of science. By his ontological approach Tillich brings God into the heart of the cosmos, for there is nothing closer to beings, nothing more fundamental than the structure of being and its ground. In more human terms, the interplay of anxiety (non-being) and courage (being) is the very stuff of life. Love, power, and justice—the profoundest positive motivations of human behavior—are rooted in God as being-itself.

In addition, Tillich's adroit theologizing on God as the power of being recovers some of the splendor of this ancient religious theme. The divine power is a thoroughly biblical doctrine, and we recite in the first article of the Creed: "I believe in God the Father almighty." In our age of power—nuclear, electronic, ballistic, to cite examples only of physical power—the God who is power-itself is especially apropos.

By finding God at the depth of life and not at its fringes, Tillich paves the way for his close union of religion and culture. But this is possible only if creation is essentially good, if there is no independent negative power which escapes the divine dominion. The objection has been raised that Tillich's non-being is "the hypostatization of a negation" which leads to a kind of Manichean dualism.[131] His answer would be that non-being is a dialectical notion, that is, it is dependent upon being and helps to explain the positive power of being and the negative weakness of finite beings, but it is not a self-sufficient evil power. While, admittedly, there may be obscurities, perhaps even deficiencies, in either his doctrine of nonbeing or his manner of expression, it appears that Tillich follows rather standard philosophical procedure in proposing a negative principle to account for the limitations of finitude and to bring into relief the positive principle of being. One recalls such non-Tillichian examples as potency, matter (in the philosophical sense), and contingency.

The suggestion has also been made that the concept of the demonic runs the same risk of dualism.[132] But, as Christoph Rhein points out, the divine and demonic are two different aspects of the same creative surge from the abyss of being. The difference is that, in the demonic, the destructive aspect predominates over the creative, while, in the divine, creativity controls the destructive tendency. But even in the latter case destructivity is not entirely absent, for the old form has to be broken and cast off so that the new creation can come to be.[133] Consequently, it is hard to see how the divine and the demonic constitute a dualism in the pejorative sense any more than do being and nonbeing.

The content of theonomy and, indeed, of all of Tillich's theology is presented to us clothed in the garments of symbolism. Earlier in this chapter, in the section "Symbol and Analogy," we attempted to unravel some of the strands which are woven together to form the fabric of Tillichian symbolism. Two of the most important are the two distinct functions of symbols: they serve as a medium of religious experience and as a medium of communication.[134] God reveals himself through finite reality, and, through that same reality, revelation is expressed. A symbol, then, is a door which opens into a religious experience and which opens out to communicate it. In both cases the pivotal hinge is analogy, the participation of the symbol in the ground of being. But the symbol primarily mediates and communicates the experience of God, not conceptual knowledge about him. Symbols yield knowledge of God only in the biblical sense of knowledge, that is, an existential relationship which enkindles the fire of love. When theology comes along with its conceptual, rational apparatus, its task is to show the relevance of the Christian symbols to the human situation, not to discover propositions which contain "revealed knowledge."[135]

It is evident that the nerve center of Tillich's symbolism is the religious experience of ultimacy. He finds in it two inseparable elements:

(1) the "point" of immediate awareness of the unconditional which *is* empty but unconditionally certain; and (2) the "breadth" of a concrete concern which is full of content but has the conditional certainty of venturing faith. Theology deals with the second element, while presupposing the first and measuring every theological statement by the standard of the ultimacy of the ultimate concern.[136]

We are now in a position to discuss some of the difficulties raised by various authors. Some argue that God as being-itself remains totally ineffable because Tillich permits no positive, literal statements about him. Analogy demands that we know what is literally affirmed and literally negated so that the symbolic assertion may have a firm footing. By making every statement symbolic, Tillich mutes theology.[137] Another is concerned about the lack of content in the "point" of the religious experience:

Unconditional certainty is surely certainty of something. An awareness, or experience, or certainty which is only a point, without content, is, it seems to me, unintelligible. It cannot be used as a basis for affirming or refuting any particular ontological or metaphysical doctrine. For the "point" does not apparently guarantee its own content. If it does, then it is more than a point. If it does not, then the criterion for the adequacy of various interpretations of the content must be derived elsewhere.[138]

And a similar criticism is launched from a Barthian viewpoint, namely, that Tillich establishes a natural theology because there is no basic distinction between an awareness of God and knowledge of God.[139] The "point" must have "breadth"; the experience must have content.

These sharp, well-argued criticisms reveal a weakness in Tillich's position: the lack of specification of the content of the revelatory experience—a problem we shall take up again later. But somehow he seems unperturbed by the difficulty, which leads us to suspect that he and his critics are on different sides of the road, and hence not on an immediate collision course. W. Norman Pittenger sympathetically refers to "Tillich's insistence on the inevitability of symbol, with its suggestiveness and its conveying of true meaning, yet with its inability to give us the neat logical precision we so desire to have."[140] Symbols do have meaning, a meaning born and developed in the Christian experience and tradition, but Tillich stresses that they can never claim to have neatly packaged the unfathomable ground of being in tidy concepts and placed it on the shelf next to other objects. To do so is demonism. His own procedure is to take the symbols of revelation and explain them with the symbols of ontology. For once we cross the frontier of ultimate concern, of revelation, of religious experience, we enter a land where the only language spoken is symbolic. And to those who remonstrate that he converts the facts and tenets of Christianity into something ethereal and unreal—in short, into "only a symbol"—Tillich replies, "He who says 'only a symbol' has completely misunderstood the meaning of symbol; he confuses symbol with sign, and ignores that a genuine symbol participates in the reality of that which it symbolizes."[141]

But the complaint of the critics cannot be so easily muffled. Granted that revelatory knowledge cannot be equated with rational knowledge, there must still be a conceptual element, a truth that enlightens our intellects. What is the content of faith, of revelation, of the Christian symbols? We have seen part of Tillich's answer: God is the symbol for man's ultimate concern and the answer to the question of being. In the following chapters we shall examine other symbols—the Christ, the Spirit, and the Kingdom of God—to determine their symbolic meaning. Only then do we have adequate evidence upon which to estimate the validity and efficacity of Tillich's symbolism to expound the Christian message.

Tillich's doctrine of symbols is almost invariably considered as a methodological or epistemological problem, that is, how to know and speak about God. However, if its ramifications are pursued to their fullest extent, symbolism is actually a restatement of theonomy,[142] for, as Tillich understands them, symbols are born in a theonomous situation by their transparency to the divine. When a person is grasped by an ultimate concern through the medium of a symbol, it means that the depths of this finite reality are opened to reveal the ground of being which sustains it. Substance shines through form, and the symbol radiates the glow of theonomy. In a perfectly theonomous culture everything is symbolic of God.

Notes

1. The only section of *Systematic Theology* not represented here in Part II is the section on revelation. This topic, however, has been treated both explicitly and implicitly in the second chapter of Part I.

2. ST, I, 163.

3. LPJ, 18.

4. *Ibid.,* 19.

5. ST, I, 163. See also *Ibid.,* 113.

6. *Ibid.,* 164–67.

7. *Ibid.,* 166.

8. *Ibid.*, 167.

9. "Reply," K and B, 330–31.

10. LPJ, 24.

11. ST, I, 164, 168–74.

12. *Ibid.*, 170.

13. *Ibid.*, 171.

14. *Ibid.*, 165.

15. CEWR, 55.

16. ST, I, 198.

17. *Ibid.*, 174–78. Cf. also CB, 86–90.

18. ST, I, 176.

19. *Ibid.*, 178–82.

20. *Ibid.*, 178.

21. *Ibid.*, 179.

22. "Everything wants to grow. It wants to increase its power of being in forms which include and conquer more nonbeing. Metaphorically speaking, one could say that the molecule wants to become a crystal, the crystal a cell, the cell a center of cells, the plant animal, the animal man, the man god, the weak strong, the isolated participating, the imperfect perfect, and so on!" LPJ, 54.

23. ST, I, 182–86.

24. *Ibid.*, 185.

25. *Ibid.*, 166.

26. *Ibid.*, 186–89. Cf. also LPJ, 35–40.

27. ST, I, 189.

28. LPJ, 37.

29. *Ibid.*, 37.

30. LPJ, 38, Cf. CB, 34.

31. ST, I, 190.

32. *Ibid.*

33. *Ibid.*, 191.

34. *Ibid.*, 192.

35. CB, 35. Cf. *Ibid.*, 32–39 where Tillich works out the ontology of anxiety.

36. ST, I, 198–201.

37. *Ibid.*, 198.

38. *Ibid.*, 165, 182, 202.

39. *Ibid.*, 203.

40. *Ibid.*, 204.

41. BR, 11.

42. ST, I, 192–98; 165–66.

43. *Ibid.*, 198.

44. *Ibid.*, 204–210.

45. On the basis of the two general types of arguments for God, Tillich distinguishes the ontological from the cosmological approach to the philos-

ophy of religion. Cf. "The Two Types of Philosophy of Religion," TC, 10–29.

46. ST, I, 205.

47. *Ibid.*

48. *Ibid.,* 206.

49. *Ibid.,* 208.

50. ST, I, 235, 237; TC, 24–26; "Reply," K and B, 341.

51. ST, I, 106–108.

52. *Ibid.,* 211.

53. *Ibid.,* 218.

54. "Jewish Influences on Contemporary Christian Theology," *Cross Currents,* II, 1952, 39.

55. *Ibid.,* 40.

56. SF, 52–63.

57. ST, III, 293–94.

58. ST, I, 155–56, 209, 237–38.

59. *Ibid.,* 238.

60. *Ibid.,* 156.

61. *Ibid.,* 79, 110, 113, 216, 237. Cf. also "Reply," K and B, 341.

62. ST, I, 180, 246.

63. *Ibid.,* 241.

64. *Ibid.,* 242–43.

65. *Ibid.,* 243–44.

66. *Ibid.,* 243.

67. BR, 21–28; TC, 131–32; ST, I, 223, 244.

68. TC, 132.

69. ST, I, 245.

70. BR, 82–85; TC, 131–32; ST, I, 244–45.

71. ST, I, 245.

72. BR, 83. In replying to Hartshorne, Tillich claims that he balances the *via eminentiae* (God has personality in an absolutely perfect way) with the *via negationis* (person in the proper sense is negated) to produce his *via symbolica.* "Reply," K and B, 334.

73. TC, 132.

74. ST, I, 238.

75. In ST, I, 238–39 Tillich practically identifies the ground of being with the structure of being: "Since God is the ground of being, he is the ground of the structure of being. He is not subject to this; the structure is grounded in him. . . . He *is* the structure; that is, he has the power of determining the structure of everything that has being." But one year later, responding to criticism, he points out that he did not intend a total identification: "I must first concede that the structure of being, although it is rooted in being-as-such, is certainly not identical with it, and should perhaps have been more sharply distinguished from it." "Reply," K and B, 335.

76. "Reply," K and B, 334; ST, II, 9–10.

77. ST, I, 238–39.

78. *Ibid.*, 240.

79. *Ibid.*, 240–41.

80. *Ibid.*, 131, 179, 239–240; "Reply," K and B, 339; GW, IV, 125–26; "Reply" to Gustave Weigel, "The Theological Significance of Paul Tillich," O'M and W, 23–24.

81. M. T.-L. Penido, *Le Rôle de l'Analogie en Théologie Dogmatique,* Paris: J. Vrin, 1931, 26.

82. ST, I, 168–69; ST, II, 31; ST, III, 20–21, 86. Tillich's analysis of self-integration, self-creativity, and self-transcendence is but one protracted example of this procedure. *Ibid.* 11–106.

83. See LPJ and CB.

84. ST, II, 115.

85. ST, I, 131. See also *Ibid.*, 239–40.

86. We are indebted to the clear and stimulating analysis of Tillich's symbolism made by Stephan Wisse, *Das Religiöse Symbol,* Essen: Ludgerus-Verlag, 1963, 151–53.

87. "Relation of Metaphysics and Theology," *The Review of Metaphysics,* X, September, 1956, 58–59.

88. See DF, 41–54 where Tillich develops the relationship between symbols and ultimate concern.

89. "Reply" to Weigel, "Theological Significance of Paul Tillich," O'M and W, 24.

90. See ST, I, 243. The discussion of Tillich's theory of symbolism has been greatly furthered by three recent publications. Lewis S. Ford unravels three of the strands: "a dialectic of affirmation and negation, an extended use of the metaphor of the transparency of the symbolic medium, and a theory of participation relevant to symbolic predication. These theories appear singly and in various combinations with one another." Cf. "The Three Strands of Tillich's Theory of Religious Symbols," *The Journal of Religion,* XLVI, January, 1966, No. 1, Part II, 104–130. Tillich's "Rejoinder," in which he suggests the metaphor "translucency" of symbols instead of their "transparency," is worthy of special note. *Ibid.* 186–89. Klaus-Dieter Nörenberg considers Tillichian symbolism as inextricably bound up with the method of correlation: "For Tillich a religious symbol is genuine and valid only if it relates to a human situation and can enter into a relation of correlation with it." Nörenberg's whole book is an attempt to understand in depth and evaluate this thesis. Cf. *Analogia Imaginis: Der Symbolbegriff in der Theologie Paul Tillichs,* Gütersloh: Gütersloher Verlagshaus Gerd Mohn, 1966, 79. Robert P. Scharlemann also locates symbolism within the problematic of the method of correlation. He concludes that ". . . statements of correlation describe the correlation between structure and depth and can be approached from the side of religion or from the side of philosophy and that the prius and structure of our being and knowing is 'God is' rather than 'being.' . . ." Cf. "Tillich's Method of Correlation: Two Proposed Revisions," *The Journal of Religion,* XLVI, January, 1966, No. 1, Part II, 92–103.

91. ST, III, 31.

92. ST, I, 252–53.

93. *Ibid.*, 253–54.

94. *Ibid.*, 253.

95. *Ibid.*, 254–56.

96. *Ibid.*, 255.

97. *Ibid.*, 256.

98. *Ibid.*, 261–63.

99. *Ibid.*, 263. See also BR, 74–75.

100. ST, I, 263–70. Cf. also the sermon "The Meaning of Providence," SF, 104–107.

101. ST, I, 264.

102. ST, III, 15; GW, IV, 118–19.

103. Why Tillich speaks of the "supranatural" in place of the more common "supernatural" is not clear. Only in one passage does he use the term "supernature." Cf. PE, 16. We suggest that, in his mind, "supra" connotes more the spatial position of "above," while "super" stresses rather a superiority in power. Thus, "supranatural" corresponds more closely to his basic objection against it, i.e., that it puts God above the world. Confer ST, III, 363 where he states, "The prefix 'supra' indicates a higher level of reality in which divine actions take place without connection with world history." Besides, "supranaturalism" is the exact duplicate of the German *Supranaturalismus* which he employed for many years.

104. PE, xxiii, 151.

105. ST, I, 65, 116–17; ST, III, 15.

106. "Reply," K and B, 341.

107. ST, III, 5.

108. *Der Begriff des Übernatürlichen, sein dialektischer Charakter und das Prinzip der Identität, dargestellt an der Supranaturalistischen Theologie vor Schleiermacher,* Part One, Königsberg/Neumark: H. Madrasch, 1915. Part Two was never published.

109. *Ibid.*, 27–30. Tillich remarks that the supranaturalists never clearly define nature. From their usage he distinguishes two concepts of nature, the formal and the material. Nature in the formal sense is the nature of things (*die Natur der Dinge*), that is, their essence, the thing that makes them what they are. Whatever flows from this nature undisturbed by interference from without is "natural." Nature in the material sense is the world of nature (*die Dinge der Natur*), the universe of time, space, and experience in which the formal definition is verified. *Ibid.*, 3–8, 27.

110. "Theologie der Kultur," 31; IH, 222–23; ST, II, 5–6.

111. ST, I, 64.

112. *Ibid.*, 116–17, 267.

113. PE, 82; ST, III, 397; ST, II, 6.

114. PE, 82.

115. *Ibid.*, xxiii.

116. IH, 223; ST, I, 65; ST, II, 6–7.

117. ST, I, 233–34, 236–38. Tillich exonerates Schelling of pantheism on the score that he never made God the totality nor the substance of nature, but rather the creative power within nature. Cf. GW, I, 44, note 9.

118. ST, I, 234.

119. "Afterword," O'M and W, 308.

120. ST, II, 7–8. Cf. also ST, I, 64–65 and "Reply," K and B, 341.

121. See Killen, *The Ontological Theology of Paul Tillich*, 241–45, 253–257; Marvin Fox, "Tillich's Ontology and God," *Anglican Theological Review*, XLIII, July, 1961, 266; Pierre Barthel, *Interprétation du Langage Mythique et Théologie Biblique*, Leiden: E. J. Brill, 1963, 194–95. Barthel cites H. Kraemer's colorful accusation that Tillich's system is a Trojan horse that introduces into Christianity a kind of Hindu monism. Kenneth Hamilton declares that Tillich is "monistic and quasi-pantheistic." *The System and the Gospel*, 194. See also *Ibid.*, 85–87, 192–94.

122. See George F. McLean, *Man's Knowledge of God According to Paul Tillich*, dissertation abstract: The Catholic University of America, Washington, D.C., 1958, 16–17, and by the same author, "Paul Tillich's Existential Philosophy of Protestantism," O'M and W, 70; Albert J. Zabala, *Myth and Symbol: An Analysis of Myth and Symbol in Paul Tillich*, dissertation: Institut Catholique de Paris, 1959, 66–67, 285–86; and Christoph Rhein, *Paul Tillich: Philosoph und Theologe*, Stuttgart: Evangelisches Verlagswerk, 1957, 63–64.

123. "God as Reality and Symbol," *Essays and Studies* (Tokyo), XI, March, 1961, 107–108. In ST, I, 245 he states: " 'Personal God' does not mean that God is *a* person. . . . He is not a person, but he is not less than personal." And he concludes his book on the relation of ontology to the personalistic religion of the Bible with the ringing declaration: "*Against* Pascal I say: The God of Abraham, Isaac, and Jacob and the God of the philosophers is the same God. He is a person and the negation of himself as a person." BR, 85.

124. William Hallock Johnson, "Tillich's Science of Being," *The Princeton Seminary Bulletin*, LVI, October, 1962, 53.

125. Guy B. Hammond, "Tillich on the Personal God," *The Journal of Religion*, XLIV, October, 1964, 293. It is worth noting that the commentators are practically unanimous in accepting Tillich's position that what concerns us ultimately cannot be less than a person. But there is one dissident voice which claims that this supposition is still problematic. Wilhelm Weischedel asks, "Why should not the impersonal be able to be experienced as our ultimate concern, for example, nothingness, when it encounters us in the fullness of its threatening character?" "Paul Tillichs philosophische Theologie: ein ehrerbietiger Widerspruch," *Der Spannungsbogen*, Karl Hennig (ed.), 37.

126. Charles Hartshorne, although not in complete agreement with Tillich on other points, has no difficulty in reconciling his two definitions of God as being-itself and God as whatever can be loved with all one's mind,

heart, soul, and strength. He shows that these two conceptions are not only consistent, but equivalent. Cf. "Tillich and the Other Great Tradition," *Anglican Theological Review*, XLIII, July, 1961, 245–46.

127. Christopher Kiesling, a Catholic writer, rejects the caricature of the supernatural as vigorously as Tillich does. Kiesling then goes on to point out supernatural elements in Tillich's theology—for example, *gratia sanans* in the sense of faith and love which close the gap between essence and existence. "The Life of the New Being," O'M and W, 269–71.

128. Henri Rondet, *Gratia Christi*, Paris: Beauchesne, 1948; Henri de Lubac, *Surnaturel*, Paris: Aubier, 1946; Karl Rahner, *Schriften zur Theologie*, Band I–V, Einsiedeln: Benziger, 1958–1962: "Über das Verhältnis von Natur und Gnade," I, 323–45; "Zur scholastischen Begrifflichkeit der ungeschaffenen Gnade," I, 347–75; "Personale und sakramentale Frömmigkeit," II, 115–41; "Über die Erfahrung der Gnade," III, 105–109; "Natur und Gnade," IV, 209–36; "Weltgeschichte und Heilsgeschichte," V, 115–35.

129. *Schriften*, IV, 209–36.

130. See Dietrich Bonhoeffer, *Letters and Papers from Prison*, London: Collins, paperback, 1959, 93, 106–108, 114–15.

131. J. Heywood Thomas, *Paul Tillich: An Appraisal*, Philadelphia: Westminster Press, 1963, 71–73, 119. A diametrically opposite judgment is rendered by Kenneth Hamilton who claims that Tillich's system is monistic. See *The System and the Gospel*, 194–96.

132. Barthel, *Interprétation du Langage Mythique et Théologie Biblique*, 171.

133. Rhein, *Paul Tillich: Philosoph und Theologe*, 64–65.

134. Tavard distinguishes the same two functions when he says that Tillich's symbols are associated with revelation and are used to speak indirectly of God. George Tavard, *Paul Tillich and the Christian Message*, 54–55.

135. See ST, I, 129 where Tillich prefers the terms "knowledge of revelation" or, even better, "revelatory knowledge" to the misleading phrase "revealed knowledge" which connotes ordinary knowledge received in an extraordinary way.

136. "The Problem of Theological Method," *Four Existentialist Theologians*, Herberg (ed.), 249.

137. See William L. Rowe, "The Meaning of 'God' in Tillich's Theology," *The Journal of Religion*, XLII, 1962, 274–86, and Bowman L. Clarke, "God and the Symbolic in Tillich," *Anglican Theological Review*, XLIII, July, 1961, 302–11.

138. Daniel D. Williams, "Tillich's Doctrine of God," *The Philosophical Forum* (Boston University), XVIII, 1960–61, 46–47.

139. Alexander J. McKelway, *The Systematic Theology of Paul Tillich*, Richmond: John Knox Press, 1964, 139–40. An interesting discussion of Tillich's views on the proofs for God is found in J. Heywood Thomas, *Paul Tillich: An Appraisal*, 58–65.

140. W. Norman Pittenger, "Paul Tillich as a Theologian: An Appreciation," *Anglican Theological Review*, XLIII, July, 1961, 274.

141. "Reply," K and B, 334–35. See also ST, I, 131, 141; ST, II, 9; TC, 64.

142. See Wisse, *Das Religiöse Symbol*, 152. Rhein also observes that Tillichian symbolism is a synthesis which expresses the paradoxical immanence of the transcendent. *Paul Tillich: Philosoph und Theologe*, 63.

5/Existence and the Christ

THEONOMY, THE SOLUTION to the union of religion and culture, is brought about only by the final revelation of the New Being in Jesus the Christ.[1] It is the power of the New Being which overcomes autonomy and heteronomy. The Christ as the bearer of final revelation is transparent to the ground of being. By overcoming estrangement he reunites the creature to its ground and thus opens up the divine depth-dimension. The emptiness of autonomy is filled by the Spiritual Presence which excludes demonic intrusions.

Heteronomy is always imposed by a group or by an institution. The church, as the community of faithful who receive the New Being, ideally should be free from heteronomous tendencies. But the church is also subject to the ambiguities of existence which tempt it to exercise heteronomous authority. Here is where the Cross of the Christ intervenes as a corrective. For in Jesus crucified the medium of revelation sacrificed himself to the content of revelation. The Cross is the church's protection against heteronomy if the members embrace it.

The power of the New Being, then, is the foundation of theonomy. "Theonomous periods do not feel split, but whole and centered. Their center is neither their autonomous freedom nor their heteronomous authority but the depth of reason ecstatically

167

experienced and symbolically expressed."[2] The ecstatic experience which gives birth to theonomy is the experience of the New Being as symbolized in Jesus who is the Christ.

The tenor and direction of a theology can usually be gauged by its Christology, since the Christ is the beginning and the end of all theologizing. How religion relates to culture will eventually depend upon how God relates to Jesus and how Jesus relates to the world. Our exposition of Tillich's Christology follows his own order; he first asks the question of existential estrangement, and then answers it with the theological doctrine of the New Being in Jesus as the Christ.

We progress from volume one to volume two of *Systematic Theology*, a progression that "mirrors the leap from man's essential nature to its distortion in existence."[3] Tillich insists that it is not a logically necessitated sequence, but a jump, for the transition from essence to existence is "irrational," the passage from God to the Christ, "paradoxical."

THE QUESTION OF EXISTENCE

The previous chapter dealt with being as opposed to nonbeing; this chapter examines existential being as opposed to essential being. The question of existence is broken down into the following considerations: the notion of existence, the fall from essence to existence, the state of estrangement and sin, and the quest for the New Being amid the tragic ruins of existence.

Existence

Etymology is one of Tillich's standard devices for clarifying his concepts, and he also applies it to "existence."[4] "To exist" means to "stand out." On the most fundamental level, to exist means to be, to stand out of nonbeing. Since nonbeing can be the absolute nonbeing of *ouk on* or the relative nonbeing of *me on,* existence can take two directions. If something stands out of absolute nothingness, it exists in the sense that it has being. If something stands out of relative nothingness, that is, potentiality, then it exists in the sense that it has actuality. Etymology, then, indicates two senses of existence: "to stand out" of either absolute nonbeing or relative nonbeing.

But in either case, the metaphor "to stand out" connotes the metaphor "to stand in," just as trees "stand out" of the earth and yet "stand in" it. A being stands out of nonbeing, but not completely, for it is a mixture of being and nonbeing. An actual being stands out of potentiality, but not completely, for it never fully realizes all its potentiality. Existence, therefore, is an imperfect state, for to exist means to have being and yet to "stand in" nonbeing, to have actuality, and yet to "stand in" potentiality.

Historically, however, attention has been focused upon the second meaning of existence and the split between potentiality and actuality.[5] If we interpret Tillich correctly, this is the overriding meaning of existence: to stand out of potentiality. Upon this meaning he builds the distinction between essence and existence. Essence is real, is actualized in existence, but only in fragments, never totally. This situation gives rise to two conflicting viewpoints which Tillich finds exemplified in Plato and Hegel. Plato viewed the gap between potential and actual being as a fall. For him, existence is a fall from essence. Hegel, on the contrary, considered the gap as merely part of the process of divine self-realization. For him existence is the expression of essence.

Tillich describes how Hegel's essentialism set the stage for the existentialist revolt.[6] Schelling, Schopenhauer, Marx, and Kierkegaard all share a common insight: that human existence is a state of estrangement from its essential nature. Existence is "dehumanization and not the expression of essential humanity."[7] This is the truth about man's predicament which existentialism has laid bare. However, it is the question of existence, not the answer. Whenever existentialists, atheistic or theistic, go beyond their analyses and provide answers, they draw upon religious sources. For the answer to existence is a matter of ultimate concern, and hence is religious, even though it be disguised in secular or atheistic garb. The religious character of existentialism stems from the very nature of philosophy which embraces both scientific detachment and the involvement of faith in an ultimate concern. Christianity proclaims the "New Being" in Christ; the merit of existentialism lies in its graphic portrayal of the "old being," namely, the tragedy and anxiety of a cosmos estranged from its essential nature.

The Fall

The transition from essence to existence, from potentiality to actuality, is a leap, a jump that is not necessitated by the inner logic of essences. Tillich refers to it as "the Fall."[8] "The Fall" as a symbol for the transition from essence to existence is broader in scope than the Fall depicted in Genesis, although the latter is its classic expression. Plato's myth of "the Fall of the souls" conveys the same notion of the tragic passage from potentiality to actuality. The Fall has "universal anthropological significance." To speak of it as the transition from essence to existence is demythologizing, but only to a limited extent, for in dealing with this question the philosopher commits himself in a matter of ultimate concern and so cannot avoid using myth and symbol. Yet a certain amount of demythologizing is necessary, since the theologian must employ philosophical ideas to explain the Fall. "The philosopher cannot avoid existential decisions, and the theologian cannot avoid ontological concepts."[9] Consequently, Tillich feels justified in using the myth of the Fall to formulate the question of existence. He finds in Genesis, chapters one to three, "the profoundest and richest expression of man's awareness of his existential estrangement,"[10] and from it he outlines the four elements of the transit from essence to existence: the possibility of the Fall, its motives, the event itself, and its implications.

The possibility of the Fall lies in the fact that man alone possesses finite freedom.[11] Creatures lower than man have only analogous freedom, and God is infinite freedom. But man is free even to the extent that he can contradict his essential nature and destroy his own humanity. Yet man's freedom is not absolute; it operates within the context of universal destiny. The Fall, although always presented as the Fall of man, is a cosmic event. But to return to the words of Genesis, the Fall is possible because man is made in the image of God, that is, he has freedom in destiny.

The motives for the Fall involve a discussion of essential being, of Adam before the Fall.[12] The difficulty is that one does not find essential being as such, but only essence in the state of existential distortion. Common procedure has been to project back into prehistory the myth of Paradise, but orthodox theology has heaped so many perfections upon Adam as to make his Fall unintelligible. Therefore, Tillich prefers the psychological analogy of "the state of dreaming innocence." A dream anticipates actuality, and, although reality differs from it, still there is a certain correspondence between the two. Innocence is the state of non-actualized potentiality characterized by the absence of experience, responsibility, and guilt, but which, if actualized, puts an end to innocence. The growth of sexual awareness is a good example of innocence and its loss. Briefly, "the symbol 'Adam before the Fall' must be understood as the dreaming innocence of undecided potentialities."[13] In the state of dreaming innocence, "freedom and destiny lie within each other, distinct but not separated, in tension but not in conflict."[14] They are held in polar unity by the ground of being in which they are rooted. The motives for the Fall are seen in the anxiety which besieges man from without and from within. From without, the command not to eat the forbidden fruit testifies both to man's aroused freedom, his desire to actualize himself, and to his instinct for self-preservation by obeying the divine prohibition. From within, man is torn by the same anxiety to actualize the freedom of which he is aware and to preserve his innocence by not realizing his potentialities. In either case, under the pressure but not the compulsion of anxiety, man decides for self-actualization.

In what sense is the Fall an event?[15] It certainly is not an historical event that happened "once upon a time." It is a fact, the original fact, in that it is an ontological condition that precedes but touches all of creation. "It means that the transition from essence to existence is a universal quality of finite being."[16] The Genesis story stresses the moral element of this quality by highlighting the ethical act of Adam. But the tragic element which involves the whole cosmos is not absent: "The serpent represents the dynamic trends of nature; there is the magical character of the two trees, the rise of sexual consciousness, the curse over the heredity of Adam, the body of the woman, the animals and the land."[17] These symbols point to a cosmic myth which teaches that the individual act of freedom is embedded in a universal destiny. The polarity of freedom-destiny is asserted. "Existence is rooted both in ethical freedom and in tragic destiny."[18]

The cosmic implications of the Fall introduce the problem of how universal existence is related to man's existence.[19] These implications are distilled into two questions: How is nature related to fallen man?; What is the relationship between creation and the Fall? As regards the first question, Tillich's insistence upon the transhistorical character of the Fall rules out a before and after, a change in the structure of nature due to the divine curse laid upon the land. The transition from essence to existence is not an event in time; Adam before the Fall and nature before the curse are states of potentiality. The only actual state is the one in which man and the world now exist, and it was never otherwise. A simple solution would be to separate innocent nature and guilty man, to speak no more of a fallen world. But to do so neglects the tragic element of destiny. For within man himself nature is implicated in the Fall.[20] First, in the course of human evolution, "there is no absolute discontinuity between animal bondage and human freedom."[21] Secondly, in the development of the human individual, who can say where and when responsibility begins and ends? Thirdly, the discovery of the unconscious reveals a hidden but determining power that influences man's decisions. And, lastly, the social dimension of the "collective unconscious" contributes to the limitation imposed by destiny. In a word, biological, psychological, and sociological factors affect the individual's decision. "But freedom is the possibility of a total and centered act of the personality, an act in which all the drives and influences which constitute the destiny of man are brought into the centered unity of a decision. None of these drives compels the decision in isolation."[22] Yet, they are effective, and in this way nature represents destiny and participates in the act of freedom. It is possible, in fact necessary, to speak of a fallen world. "The tragedy of nature is bound to the tragedy of man, as the salvation of nature is dependent on the salvation of man . . . for man is in nature and nature is in man."[23] In the words of Schelling, "Nature, also, mourns for a lost good."[24]

The second question is the coincidence of creation and the Fall.[25] Despite their logical differences, how does one explain finite freedom, the point at which they coincide? Or to put it another way, does Tillich's doctrine make sin ontologically necessary? Fundamental to his position is the view that creation and Fall are not historical events, but ontological states. Consequently, "there is no point in time and space in which created goodness was actualized and had existence."[26] There was no paradise just as there will be no utopia. "Actualized creation and estranged existence are identical."[27] For example, the newly created infant falls into the state of existential estrangement. Creation and Fall coincide, but not logically, for, when the child matures, it affirms its existential condition by free acts which incur guilt. The child is essentially good, but its self-actualization through freedom and destiny results in sin. But this sin is not a structural necessity; the transition from essence to existence is a leap. Existence can never be derived from essence.[28]

Reinhold Niebuhr questions whether Tillich's "ontological speculations" about creation and the Fall have betrayed the

biblical picture of man.[29] Niebuhr maintains that the paradox of
fate and freedom in the Bible is weighted on the side of freedom
and responsibility. He objects:

> In Tillich's thought the emphasis upon the ontological basis of this para-
> dox seems subtly to shift the meaning of the fate, contained in the idea
> of "original sin" from a historical to an ontological one. With this shift
> the emphasis falls upon the fatefulness of sin rather than upon our
> responsibility.[30]

In Niebuhr's opinion, Tillich goes too far in eliminating all historical import from the Genesis myth and in replacing it with
ontological insights. The danger is that the mystery of evil is
solved too neatly, with the result that temporal existence itself is
considered evil.

Responding to Niebuhr's criticism, Tillich defends the use of
ontology on the score that it is as open to freedom as it is to
destiny.[31] If Niebuhr accepts his definition of man as finite freedom, surely he cannot object to an ontological analysis of what
this means. Perhaps he does not care for the particular analysis,
but he cannot reproach ontology as such. Furthermore, Tillich
denies the charge that his ontology identifies finitude and evil.[32]
Creation is not an unfinished work that can be completed only by
a touch of evil. Created finite freedom falls universally, and hence
unavoidably, but not logically. "The universality and consequently
the unavoidability of the fall is not derived from 'ontological
speculation,' but from a realistic observation of man, his heart, and
his history."[33] Some of the greatest philosophers (Plato, Origen,
Kant, and Schelling), attempting to reconcile freedom and evil,
conceived the myth of the transcendent fall. Theology, once it
rejects a literal interpretation of Genesis, must boldly re-examine
universal sinfulness. The supralapsarian Calvinists had the courage
to affirm that if God creates, his creation will turn against him,
although their position is tainted with the demonic when they
make Adam fall by divine decree.[34] The point is that theology

must take seriously, and thus ontologically, the universality of sin.

If the problem is posed in terms of guilt, we find that Tillich considers the inevitability of a guilty conscience the normal consequence of man's finite freedom: "Even in what he considers his best deed nonbeing is present and prevents it from being perfect."[35] A good conscience is impossible: "Only self-deception can give a moral conscience, since it is impossible *not* to act and since every action implies guilt."[36] But again, the cause of guilt is not finitude as such, but rather "the self-assertiveness of the finite being in its pride, concupiscence, and separation from its ground."[37] A down-to-earth example of the guilt which attaches to the transition from essence to existence is the severing of family connections:

We cannot cut the ties with our family without being guilty. But the question is: Is it willfulness which demonically disrupts the family communion, or is it the step toward independence and one's own understanding of the will of God which divinely liberates us from the bondage to our family? We never know the answer with certainty. We must risk tragic guilt. . . .[38]

Estrangement and Sin

What are the characteristics of human existence as a result of the Fall?[39] In general terms they are as follows: "The state of existence is the state of estrangement. Man is estranged from the ground of his being, from other beings, and from himself. The transition from essence to existence results in personal guilt and universal tragedy."[40] In more specific terms, they are estrangement and sin, two closely related, but not identical concepts. Estrangement means that "man as he exists is not what he essentially is and ought to be."[41] But the special force of estrangement is the connotation that man *belongs* to that from which he is cut off. "For separation presupposes an original unity. . . . It is impossible to unite that which is *essentially* separated. Without an ultimate belongingness no union of one thing with another can be conceived."[42] Just as nonbeing depends upon being, and the negative depends upon the positive, so estrangement depends upon union. Unity embraces both itself and estrangement, and the latter is overcome by *reunion*.

Sin is estrangement with the addition of one extremely important factor, namely, "the personal act of turning away from that to which one belongs."[43] Sin is "separation," "estrangement from one's essential being."[44] Sin is "the unreconciled duality of ultimate and preliminary concerns, of the finite and that which transcends finitude, of the secular and the holy."[45] Because of sin, man's essential nature stands against him as law, not as a strange law, but as a natural law, for it represents his true nature from which he is separated.[46] In strict Tillichian usage, therefore, estrangement is a broader notion than sin, but when he refers to human estrangement, as is usually the case, sin and estrangement are equivalent.

Man's predicament is one of estrangement, but this is not to say that it is a state of things like the law of gravity. For estrangement always combines the two factors of personal freedom and universal destiny. Nor must sin be understood as "sins," that is, particular acts which are considered morally evil. "Sins" are expressions of sin; their sinfulness lies not in disobedience to a law, but in the estrangement from God, from men, and from self to which they bear witness.

In his portrayal of man's existential situation, Tillich develops what he calls "the marks of estrangement."[47] We mention them to show the ramifications of his thought on sin. "Unbelief" is a mark of estrangement because it is "the act or state in which man in the totality of his being turns away from God."[48] "Hubris" is another sign of estrangement, for by it man distorts his naturally good centeredness of self-consciousness by elevating himself as the absolute center of his world. He usurps the place of the divine. The last mark of estrangement is "concupiscence," "the unlimited desire to draw the whole of reality into one's self."[49] Concupiscence is seen in man's unbounded, insatiable strivings for knowledge, sex, and power.

Tillich understands the classic distinction between original sin and actual sin as the difference between sin as fact and sin as act.[50] Adam represents essential man, and his fall symbolizes the transition from essence to existence. Consequently, sin as the universal fact embracing both freedom and destiny precedes sin as an individual act. The individual act of sin actualizes the universal fact of estrangement. Tillich is sympathetic toward the Catholic distinction between mortal and venial sin, pointing out that Protestantism's insistence upon the absoluteness of turning from God results in a loss of psychological insight and of educational flexibility.

Thus far Tillich has dealt exclusively with the estrangement of the individual person. Is there such a thing as collective estrangement?[51] Strictly speaking, no, because a social group has no natural center of decision corresponding to the self of the individual person. Therefore, there is no collective sin, no collective guilt. However, since freedom and destiny work together, members of a social group could be guilty, "not of committing the crimes of which their group is accused, but of contributing to the destiny in which these crimes happened."[52]

The Quest for the New Being

"Existence is always both fact and act."[53] Although freedom is not destroyed, it is always in bondage to destiny. Therefore, no individual act within existence can overcome estrangement; existence itself becomes destiny. In spite of his finite freedom, man cannot achieve reunion with God. Certain individual acts can be performed which express fleetingly and fragmentarily man's essential goodness, but these reveal only what is indispensable for victory over existence, namely, reunion with the ground of being. In order to overcome the old state of estrangement, man needs to receive new being, for new being precedes new acting just as estrangement precedes sin. Union with God, with the power of being, must be re-established. This is the quest for the New Being. In discussing it, we shall touch upon man's efforts at self-salvation, his expectation of the New Being, the meaning of the symbol "Christ," and certain concepts which interpret it.

The history of religion records man's attempts and failures to find the New Being, to save himself.[54] Religion is the sphere where the New Being is sought; it is contrasted with the split between essence and existence. Myth and cult are indispensable for existential man, because, in the state of existence, reason cannot penetrate to its depth in the ground of being.[55] But religion is ambiguous, for the very fact of the quest indicates the presence, at least germinally and fragmentarily, of the New Being, and at the same time the quest degenerates into futile efforts at self-salvation. These vain attempts, which are found in all religions and not only in particular ones, can be listed as follows: legalism, asceticism, mysticism, sacramentalism, doctrinalism, and emotionalism. Yet, even in their inadequacy they are salutary in a minimal way, for awareness of estrangement and desire for reunion indicate the presence of a saving power.

"The quest for the New Being is universal because the human predicament and its ambiguous conquest are universal."[56] This utopian expectation, religious in substance, is often cloaked under a secular form. Although the character of the quest constantly changes, Tillich distinguishes two major types: the non-historical and the historical expectation of the New Being. The non-historical attitude, exemplified primarily in Far Eastern religions, does not expect salvation through history, but rather in "the negation of all beings and the affirmation of the Ground of Being alone."[57] The historical attitude, on the other hand, asserts the essential goodness of being and awaits the New Being as a transformation of reality "through a historical process which is unique, unrepeatable, irreversible."[58]

The symbol "Christ" or "Messiah" expresses the universal expectation of the New Being.[59] Although the messianic idea is thoroughly historical, it is capable of incorporating the non-historical type. The cosmic Messiah of apocalyptic literature, the personification of divine Wisdom, the Son of Man, the Logos of the Fourth Gospel, the mysticism of Paul and his doctrine of the Spirit—all these transhistorical elements build a bridge across which non-historical expectations can enter into Christianity. The non-historical type, however, is unable to embrace the historical type. Consequently, Christianity is the universal type of the universal quest for the New Being set in motion by a universal revelation. Yet it is not universally acknowledged as such, for man's estrangement, futile self-salvation, and consequent despair generate a self-understanding and an expectation which is contradicted by the New Being in Jesus as the Christ. The New Being of Christianity is "paradoxical" in the root meaning of the word; it runs counter to the expectations of the whole of human experience.[60]

The Christ is the symbol for the expectation of the New Being. How is it to be interpreted?[61] Traditionally he has been called the "mediator" in that he makes the ultimate concrete and saves by reuniting. The mediator, however, is not a third reality between God and man, for all mediation and salvation is from God. The Christ is essential man. He represents man to man, that is, he shows what man essentially is. But he also represents God to man, because essential man has embedded within him the image of God. Therefore, essential manhood and essential God-manhood are identical. It is important to note that, for Tillich, "the paradox of the Christian message is not that essential humanity includes the union of God and man . . ." but rather, "that in *one* personal life essential manhood has appeared under the conditions of existence without being conquered by them."[62]

Another term often used to interpret the symbol of the Christ is "incarnation." It is a concept commonly found in pagan religions, and Tillich has grave reservations about it because it is so vulnerable to misunderstanding. For instance, if incarnation is taken to mean "God has become man," then it is nonsense, because the words do not mean what they say. Obviously, God does not change into something that is not God. Again, incarnation carries polytheistic connotations of divine beings besides God and mythological connotations of anthropomorphism. Tillich does, however, accept incarnation in the Johannine sense of "the Logos became flesh." "Logos" is the principle of divine self-manifestation, "flesh" signifies historical existence, and "became" indicates that God participates in that which is estranged from him. Thus, the Johannine phrase means that "God is manifest in a personal life-process as a saving participant in the human predicament."[63]

The question of existence terminates in the quest for the New Being. We have remained on the level of expectation, even though it has been described in Christian terminology. The next step is the actual appearance of the Christ in Jesus, the event which fulfills all expectations.

THE REALITY OF THE CHRIST

Man's quest for the New Being which overcomes existential estrangement ends in the acceptance of Jesus of Nazareth as the Christ.[64] Peter's confession at Caesarea Philippi—"Thou art the Christ"—marks the birth of Christianity, for it contains the two basic elements of the Christian message: the fact of Jesus of Nazareth and his reception as the Christ in an act of faith.[65] "The receptive side of the Christian event is as important as the factual side. And only their unity creates the event upon which Christianity is based."[66] Tillich's absolute refusal to use the name "Jesus Christ" is founded upon this distinction between the man from Nazareth and the mythological title "the Christ" which is paradoxically attached to him by faith. He therefore employs such phrases as "Jesus who is called the Christ," or "Jesus who is the Christ," or "Jesus as the Christ," or "Jesus the Christ."[67]

The reality of the Christ will be discussed under the following headings: historical research and the Christ, the New Being, theories of Christology, the significance of the Cross and the Resurrection, and the meaning of salvation.

Historical Research and the Christ

The application of scientific methods of historical criticism to biblical literature produced, among other results, the ill-fated search for the historical Jesus.[68] Its failure is due not to defective methods or faulty applications of sound ones, but to the nature of the sources themselves. The gospels are reports of faith about Jesus as the Christ, not about Jesus of Nazareth. The attempt to sift fact from faith yields, at best, a sketchy, conjectural picture. The result of the search is "not a picture of the so-called historical Jesus but the insight that there is no picture behind the biblical one which could be made scientifically probable."[69] Since it is impossible to found the Christian faith upon a factual biography of Jesus, some theologians seek its historical foundation in the words of Jesus. "As the teachings of Jesus, they are understood as refined interpretations of the natural law or as original insights into the nature of man."[70] But though their power of expression is remarkable, they leave Jesus on the same level as the Old Testament. The latest approach to the words of Jesus, that of Bultmann, considers them not as general rules, but as a message that demands a decision. However, "it does not show how the requirement of deciding for the Kingdom of God can be fulfilled."[71] Neither the teachings of Jesus nor his demands provide the power to follow him, for that can come only from a new reality, from the New Being which is first a gift before it is a demand.

Much of the confusion that accompanied the search for the Jesus of history could have been dispelled by a distinction in the term "historical Jesus." It can refer to the fragmentary and hypothetical results of historical investigation into the person behind the gospel story. It can also refer to the indispensable factual element in the Christian event which lies in the sphere of faith and cannot be touched by the skepticism of critical history. "Faith cannot even guarantee the name 'Jesus' in respect to him who was the Christ. . . . But faith does guarantee the factual transformation of reality in that personal life which the New Testament expresses in its picture of Jesus as the Christ."[72]

Although the search for the historical Jesus failed to establish Christianity upon a foundation of undisputed fact, Tillich by no means underestimates the impact of historical research upon theology.[73] He credits Protestantism with being the first religion to subject its sacred writings to the criticism of historical method and to draw out the consequences in its theology. Historical criticism enables the theologian to distinguish between "the empirically historical, the legendary, and the mythological elements" in the Bible.[74] This knowledge leads to a deeper insight into the growth and meaning of the Christological symbols. Tillich outlines the four steps of their development: (1) the origin of the symbols in religious culture and language; (2) the vital use of the symbols to express the question and answer of existence; (3) their transformation when used to interpret the Christian event; and (4) their distortion by popular superstition, abetted by theological literalism and supranaturalism. Although theology does not depend upon historical research, the latter protects it against literal and superstitious interpretations of the Christian symbols.

Illuminating as it is theologically, historical criticism of the Bible leaves a nagging doubt in regard to faith.[75] Tillich poses the question in extreme but sharp terms: What if historical research should demonstrate that Jesus of Nazareth never lived?[76] It is insufficient to say that historians have not yet done so and that it is very unlikely they ever will. "Not yet" and "unlikely" still leave room for doubt. If one replies that "the historical foundation of Christianity is an essential element of the Christian faith itself," it must be made quite clear just exactly what faith does guarantee.[77] In the last analysis, "faith can guarantee only its own foundation, namely, the appearance of that reality which has created the faith."[78] The New Being is the reality that gives birth to faith by conquering existential estrangement. Therefore, the presence of faith is identical with the presence of the New Being, and this presence is what is guaranteed by faith. For "no historical criticism can question the immediate awareness of those who find themselves transformed into the state of faith."[79] Faith is a given, not a deduction from logical or historical premises. "By analogy, one must say that participation, not historical argument, guarantees the reality of the event upon which Christianity is based."[80] By faith one is assured that in a personal life the New Being has overcome the estrangement of existence, that the New Being was and is actualized in him. "But it does not guarantee his name to be Jesus of Nazareth."[81] That is an historical question open to historical doubt.

The final difficulty that Tillich handles is the problem of how the New Being as the Christ can excite faith if history provides no concrete picture of him, for faith is not founded on an abstract statement, but on a concrete encounter. The reality of the New Being with all his individual characteristics was experienced by the disciples. Their experience is expressed in the biblical picture of the Christ which is now the medium for the transforming power of the New Being. Tillich proposes an *analogia imaginis* between the actual personal life and the gospel image which arises from it. The situation is compared to the *analogia entis*, which is not a method of knowing God, but the way of talking about him. The gospel image is the symbolic or analogical way of describing Jesus as the Christ. Consequently, the empirical traits of the biblical picture of the Christ are not guaranteed by faith, but the picture itself is guaranteed "as an adequate expression of the transforming power of the New Being in Jesus as the Christ."[82]

The New Being

The New Being will first be considered under the aspect of "newness." The old eon is estrangement, the split between essential and existential being. The Christ as the New Being ushers in the new eon by manifesting undistorted essential being within the conditions of existence. The New Being is new "in contrast to the merely potential character of essential being; and it is new over against the estranged character of existential being."[83] In St. Paul's words, those who are "in Christ" are "new creatures." "In Christ" means participation in him. "Those who participate in him participate in the New Being, though under the condition of man's existential predicament and, therefore, only fragmentarily and by anticipation."[84] The real, but imperfect, state of participation can be explained as the interim period between the first and second coming of the Christ. In this period the New Being is present in the Christ; "in him the eschatological expectation is fulfilled in principle."[85]

The appearance of the New Being is the beginning of fulfilment, and, consequently, it marks the end of the old situation. It signals the end of the reign of law, the law of "man's essential being standing against his existence, commanding and judging it."[86] It means the end of existence, the existence which is estrangement, ambiguity, and disintegration. It announces the end of history in the sense that "nothing qualitatively new in the dimension of the ultimate can be produced by history which is not implicitly present in the New Being in Jesus as the Christ."[87] The end of history is here understood not as a temporal terminal point, but as the ultimate aim that imparts meaning to the whole process.

Tillich is at pains to point out that the newness of the New Being, the beginning that heralds the end, has appeared in a *personal* life, and it could not have been otherwise. For the only being which has finite freedom is a person. "Only where existence is most radically existence—in him who is finite freedom—can existence be conquered.[88] But the manifestation of the New Being in a personal life still has cosmic significance, not quantitatively, but qualitatively, since in man all levels of being are present. The New Being inaugurates a new cosmos.

The next step is to consider the "beingness" of the New Being. Tillich insists that the Christ is the bearer of the New Being in the totality of his being which must be distinguished from its modes of expression.[89] The biblical picture of the Christ expresses his being in his words, deeds, and sufferings. But underlying these expressions is the very being of the New Being. Hence, "as the Word, he is more than all the words he has spoken," for being precedes speaking.[90] His deeds are not models to be piously imitated, but rather actions which render his being transparent. His sufferings are not works of supererogation that effect atonement, but "an inescapable implication" of his appearance *within* the sphere of existence. The New Being which shines through its concrete expressions in the New Testament is analogous to divine being as the power of being. The power of being conquers non-being. The New Being in Jesus as the Christ overcomes the non-being which is existential estrangement.

In his essay "A Reinterpretation of the Doctrine of the Incarnation" Tillich elaborates upon the precise meaning of the New Being.[91] The key to his position is the concept "essential God-manhood." It expresses the dialectical relationship of finiteness and infinity in man. "Man is the only being who possesses a genuine finiteness because he is the only being who possesses a potential infinity; for finiteness has meaning only in correlation with infinity."[92] Barth errs in simply juxtaposing the creator and the creature without showing the dialectical interdependence between them. In essential man finitude and infinity are related. Consequently, the phrase "essential God-manhood" should not come as a shock. "It simply indicates that divine self-objectification and essential manhood belong together, because man is essentially the divine image, and anthropomorphism contains an indestructible element of truth."[93] Tillich logically concludes that the Incarnation could take place only in the personal life of a human being. In the man Jesus, whom faith accepts as the Christ, essential God-manhood appears in history and not only does not succumb to the disruptive forces of existence, but unleashes the power to transform them. In brief, "the New Being, manifest in the picture of Jesus as the Christ, represents the essential unity between finiteness and infinity, or the undisrupted unity between man and God."[94] Essential God-manhood means that "there is one man in whom God found his image undistorted, and who stands for all mankind—the one, who for this reason, is called the Son and the Christ."[95]

It must be emphasized, however, that, for Tillich, the paradox lies not in the essential union of the divine and the human, but in the maintenance of this union within and under the conditions of existence.[96] Jesus as the Christ is in permanent unity with God, a unity which does not exclude the consequences of existence, not even death, but transcends them.

Christological Dogma

The Christological problem begins when men realize they are estranged and wonder about a new reality with the power to conquer existence, but it does not end with the simple acceptance of Jesus as the Christ. "The baptismal confession that Jesus is the Christ is the text of which the christological dogma is the commentary."[97] Tillich finds in dogma a twofold purpose: to affirm and defend the Christian message against distortion, and to express it in conceptual terms.[98] The first function guards the substance; the second function imparts form.

The aim of the early conciliar Christological formulas was to preserve both the Christ-character and the Jesus-character of the event of Jesus as the Christ.[99] The *homoousion* of Nicaea maintained the Christ-character against the Arians who would make Jesus a semi-divine being. Chalcedon warded off the attacks of the monophysites upon the Jesus-character of the Christ. Both councils succeeded in affirming and defending the substance of the Christian message, but they did so in spite of the inadequate intellectual tools of the two-natures theory.

Tillich envisions the task of present-day Protestant Christology as the development of new forms to express the substance of Nicaea and Chalcedon.[100] He rejects as obsolete the traditional two-natures doctrine. "The basic inadequacy lies in the term 'nature.' When applied to man, it is ambiguous; when applied to

God, it is wrong."[101] "Human nature" can mean three things: (1) essential or created nature, (2) existential or estranged nature, and (3) an ambiguous unity of the two. All three meanings can be applied to Jesus as the Christ, although the second must be qualified insofar as estrangement, while remaining a real possibility, is taken into the unity with God.[102] Because of this ambiguity and need for qualification, Tillich concludes that "it is imperative to dismiss altogether the term 'human nature' in relation to the Christ and replace it by a description of the dynamics of his life. . . ."[103]

The term "divine nature" must be understood as that which makes God what he is, his essence. But God also has existence, or, more exactly, he is beyond both essence and existence. "Divine nature" cannot be applied to the Christ precisely because the New Being is not beyond essence and existence, but *in* existence. The Christ is a personal life in a definite period of history, subject to birth and death, temptation and finitude. "The assertion that Jesus as the Christ is the personal unity of a divine and a human nature must be replaced by the assertion that in Jesus as the Christ the eternal unity of God and man has become historical reality."[104] Tillich claims that his approach is dynamic and relational, whereas the old two natures "lie beside each other like blocks and whose unity cannot be understood at all."[105]

In the third volume of *Systematic Theology* Tillich expounds a "Spirit Christology" which he derives from the synoptic gospels.[106] God was in Jesus the Christ because the divine Spirit totally grasped his human spirit. In this sense, one can speak of the faith of the Christ which is "the state of being grasped unambiguously by the Spiritual Presence."[107] But, although the Spirit is unambiguously present in the Christ, his faith still has a fragmentary character due to the fact that he is subject to the conditions of existence. Two important implications follow from Spirit Christology. First, it is not the spirit of the man Jesus that makes him the Christ, but the Spirit of God, and thus the dangers of a Jesus-theology are avoided. And, secondly, the Spiritual

Presence in history is the same as the Spiritual Presence in the Christ; hence, he is not an isolated event, but touches the whole of history through the activity of the Spirit.

The Cross and the Resurrection

"Christology is a function of soteriology."[108] The Christ who brings the New Being is a unique event which saves the whole of humanity and the whole of the universe. The task of Christology is to work out the universal significance of this single and unrepeatable historic fact. The New Testament account supplies the concrete details of an individual, personal life, while the Christological symbols convey the universal significance of the Christ. Thus, Tillich holds for a "deliteralization" of the gospels, but not for a demythologization. Myth and symbol are the very language of religion, and to demythologize "would silence the experience of the holy."[109] Two central Christological symbols reveal the significance of Jesus as the Christ: the Cross, which symbolizes his subjection to existence, and the Resurrection, which symbolizes his victory over it.

The Cross and the Resurrection are mutually interdependent, for the triumph of the Resurrection supposes the death on the Cross, and the Cross would have been no different from the death of any other man if the Christ had not risen. Building on this close relationship, Tillich establishes the Cross as the paradigm according to which the Resurrection is to be understood. The Cross is both an event and a symbol or, better, a symbol based on an event. As the crucifixion story of Jesus, it enjoys a comparatively high degree of historical probability. As the Cross of Jesus who is the Christ, "it is the myth of the bearer of the new eon who suffers the death of a convict and slave under the powers of that old eon which he is to conquer."[110]

The Resurrection must be viewed in the same way, as event and symbol, but with this difference, that the New Testament reports of the factual element of the Resurrection are far more mysterious and uncertain than those of the crucifixion. The resurrection symbol was a familiar one in ancient religions, but "a real experience made it possible for the disciples to apply the known symbol of resurrection to Jesus, thus acknowledging him definitely as the Christ." This experienced event brought the certainty "that he who is the bringer of the new eon cannot finally have succumbed to the power of the old eon. . . ."[111]

What is this event, this experience upon which the symbol of the Resurrection is founded? Tillich reviews and rejects three theories before proposing his own.[112] The first theory is that of the physical resurrection of the body of Jesus, but he considers it historically questionable and a theological rationalization that leads to scientific absurdities. The second theory is the spiritualistic theory which holds that the soul of Jesus appeared to his disciples. However, this is a weak analogy drawn from spiritualistic attempts to communicate with the dead, and it does not account for the totality of the Resurrection symbol which includes the whole personality, body and soul. The third theory is the psychological one which makes the Resurrection "an inner event in the minds of Jesus' adherents." But this theory does not do justice to the objective reality demanded by the symbol.[113]

Tillich's own theory of the Resurrection event is what he calls the "restitution theory." The Resurrection supposes a negativity which is overcome, and this negativity is not the death of one man, but the disappearance of him in whom the New Being was manifest. By his death he disappeared from the present experience of the disciples. But the New Being cannot be transitory! Therefore, the apostles were faced with a choice: either Jesus is not the New Being, or he is still present. Their decision was made as follows:

In an ecstatic experience the concrete picture of Jesus of Nazareth became indissolubly united with the reality of the New Being. He is present wherever the New Being is present. . . . In this way the concrete individual life of the man Jesus of Nazareth is raised above transitoriness into the eternal presence of God as Spirit.[114]

The experience of his living presence, from the disciples and St. Paul to the Christians of our own day, is the Resurrection event. Following upon despair and loss and meaninglessness, it is "the ecstatic confirmation of the indestructible unity of the New Being and its bearer, Jesus of Nazareth."[115] In contrast to the physical, spiritual, and psychological theories, Tillich dubs his own the "restitution theory" because, according to it, "the Resurrection is the restitution of Jesus as the Christ, a restitution which is rooted in the personal unity between Jesus and God and in the impact of this unity on the minds of the apostles."[116] In other words, the experience of the New Being in Jesus as the Christ had to come first, but, after the death of Jesus, the disciples' experience of his living presence restored him to his Christhood.

Tillich assigns only probability to his theory, but he feels it is adequate to the facts and in accordance with the New Testament, especially St. Paul. Faith in the Resurrection of the Christ does not depend upon historical research or theological theories. Certainty can come only from faith, and faith assures us of the victory of Jesus the Christ over the conditions of existence. Ultimately, the Resurrection is a mystery of faith:

Faith is based on the experience of being grasped by the power of the New Being through which the destructive consequences of estrangement are conquered. It is the certainty of one's own victory over the death of existential estrangement which creates the certainty of the Resurrection of the Christ as event and symbol; but it is not historical conviction or the acceptance of biblical authority which creates this certainty.[117]

Although Tillich does not stress this point in his systematic exposition of Christology, there is another very important meaning which he attaches to the Cross of the Christ. In presenting Jesus the Christ as the bearer of God's final revelation, he states, "Jesus of Nazareth is the medium of the final revelation because he sacrifices himself completely to Jesus as the Christ.[118] The Christ possesses perfect unity with God. However, since Jesus of Nazareth is only the bearer of this revelation, he must not point to himself, but to the ground of being. The Cross says No to Jesus while revealing the Yes of the Christ's unbroken union with God. In other words, the Cross is the symbol of the Protestant principle.

This theme runs all through Tillich's writings. For instance, in discussing the criterion of faith, he says, "That symbol is most adequate which expresses not only the ultimate but also its own lack of ultimacy. . . . Jesus could not have been the Christ without sacrificing himself as Jesus to himself as the Christ."[119] Again, in regard to world religions:

What is particular in him (Jesus) is that he crucified the particular in himself for the sake of the universal. This liberates his image from bondage both to a particular religion . . . and to the religious sphere as such. . . . With this image, particular yet free from particularity, religious yet free from religion, the criteria are given under which Christianity must judge itself. . . .[120]

Moreover, the No of the Cross applies equally to the followers of the Christ: "No finite being can attain the infinite without being broken as He who represented the world, and its wisdom and its power, was broken on the Cross."[121] And, finally, of special interest to us, theonomy is based upon the Protestant principle, the Yes and the No of the Cross. For Jesus the Christ overcomes autonomy by his transparency to the ground of being (the Yes), and he resists heteronomy by the humiliation of his death (the No).[122]

Salvation

The significance of the Cross and the Resurrection of Jesus as the Christ can be summed up in one word: salvation.[123] One can be saved from many things, but Tillich understands salvation as salvation from "ultimate negativity." To put it more positively, salvation is "healing," for "healing means reuniting that which is estranged, giving a center to what is split, overcoming the split between God and man, man and his world, man and himself."[124] It is the revelation of the New Being in Jesus as the Christ which brings salvation. Consequently, "where there is revelation, there is salvation," for the revelation of the ground of being transforms and heals.[125] Revelation and salvation are identified. The revelational history of mankind—preparatory revelation before the appearance of the New Being, and receiving revelation afterwards—testifies that men have shared in the healing power of the New Being, or else they would have succumbed to the destructive tendencies of existential estrangement and have ceased to exist. Traditional theology has presented the rigid alternatives of total condemnation and total salvation. But Tillich rejects them both, for, although the healing power of the New Being is never absent, even those who experience it are healed but fragmentarily.

In his doctrine of atonement, which describes the effect of the New Being on those who are grasped by it, Tillich distinguishes between an objective and a subjective element, between a divine act and a human reaction.[126] The divine act overcomes estrangement by removing guilt, and man reacts by accepting reconciliation.

The effects of atonement are threefold, and together they constitute the meaning of salvation: Regeneration, Justification, and Sanctification, or, in Tillichian terminology, participation, acceptance, and transformation.[127] Regeneration stresses the objective power of the New Being to grasp estranged mankind and draw it into itself. Man participates in the new reality revealed in the Christ only by being seized by it. Thus, Regeneration is "the new state of things, the new eon, which the Christ brought; the individual 'enters it,' and in so doing he himself participates in it and is reborn through participation."[128]

Since Regeneration is participation in the objective power of the New Being, it precedes Justification, for faith as the state of being grasped by the divine presence is not a human act, but the work of the Spirit. Justification is acceptance. It is the act of God by which he accepts sinful man in spite of his guilt. It is also the act of man by which man accepts God's saving mercy. "Indeed, there is nothing in man which enables God to accept him. But man must accept just this. He must accept that he is accepted; he must accept acceptance."[129] This "in spite of" element is precisely the core of Tillich's doctrine of salvation. In spite of man's estrangement, God accepts him; and in spite of his anxiety, man accepts God's justifying act. "In spite of" is the paradox of *simul peccator, simul justus.*

"As a divine act, Regeneration and Justification are one," for Regeneration is the actual reunion of the estranged, and Justification is its paradoxical character.[130] Sanctification is distinct from both of them in the sense that "a process is distinguished from the event in which it is initiated."[131] Sanctification is the process in which the New Being transforms both individuals and communities. Sanctification, as transformation, takes place both within religion and outside it in the secular realm.

Up to now emphasis has been laid upon the individual man as the one who is saved. But Tillich's vision is broader than that. At the crucifixion of Jesus the sun was darkened, the temple veil split, rocks cracked, and the dead rose. Nature was in an uproar, and Tillich interprets this to mean that "the event at Golgotha is one which concerns the universe, including all nature and history."[132] The Christ cannot be restricted to one area; Christology must be cosmic.[133] Salvation extends to the whole world, "and *world* means nature as well as man."[134] It is through man, the microcosm, that the saving power of the New Being reaches out to the universe. "The tragedy of nature is bound to the tragedy of man, as the salvation of nature is dependent on the salvation of man . . . for man is in nature and nature is in man."[135] Consequently, the impact of the Spiritual Presence upon beings inferior to man is indirect and, in a quantitative sense, severely limited. However, in a qualitative sense it is enormous.[136] Salvation is found within the Kingdom of God which embraces the universe. It is "the place where there is complete transparency of everything for the divine to shine through it. In his fulfilled kingdom, God is everything for everything."[137]

Salvation, the healing of the disrupted, is brought about by love, for "love is the drive towards the unity of the separated."[138] Tillich has constructed an impressive ontology of love in his book *Love, Power, and Justice,* and a series of seven sermons in *The New Being* describes how the love revealed in Jesus who is the Christ reunites estranged mankind with its ground. And in the third volume of *Systematic Theology* he discusses how the Spiritual Presence manifests itself as love.[139] After distinguishing divine love from human love, he sums up man's love for God as "the drive toward the reunion of the separated."[140] But since salvation is an act of God, God's love must first extend to man and grasp him. In other words, "the distinction between faith and love disappears," for "being grasped by God in faith and adhering to him in love is one and the same state of creaturely life."[141]

We conclude this presentation of Tillich's Christology with a medley of quotations from one of his most powerful sermons, "The New Being."[142]

For neither circumcision counts for anything nor uncircumcision, but a new creation (Gal. 6:15). If I were asked to sum up the Christian message for our time in two words, I would say with Paul: It is the message of a "New Creation.". . . We belong to the Old Creation, and the demand made upon us by Christianity is that we *also* participate in the New Creation. . . . What is this New Being? Paul answers first by saying what it is *not* . . . that neither to be a Jew nor to be a pagan is ultimately important; that only one thing counts, namely the union with Him in whom the New Reality is present. . . . No religion matters—only a new state of things. . . . The New Creation—this is our ultimate concern; this should be our infinite passion—the infinite passion of every human being. This matters; this alone matters ultimately. In comparison with it everything else, even religion or non-religion, even Christianity or non-Christianity, matters very little—and ulti-

mately nothing. . . . And now we ask again: What is this New Being?
. . . It is a renewal of the Old which has been corrupted, distorted,
split and almost destroyed. . . . Therefore, we can speak of the New
in terms of a *re*-newal: The threefold *"re,"* namely, *re*-conciliation,
re-union, *re*-surrection. . . . The word "resurrection" has for many
people the connotation of dead bodies leaving their graves or other
fanciful images. But resurrection means the victory of the New state of
things, the New Being born out of the death of the Old. Resurrection
is not an event that might happen in some remote future, but it is the
power of the New Being to create life out of death, here and now,
today and tomorrow. . . . Resurrection happens *now*, or it does not
happen at all. It happens in us and around us, in soul and history, in
nature and universe. . . . The message of Christianity is not Christianity,
but a New Reality. A New state of things has appeared, it still appears;
it is hidden and visible, it is there and it is here. Accept it, enter into it,
let it grasp you.

REFLECTIONS AND APPRAISAL

The response evoked by Tillich's Christology is sometimes fa-
vorable, sometimes hostile, and more often respectful but decid-
edly reserved. The commentators are impressed by his adroit use
of concepts with contemporary appeal, such as estrangement,
healing, and acceptance. Although some pronounce all but whole-
hearted approval of his theory of the New Being,[143] others voice
serious reservations about either its general tenor or the treatment
of specific points. Gustave Weigel calls Tillichian Christology
"Nestorian."[144] J. Heywood Thomas senses the danger of adop-
tionism,[145] while Kenneth Hamilton feels that Tillich never
bridges the gap between the universal significance of the New
Being and the factual life of Jesus.[146] Some find that he neglects
the historicity of the divine revelation in the Christ,[147] and others
have difficulty in seeing how he reconciles estrangement and
freedom.[148] George Tavard concludes that Tillich's Christology is
not in accord with orthodox Christian teaching; nevertheless, he
finds many solid values in it.[149] Finally, R. Allan Killen states

flatly: "The Christ which Tillich produces is not the Christ of the Bible. He is a human man who becomes divine, while the Biblical Christ is a divine person who becomes man by taking upon Himself a complete human nature."[150]

These samplings of criticism indicate the complexity of the problems which a completely thorough discussion of Tillich's Christology comprises. However, there is one approach which cuts across all these problems and which, if it does not solve them, at least puts them into their proper context: one must determine precisely what is the core of the Christological paradox as Tillich sees it.

In Tillich's system, we recall, God is the ground and the power of being. The more fully a creature actualizes its essence, the more closely it is united to the divine ground and the more profoundly it participates in the power of being. But the very process of actualization inevitably results in estrangement from essential being, for potentialities are not realized and essence is distorted in existence. The most electrifying and the most paradoxical event that could possibly occur would be the perfect and total actualization of essential humanity, the microcosm which embraces the macrocosm. If essential manhood were perfectly realized in a personal life, despite the conditions of existence, then the universe itself would, in a sense, be fulfilled. This actualization of essential humanity is the New Being, for in contrast to it everything else is old, unfinished, distorted, and without promise. In Jesus of Nazareth the New Being is manifest, thus constituting him the Christ. For Tillich, then, the astounding paradox of Christology is the appearance of essential manhood under the conditions of existence, but without being eroded by them.

Thus, Tillich's problematic is not the same as that of traditional Christology. Theologians usually formulate it as a two-pronged question: How is Jesus related to God, and how are men saved by Jesus? The first question concerns the person of the Christ; it is Christology in the strict sense. The traditional answer has been the two-natures explanation. The second question deals with the salvific work of Jesus, soteriology as it is generally known, and it involves the theology of atonement and of the Cross. The difference between Tillich and the traditional approach lies in the first question: How are God and man united in Jesus the Christ? For Tillich, this is not the Christological problem at all, as he states quite clearly:

It is essential man who represents not only man to man but God to man; for essential man, by his very nature, represents God. He represents the original image of God embodied in man, but he does so under the conditions of estrangement between God and man. This belongs to the dialectics of the infinite and the finite. The paradox of the Christian message is that in *one* personal life essential manhood has appeared under the conditions of existence without being conquered by them. One could also speak of essential God-manhood in order to indicate the divine presence in essential manhood; but this is redundant, and the clarity of thought is served best in speaking simply of essential manhood.[151]

One cannot refrain from wishing that Tillich had explained more fully "the original image of God embodied in man," for it is not immediately evident just how "essential humanity includes the union of God and man." Nor do "the dialectics of the infinite and the finite" provide a ready clarification. "Essential God-manhood" is the key concept, but it remains a stumbling block. Tillich seems to say that man is united to God simply because he is man, that is, the freedom-bearing image of God. While there is much to commend this view, it scarcely suffices to bear the whole weight of Christology. Jesus the Christ is united to God by something more than his perfect manhood. Christians consider the union of God and man in Jesus as paradoxical, a mystery of faith which the theologians attempt to articulate in their various Christologies. The fact that Tillich finds no paradox here at all throws the burden of proof upon him, for it is inconceivable that, for centuries, theologians have missed the point of the paradox of their faith. At least they must know where the central mystery lies.

Tillich's doctrine of the appearance of essential manhood in Jesus the Christ does not entirely succeed in relating Jesus to God, or, rather, it makes no serious attempt to do so. However, it is useful for relating the New Being to the human existential situation. George Tavard, who has written extensively and perceptively on Tillich's Christology, points out the contribution which Tillich makes toward a Christology of man. Tavard even suggests a rough outline of such a Christology in which the two-natures doctrine of Chalcedon is replaced by a double-humanity theory: the divine humanity and the creaturely humanity of Christ.[152] This novel proposal bristles with problems, but it is nonetheless intriguing. The key to it is the notion of "divine humanity," just as the key to Tillich's Christology is "essential God-manhood." Whether or not these difficult concepts can be satisfactorily explained is a further question. Tillich's treatment leaves too many obscurities unclarified and too many problems unresolved, but the momentum which he imparts to a Christology of man is some measure of the creativeness and the stimulating vigor of his thought.

Tillich's understanding of the Cross and Resurrection proceeds quite consistently from his problematic that the significance of Jesus the Christ is the undistorted manifestation of essential manhood. The Cross is the symbol of the Christ's total immersion in the existential situation, and the Resurrection is symbolic of his total victory over it. We do not deny that these meanings are contained in the Cross and Resurrection, but we question the role and interpretation Tillich assigns to them. For instance, he has no room whatsoever for the sacrificial aspect of the crucifixion, for sacrifice, in his perspective, is irrelevant. Salvation is assured by the manifestation of the New Being within existence, and the Cross is the guarantee that Jesus the Christ experienced existence to its most terrifying degree. The works of Jesus, including his sacrificial death, do not bring release from sin, but the New Being in him is the source of salvation, and so Tillich sweeps away the threefold work of Christ the prophet, priest, and king as inconsequential.[153]

It should now be clear that any attempt by more traditional Christology to dispute particular points of Tillichian Christology is next to useless, for the disputants are not even fighting in the same arena. As we have seen, their problematics are different. But how determine the proper one? Although there may be other methods, it seems that one way to establish a correct problematic is to make sure that it accounts for all the data of the theological sources, especially the Bible. In this case, one can only ask if Tillich faithfully incorporates all the evidence of the biblical sources—for example, the sacrificial theme of the Old Testament and its fulfilment by the crucifixion of Jesus as testified to by the Epistle to the Hebrews. No Christology or soteriology can impugn the Christian's prerogative to say, "Jesus died for me"—and this statement contains an inescapable sacrificial element.

The far-reaching effects of Tillich's starting point are again demonstrated in his understanding of the Resurrection. The Resurrection symbolizes the conquest of existence by the manifestation of essential manhood in Jesus the Christ. Now, according to Tillich's views on revelation, the Christ cannot be the Christ unless he is received as such in an act of faith. Before the crucifixion the disciples had faith in the Christhood of Jesus, but the catastrophe of the Cross shattered their faith. After the death and burial of Jesus, in an ecstatic experience of the New Being, they realized that the power of the Christ was still operative, and so their faith was restored. This is the restitution theory by which Tillich explains the Resurrection event.

There are at least two grave difficulties with this theory. First, the New Testament presents the Resurrection as an act of Jesus; he does something. In Tillich's view, however, Jesus does nothing in the Resurrection event, for he is dead and buried, and it is the power of the New Being which grasps the disciples in an ecstasy of faith. Apparently the New Being can be separated from Jesus, and the Resurrection is an act of the New Being, but not an act of Jesus. Secondly, the biblical material insists that it is the Resurrection of Jesus which vivifies our faith, that we have risen because he has risen. But Tillich reverses the direction of causal influx: it is the resuscitation of the disciples' faith which accounts for the Resurrection event; it is their faith which restores Christhood to Jesus.

To put it concisely, Tillich admits the Resurrection is both event and symbol. The event is the restoration of the disciples' faith, and the symbolic element is the triumph of essential manhood over the estranged conditions of existence. The rub is that the New Testament presents the reverse of this scheme: the event is the triumphal Resurrection of Jesus which, in turn, symbolizes the rebirth of our life of faith.

Fundamental to Tillichian Christology is the notion of estrangement, for it is from our estranged human situation that the New Being rescues us. The force of the method of correlation is nowhere more powerfully evident than in Tillich's portrayal of man's estrangement and the power of the New Being which overcomes it. However, it is sometimes objected that he pushes estrangement too far; he defines original sin as the state of estrangement and then makes Creation and the Fall coincide. To some critics, this renders finitude inherently evil, and sin ontologically necessary. Admittedly, Tillich's explication of this point is not outstanding for its clarity, but in our opinion he manages to avoid these obvious traps. Creation and Fall are states, not events. Creation is the state of finitude, and the Fall is the state of estrangement. Creation, and hence finitude, is good, although the mixture of being and nonbeing which constitutes it is always charged with tension. The Fall is the state of existence in which the potentialities of finite essences are actualized, but the nonbeing of the essence takes its toll also, and the creature does not perfectly live up to its essence. It is always in some degree estranged from it and, consequently, from the ground of being. However, inevitability is not the same as necessity.[154] What Tillich seems to mean is that finitude is good, but not perfect, and when it seeks to perfect itself by actualizing its potencies, it falls, because, after all, it is finite.

It would be in bad taste to end a comment on estrangement with hair-splitting subtleties, for it is a deeply meaningful concept which Tillich uses boldly. With George Tavard we prefer to underscore the existential value of Tillichian Christology which derives in great part from the notion of estrangement:

. . . that Christ is the answer to existential anguish, is a fundamental insight which Catholics have tended to neglect in a smug unconcern for those who have brought this anguish to the fore of modern thought. We should be grateful that we can learn something about Christ, that at least some aspects of Christology can be emphasized with the help of modern thinkers, be they Protestant like Tillich or agnostic like many philosophers of existentialism. . . . whatever label we give it, and how much we may wish to rewrite his thought for the sake of orthodoxy, we should heed Paul Tillich's eagerness to interpret Christianity for the man of today, for the estranged, the puzzled, the frightened man of today.[155]

Theonomy means union with God, the ground of being. Finite beings can achieve it only by actualizing their essences in such a way that they are transparent to their ground. However, the universal fact of existence is estrangement, separation of beings from God, from themselves, and from one another. A new power, a New Being is needed to overcome estrangement, and in Jesus the Christ it has appeared. To whatever extent religion animates culture, this theonomous union is realized by the power of the New Being which grasps us in the ecstasy of faith. But one of the potentialities of man is his drive toward community. We must now examine the church, the community of those who receive Jesus the Christ as the New Being.

Notes

1. ST, I, 147–50.
2. *Ibid.*, 148.
3. ST, II, 4.
4. *Ibid.*, 19–21. For a thorough discussion of the meaning and history of the term "existence," see his essay "Existential Philosophy: Its Historical Meaning," TC, 76–111.
5. ST, II, 21–24. See also ST, I, 202–204.
6. ST, II, 24–28. Tillich distinguishes between "existential" and "existentialist." The former refers to an attitude of involvement; its opposite is detachment. The latter designates a philosophical school which is opposed to essentialist philosophy. *Ibid.*, 26. See also CB, 123–26.
7. ST, II, 25.
8. *Ibid.*, 29–31.
9. *Ibid.*, 30–31.
10. *Ibid.*, 31.
11. *Ibid.*, 31–33.
12. *Ibid.*, 33–36.
13. *Ibid.*, 34.
14. *Ibid.*, 62.
15. *Ibid.*, 36–39.
16. *Ibid.*, 36.
17. *Ibid.*, 37.
18. *Ibid.*, 38.
19. *Ibid.*, 39–44.
20. Schelling's influence is especially discernible in Tillich's doctrine of the participation of nature in the transcendental Fall. See "Autobiographical Reflections," K and B, 4; the sermon "Nature also Mourns a Lost Good," SF, 76–86; TC, 102; GW, I, 92–93; and *Die Religionsgeschichtliche Konstruktion in Schellings positiver Philosophie*, 133.
21. ST, II, 41.
22. *Ibid.*, 42–43.
23. SF, 83–84.
24. *Ibid.*, 82.
25. ST, II, 43–44; ST, I, 254–61.
26. ST, II, 44.
27. *Ibid.*
28. See also Tillich's essay "Existentialist Aspects of Modern Art," *Christianity and the Existentialists*, Carl Michalson (ed.), 129.
29. Reinhold Niebuhr, "Biblical Thought and Ontological Speculation," K and B, 216–27.
30. *Ibid.*, 219.
31. "Reply," K and B, 338–39.

32. *Ibid.*, 342–44.
33. *Ibid.*, 343.
34. See also ST, I, 256.
35. CB, 52.
36. PE, 148.
37. *Ibid.*, 165.
38. NB, 107–108.
39. ST, II, 44–47.
40. *Ibid.*, 44–45.
41. *Ibid.*, 45.
42. LPJ, 25.
43. ST, II, 46.
44. SF, 154–155; TC, 123.
45. ST, I, 218.
46. LPJ, 76–77.
47. ST, II, 47–55.
48. *Ibid.*, 47.
49. *Ibid.*, 52.
50. *Ibid.*, 55–58.
51. *Ibid.*, 58–59.
52. *Ibid.*, 59. In one passage Tillich appears to affirm explicitly the reality of collective guilt: "The perversion of human existence is real in social, just as strongly as in the individual, distortions and with even more primitive force; and collective guilt is just as real and perceptible as individual guilt; neither can be separated from the other." PE, 166. But even here "collective guilt" is a description of estrangement whose explanation leads back to the polarity of individual freedom and universal destiny.
53. ST, II, 78. See *Ibid.*, 78–80.
54. *Ibid.*, 80–86.
55. See ST, I, 79–81.
56. ST, II, 86.
57. *Ibid.*, 87.
58. *Ibid.*, 88.
59. *Ibid.*, 88–90.
60. *Ibid.*, 90–92.
61. *Ibid.*, 93–96.
62. *Ibid.*, 94.
63. *Ibid.*, 95.
64. *Ibid.*, 97–99.
65. See Tillich's homily "He Who Is the Christ" for fuller details on the scene at Caesarea Philippi. SF, 141–48.
66. ST, II, 99. The stress upon reception raises a speculative problem: if the Christ is not the Christ unless he is received as the Christ, what happens to the validity of the Christian message if the group who accepts him is destroyed? Tillich answers that "Jesus is the Christ for us, namely, for

those who participate in the historical continuum which he determines in its meaning." *Ibid.,* 101. Other divine self-manifestations could occur before or after this continuum.

67. *Ibid.,* 98.
68. *Ibid.,* 101–107.
69. *Ibid.,* 102.
70. *Ibid.,* 105.
71. *Ibid.,* 106.
72. *Ibid.,* 107.
73. *Ibid.,* 107–13.
74. *Ibid.,* 108.
75. *Ibid.,* 113–17.
76. As early as 1911, Tillich took a position on how to interpret Christian doctrine if the non-existence of the historical Jesus should be proved historically probable. His solution has remained the same over the years: "The foundation of Christian belief is not the historical Jesus, but the biblical picture of Christ." IH, 33–34. The influence of Martin Kähler is quite evident here.
77. ST, II, 113–14.
78. *Ibid.,* 114. Tillich's position is expounded and criticized by D. Moody Smith, Jr., "The Historical Jesus in Paul Tillich's Christology," *The Journal of Religion,* XLVI, January, 1966, No. 1, Part II, 131–47. In his "Rejoinder," Tillich indicates his agreement and disagreement with Smith's analysis: "Can faith guarantee the historical events through which it came into existence and to which it remains related? He says 'No!' I answer: 'No and yes!' If I am asked, 'Is Christian faith certain of the continuity of the development from Jesus to Paul?' I, obviously, must say 'No!' If I am asked, 'Does Christian faith guarantee a historical event that can be described as the work of the divine Spirit creating the spiritual community that is called church, and in it individuals who, at least in moments, are Spirit-determined, creating both through a bearer of the Spirit in whom the power of "new creation" in both respects was present and is effective even today?' I would say 'Yes!' If I am asked, 'Does Christian faith guarantee that the synoptic picture of this man is guaranteed as historically correct—including his name?' I would say 'No!' If I am asked, 'Does Christian faith guarantee that this picture is an expression of the bearer of the Spirit who, through this picture, creates and recreates human beings spiritually?' I would say 'Yes!' If the Christian faith can guarantee as much as this, it does not need to call for the support of human work, namely historical research. And it does not need to be afraid of it." *Ibid.,* 192.
79. ST, II, 114.
80. *Ibid.*
81. *Ibid.*
82. *Ibid.,* 115.
83. *Ibid.,* 119.
84. *Ibid.,* 118.

85. *Ibid.*
86. *Ibid.*, 119.
87. *Ibid.*, 119–20.
88. *Ibid.*, 120.
89. *Ibid.*, 121–25.
90. *Ibid.*, 121.
91. "A Reinterpretation of the Doctrine of the Incarnation," *Church Quarterly Review*, CXLVII, January, 1949, 133–48. Hereinafter referred to as "Doctrine of the Incarnation."
92. *Ibid.*, 143.
93. *Ibid.*
94. *Ibid.*, 144.
95. EN, 76.
96. ST, II, 125, 135.
97. *Ibid.*, 139.
98. *Ibid.*, 138–42. See also ST, I, 32.
99. ST, II, 142–45.
100. *Ibid.*, 145–50.
101. *Ibid.*, 142.
102. Tavard interprets Tillich in this section to mean that the second meaning of human nature, existential nature, cannot be applied to Jesus the Christ. Cf. *Paul Tillich and the Christian Message*, 126. McKelway claims that only the first meaning, essential human nature, can be applied to the Christ. Cf. *The Systematic Theology of Paul Tillich*, 165. However, it seems to us that Tillich intends that all three meanings apply, and that therein lies the source of ambiguity in the use of the term. In any case, the variety of interpretations indicates that his argument against the two-natures doctrine suffers from obscurity and overbrevity.
103. ST, II, 147.
104. *Ibid.*, 148.
105. *Ibid.*
106. ST, III, 144–49.
107. *Ibid.*, 146.
108. ST, II, 150.
109. *Ibid.*, 152.
110. *Ibid.*, 153–154.
111. *Ibid.*, 154.
112. *Ibid.*, 155–56.
113. *Ibid.*, 156.
114. *Ibid.*, 157.
115. *Ibid.*
116. *Ibid.*
117. *Ibid.*, 155.
118. ST, I, 136. See also *Ibid.*, 147–48, and ST, II, 123.
119. DF, 97–98, 125.

120. CEWR, 81–82.
121. NB, 112.
122. Cf. ST, I, 147; ST, III, 380, PE, xii.
123. ST, II, 165–68.
124. *Ibid.*, 166. Tillich has often elaborated upon the theme of salvation as healing. See ST, III, 275–82; NB, 34–45; EN, 112–21.
125. ST, II, 166. See also ST, I, 144–47.
126. ST, II, 170–73.
127. *Ibid.*, 176–80.
128. *Ibid.*, 177.
129. *Ibid.*, 179. See also the sermon "You Are Accepted" in SF, 153–163.
130. ST, II, 179.
131. *Ibid.*
132. NB, 176.
133. "Rechtfertigung und Zweifel," 31.
134. SF, 77.
135. *Ibid.*, 89.
136. See ST, III, 275–77.
137. ST, I, 147.
138. LPJ, 25.
139. ST, III, 134–38.
140. *Ibid.*, 138.
141. *Ibid.*
142. NB, 15–24.
143. See for instance, W. Norman Pittenger, "Paul Tillich as a Theologian: An Appreciation," *Anglican Theological Review*, XLIII, July, 1961, 277–78, and A. T. Mollegen, "Christology and Biblical Criticism in Tillich," K and B, 230–45.
144. "Contemporaneous Protestantism and Paul Tillich," *Theological Studies*, XI, 1950, 194.
145. *Paul Tillich: An Appraisal*, 97.
146. *The System and the Gospel*, 158–73.
147. Reinhold Niebuhr, "The Contribution of Paul Tillich," *Religion in Life*, VI, 1937, 578; Avery Dulles, "Paul Tillich and the Bible," O'M and W, 129; and Hermann Herrigel, "Die Philosophische Theologie Tillichs," *Die Sammlung* (Göttingen), XIII, May, 1958, 236.
148. Eugene H. Peters, "Tillich's Doctrine of Essence, Existence, and the Christ," *The Journal of Religion*, XLIII, October, 1963, 298–99, and George F. McLean, "Paul Tillich's Existential Philosophy," O'M and W, 59–60.
149. *Paul Tillich and the Christian Message*, 137–39, 172–74.
150. *The Ontological Theology of Paul Tillich*, 240.
151. ST, II, 94. Cf. also "Doctrine of the Incarnation," 144.
152. *Paul Tillich and the Christian Message*, 171.
153. ST, II, 168.
154. A parallel case of the same principle in Catholic theology is the com-

mon doctrine that without grace one cannot long avoid sin. Yet the lack of grace does not necessitate the sin.

155. "Christ as the Answer to Existential Estrangement," O'M and W, 235–36. This article is copyrighted by and published in *Continuum* (Chicago), IV, Spring, 1966, 3–12.

6/Life, the Spirit, and the Spiritual Community

IN ANY SCHEME of Christian theology the church is an indispensable agent for the harmonizing of religion and culture. Society, the bearer of culture, encounters in the church the wellsprings of the Christian religion, the abiding presence and power of Christ. In Tillichian terminology, the church in its evangelizing role must "show to the people outside the Church that the symbols in which the life of the Church expresses itself are answers to the questions implied in their very existence as human beings."[1] And, in its prophetic role, "the Church is the guardian who reveals dynamic structures in society and undercuts their demonic power by revealing them, even within the Church itself."[2] Therefore, one can say that "the Church judges culture, including the Church's own forms of life. For its forms are created by culture, as its religious substance makes culture possible. The Church and culture are within, not alongside each other."[3]

The importance of the church is measured by the importance of the New Being, for "the Church is the historical embodiment of the New Being created by the Incarnation."[4] Consequently, "the church as the community of the New Being is the place where the new theonomy is actual. But from there it pours into the whole of man's cultural life and gives a Spiritual center to man's spiritual life."[5] Final revelation appeared in Jesus as the

208

Christ, but it is the church "which is supposed to receive it in a continuous process of reception, interpretation, and actualization."[6] The history of the church is "the locus of continuous dependent revelations."[7] But Tillich's enthusiasm for the church never develops into triumphalism in regard to individual churches. Far from it! "The Church is the place where the reunion of man with man is an actual event, though the Church of God is permanently betrayed by the Christian churches."[8] Yet, "the church is the Community of the New Being, even if its organization seems always a betrayal of the New Being."[9] Although Tillich is hard on the churches, he confesses, "The Church has always been my home in spite of all criticisms, which I had to exercise at an early time upon Church doctrine and upon Church practice."[10]

In the third volume of *Systematic Theology*, Tillich treats the church under the rubric of the Spirit; it is the Spiritual Community established by the Spiritual Presence. Since the Spirit is the symbolic answer to an existential question, we begin our exposition of his ecclesiology with a sketch of the quest for unambiguous life. Then follows his notion of the Spiritual Presence and the Spiritual Community, the nature and paradox of the churches, and, lastly, his interpretation of Protestantism.

THE QUEST FOR UNAMBIGUOUS LIFE

Adhering rigorously to his method of correlation, Tillich develops an existential analysis of life, its ambiguities, and the quest for unambiguous life before he introduces the symbol of the Spirit.

Life

He defines life ontologically as the "actuality of being."[11] It is a mixture of essence and existence, of actualized potentiality and existential distortions, of being and estrangement. Since the process of actualization is ontological, life is a universal concept applicable to all real beings, organic and inorganic, stars and rocks, animals and men.

Life can be considered from the viewpoints of its two constitutive factors, essence and existence. Essentially, life exhibits a unity amid diversity that Tillich describes as "the multidimensional unity" of life. Existentially, life is ambiguous.

The metaphor "dimension" should replace "level" in depicting the diversity of life, for levels so divide life into watertight compartments that its essential unity is destroyed.[12] A plurality of dimensions reflects the differences in life, but, because dimensions can meet in a point without excluding one another, they accurately express the essential unity of life. Since life is the gradual actualization of potentialities, some dimensions are called "realms." "In this sense one speaks of the vegetable realm or the animal realm or the historical realm. In all of them, all dimensions are potentially present, and some of them are actualized."[13] But in man all dimensions, especially the spiritual and historical, are actual; in him is found the fullness of the essential multidimensional unity of life.

Functions and Ambiguities of Life

Life as the actualization of potential being is a process, a movement out and away from a center and then back toward it.[14] Thus, the life-process is made up of three basic functions. The circular movement of *self-integration* is the actualization of the ontological polarity of individualization and participation. Secondly, the horizontal direction of life is *self-creativity*, which is the actualization of the dynamics–form polarity. Thirdly, the vertical movement toward the ultimate and infinite is *self-transcendence* which actualizes the polarity of freedom-destiny.

Although these functions of life in themselves are unified and harmonized, they are subject to the disruptions that follow upon existential estrangement. When separation becomes actual, their negative effects come into play, and ambiguity sets in. "To the degree in which this disruption is real, self-integration is countered by disintegration, self-creation is countered by destruction, self-transcendence is countered by profanization."[15] In the life-process these positive and negative elements are inseparably entwined, "for life is neither essential nor existential but ambiguous."[16]

The Dimension of Spirit

The multiple dimensions of life are all found in man, but the dimension of spirit is proper to him. After airing the etymological and semantic problems connected with the word,[17] Tillich settles upon a definition of spirit as the union of the power of being with meaning, "the actualization of power and meaning in unity."[18] Spirit is the power that perceives meaning, and the participation in meaning that imparts power.

Within the spiritual dimension the functions of life are operative: self-integration appears as morality, or the constitution of the personal self; self-creativity is seen as culture; and self-transcendence is religion, although, strictly speaking, religion is not a separate function, but a quality of the others.[19] However, even in the dimension of spirit the law of life is inexorable: morality, culture, and religion are subject to ambiguity.

The Quest

The life of every creature is an ambiguous mixture of essential and existential elements, but creation yearns for an unambiguous fulfilment of its essential potentialities.[20] Thus arises the quest for unambiguous life. Three symbols represent the perfect life: the Spirit of God, the Kingdom of God, and Eternal Life. In this chapter we are concerned with only the first, the Spirit of God.

It is the self-transcendent character of life that makes the quest possible, "but under no dimension does it reach that toward which it moves, the unconditional."[21] Therefore, "the answer to this quest is the experience of revelation and salvation; they constitute religion above religion, although they become religion when they are received."[22] The hope for unambiguous life pulsates in all the religions of the world, and somehow they receive the answer which sustains them. The quest never ceases.

But both quest and answer become matters of ambiguity if expressed in the terms of a concrete religion. It is an age-old experience of all religions that the quest for something transcending them is answered in the shaking and transforming experiences of revelation and salvation; but that under the conditions of existence even the absolutely great— the divine self-manifestation—becomes not only great but also small, not only divine but demonic.[23]

THE SPIRITUAL PRESENCE

The answer to the quest for unambiguous life is the divine Spirit (capital "S"). It invades the human spirit (small "s") and dwells there, a phenomenon which Tillich terms "the Spiritual Presence."[24] But this presence is not a static condition. Under the divine impulse, the human spirit is driven beyond itself to the ultimate, the unconditional. It transcends itself by this *ex-stasis*, the ecstasy of being grasped by the Spirit.

In the ecstatic state created by the Spiritual Presence, the essential and existential elements of being are unambiguously united. More exactly, they are *re*united, since the union occurs only after existential estrangement has been overcome. This effect of the Spiritual Presence is what Tillich calls "the transcendent union of unambiguous life." According to which facet is considered, it is faith or love, faith as "the state of being *grasped* by the transcendent unity of unambiguous life," love as "the state of being *taken into* that transcendent unity."[25] In faith one is grasped by God; by love one adheres to him. But faith and love are one and the same state, "participation in the transcendent unity of unambiguous life."[26]

Up to now Tillich has been expounding what might be called

the mechanics of the Spirit as it impinges upon the individual human spirit. They can be summed up as follows: "The Spiritual Presence, elevating man through faith and love to the transcendent unity of unambiguous life, creates the New Being above the gap between essence and existence and consequently above the ambiguities of life."[27] The Spiritual Presence, however, is manifest, not abstractly, but within historical mankind, not in isolated individuals, but in communities. This brings us to the church as the Spiritual Community.

THE SPIRITUAL COMMUNITY

In accordance with his division of revelation into preparatory, final, and receiving revelation, Tillich treats of the Spiritual Presence in these three stages. The history of world religions manifests the Spiritual Presence as an anticipation of the New Being.[28] Spirit Christology elucidates the unique presence of the Spirit in Jesus who is the Christ.[29] But our concern here is with the Spiritual Community, with those who receive the New Being.

Unambiguous, but Fragmentary

Tillich prefaces his development of the manifestation of the Spiritual Presence with an extremely important distinction between ambiguity and fragment.[30] If we recall that "all ambiguities of life are rooted in the separation and interplay of essential and existential elements of being,"[31] it would seem that, once a transcendent reunion of these elements is achieved by the Spiritual Presence, then ambiguity vanishes, and all that remains is the Yes of unambiguous life. Furthermore, "since mankind is never left alone by God, since it is continuously under the impact of the Spiritual Presence, there is always New Being in history."[32] Ambiguity seems banished; in fact, rendered impossible. But such is not the case, for existence cannot be denied, and the conditions of existence postulate ambiguity.

Tillich reconciles unambiguous life with *de facto* existential ambiguity by pointing out the fragmentary character of the unambiguous life produced by the Spirit. It is fragmentary because subject to time and space. It is incomplete in the sense that it is anticipatory. Thus, the No of the existential condition is maintained, not by injecting ambiguity into unambiguous life, but by showing the anticipatory and hence fragmentary nature of our reception of and participation in the New Being. The possession of unambiguous life integrally, i.e., beyond time and space, is the problem of eschatology.

New Being and the Spiritual Community

For the moment Tillich avoids the word "church" since it is too closely associated with the ambiguities of religion. Instead, he speaks of the Spiritual Community which is "the community of the New Being." "It is created by the divine Spirit as manifest in the New Being in Jesus as the Christ."[33] In other words, the Community of the New Being is neither organized religion, nor hierarchical authority, nor another social organization; "it is primarily a group of people who express a new reality by which they have been grasped."[34] The clue to understanding the connection between the New Being and the Spiritual Community is the nature of revelation, which includes a divine manifestation *plus* its reception as such by an individual or a group. Christology emphasizes final revelation in the Christ; ecclesiology, its reception in faith. "As the Christ is not the Christ without those who receive him as the Christ, so the Spiritual Community is not Spiritual unless it is founded on the New Being as it has appeared in the Christ."[35] The Spiritual Community is the creation of the Spirit which opens the eyes of faith to a recognition of the New Being. But it is the New Being in Jesus as the Christ that is the criterion of the Spiritual Presence and the measure of the marks of the Spiritual Community.

Tillich sees in the story of the ecstatic event of Pentecost a graphic illustration of the marks of the Spiritual Community.[36] The first mark is faith, for the individuals who constitute the community are grasped by the Spiritual Presence. Within the Spiritual Community there is room for an unlimited variety of "faiths," even conflicting ones, as long as they are all animated by the Spirit. The second mark is love, for the New Being manifest in the Spiritual Community reunites those who are separated. The third and fourth marks, unity and universality, follow naturally upon the faith and love generated by the Spirit.

The Spiritual Community, holy though it is, is not the ultimate fulfilment of the Kingdom of God. In the Spiritual Community one participates in unambiguous life, but only fragmentarily.

Latent and Manifest Stages

The nature of the Spiritual Community is further clarified by Tillich's distinction between its manifest and latent stages.[37] To put it simply, the difference between the latent and manifest community is the difference of "before" and "after" the encounter with the New Being in Jesus as the Christ. Before an individual or a group—be they ancient Hebrews or modern humanists—receives the gospel message, they are in a period of preparatory revelation. They are not destitute of the Spiritual Presence, for "there are elements of faith in the sense of being grasped by an ultimate concern, and there are elements of love in the sense of a transcendent reunion of the separated."[38] Therefore, they belong to the Spiritual Community, but in a latent manner. The latent Spiritual Community lacks the ultimate criterion of the Cross of the Christ which is the principle of resistance against profanization and demonization. The manifest Spiritual Community is the community of those who have encountered and accepted Jesus as the Christ and, consequently, in the Cross possess the means of constant self-negation, reformation, and transformation.

The Spiritual Community in its totality is thus seen to extend far beyond the Christian churches, though it embraces them. The "before" and "after" the encounter with Jesus the Christ is not demarcated by the year 33 A.D. For the Spiritual Community in its latency is created by the Spiritual Presence which is operative in all of history, including the present moment.

Tillich takes care to point out that the distinction between the latent and manifest Spiritual Community is not the same as the time-honored distinction between the visible and invisible church, for "visible" and "invisible" apply to both the latent and manifest community. By this he seems to mean that the latent Spiritual Community is visible if its faith is expressed in an organized system of symbols and ritual. Non-Christian religions, for example, form part of the latent Spiritual Community, but they are certainly visible. The invisible latent community would seem to be those individuals who, although grasped by the Spiritual Presence, do not articulate their faith by adopting the symbols and cult of a recognizable, organized religion. "Visible" and "invisible" would apply to the manifest Spiritual Community in much the same way, the invisible manifest community being those who consciously and explicitly accept Jesus as the Christ, but shun the Christian churches.

Tillich's views on the latent and manifest Spiritual Community, or the latent and manifest church, as he frequently calls it, date back to at least 1931. He describes the motives for this distinction:

The problem of the Church and society prompted me to distinguish in an essay on "Church and Humanistic Society" between a "manifest" and a "latent" Church. . . . The existence of a Christian Humanism outside the Christian Church seems to me to make such a distinction necessary. It will not do to designate as non-churchly all those who have become alienated from the organized Churches and traditional creeds. My life in these groups for half a generation showed me how much latent Church there is in them: the experience of the finite character of human existence; the quest for the eternal and the unconditioned, and absolute devotion to justice and love; a hope which is more than any Utopia; an appreciation of Christian values; and a most delicate apprehension of the ideological misuse of Christianity in the

Church and State. It often seemed to me as if the latent Church, which I found in these groups, were a truer church than the organized Churches, because its members did not assume to be in possession of the truth.[39]

Powerful as the latent church is—"Not even communism could live if it were devoid of all elements of the Spiritual Community"[40]—Tillich admits that it is deficient in two ways: it lacks the criterion of the Cross to guard against demonization from within, and the organizational strength to fend off the attacks of modern paganism.

Religion and the Spiritual Community

Life in the Spiritual Community is unambiguous life. Religion, culture, and morality, essentially united but existentially disrupted, are reunited by the Spiritual Presence.[41] Consequently, religion in the narrow sense has no place in the Spiritual Community. Religion in the broad sense of faith animates every cultural creation at its depths:

There are no religious symbols in the Spiritual Community because the encountered reality is in its totality symbolic of the Spiritual Presence, and there are no religious acts because every act is an act of self-transcendence. Thus, the essential relation between religion and culture—that "culture is the form of religion, and religion the substance of culture"—is realized in the Spiritual Community.[42]

Although the Spiritual Community unambiguously fulfills the biblical vision of the holy city without a temple, nevertheless, the fulfilment is not ultimate. It is fragmentary and anticipatory because of the temporal-spatial process of its realization.

The Spiritual Community is as manifest and as hidden as the New Being in Jesus as the Christ. It is manifest to the Spirit and hidden to all but the Spirit. "It is open only to faith as the state of being grasped by the Spiritual Presence. As we have said before: Only Spirit discerns Spirit."[43]

THE CHURCHES

The Spiritual Community is "the assembly of God" of the Old Testament, "the body of Christ" of the New Testament, and "the church invisible or Spiritual" of the Reformers. It is the "invisible essence of the religious communities," both non-Christian and Christian alike. But those religious groups which are consciously founded upon the reception of Jesus as the Christ are "the churches." The Christian churches constitute the manifest Spiritual Community. Tillich insists that the Spiritual Community, although broader than the churches, does not exist beside them as a separate entity. For the Spiritual Community is "the invisible essence," "the inner *telos*," "the essential power in every actual church."[44]

The Paradox of the Churches

The spiritual essence of the churches permits them to participate in unambiguous life under the Spiritual Presence. However, they are also groups of human beings under the conditions of existence. They are simultaneously "both the actualization and the distortion of the Spiritual Community."[45] Consequently, there are two aspects to the churches which make them a paradox: the theological aspect, which points to their spiritual essence, and the sociological aspect, which reveals their ambiguities.[46] Tillich spells out in detail the worldly side of the churches:

Every church is a sociological reality. As such it is subject to the laws which determine the life of social groups with all their ambiguities. The sociologists of religion are justified in conducting these inquiries in the same way as the sociologists of law, of the arts, and of the sciences. They rightly point to the social stratification within the churches, to the rise and fall of elites, to power struggles and the destructive weapons used in them, to the conflict between freedom and organization, to aristocratic esotericism in contrast to democratic exotericism, and so forth. Seen in this light, the history of the churches is a secular history with all the disintegrating, destructive, and tragic-demonic elements which make historical life as ambiguous as all other life processes.[47]

In the third volume of *Systematic Theology*, Tillich seldom refers to the Spiritual Community as "the church," the term logically applicable to it, because "church" connotes the ambiguities of the churches. When he does use the term "the church," it usually, although not always, means one of the churches.

Despite the sociological trappings which envelop the churches, at their core lies the Spiritual Community. It supplies the "in spite of" element in their paradoxical character, the dynamism which does not eliminate, but conquers the ambiguities of religion at least in principle.[48] By the phrase "in principle" Tillich means "the power of beginning, which remains the controlling power in a whole process. In this sense, the Spiritual Presence, the New Being, and the Spiritual Community are principles (*archai*)."[49]

Since our primary interest is the mutual relationship between religion and culture, we shall not delay to describe how the Spiritual Presence overcomes the ambiguities of religion within religion itself. Instead, we consider the influence of the churches upon individuals and upon society. As regards the ambiguities of religion, it suffices to note the operative factor, the Protestant principle: "The Protestant principle is an expression of the conquest of religion by the Spiritual Presence and consequently an expression of the victory over the ambiguities of religion, its profanization, and its demonization."[50] In this sense, Tillich can speak of "the victory of the Spirit over religion."[51]

The Individual and the Churches

The conversion of an individual to one of the churches is a gradual process that finally ends in the ecstatic moment of Christian faith.[52] Conversion is the transition from the latent stage of the Spiritual Community to its manifest stage. Thus it is relative, not absolute, conversion, for men are never completely without faith, without an ultimate concern through which they participate in the Spiritual Community. The missionary and evangelistic efforts of the churches must take this fact into account.[53] The lost sheep are never completely lost; the manifest church builds upon the latent church.

The Spiritual Community is a community of Spiritual personalities, of individuals determined by the Spiritual Presence in a state of faith and love. One is either grasped by the Spirit or one is not; there is no special status within the Spiritual Community. Everyone is a priest. However, for the sake of efficiency and orderly procedure, certain individual experts "may be called to a regular and trained performance of priestly activities."[54]

Though the convert in his actual being is subject to the ambiguities of the churches, in his essential being he is a Spiritual personality, a participant in the Spiritual Community. Tillich calls this situation "the experience of the New Being." By "experience" he means the "awareness of something that happens to somebody, namely, the state of being grasped by the Spiritual Presence."[55] According to the three elements of salvation, the New Being is experienced as creative (Regeneration), as paradox (Justification), and as process (Sanctification).

The Churches and Society

Tillich treats the relationship between the churches and society within the context of the functions of the churches. Certain functions flow from their very nature. But a function of the church is not the same as that of an institution.[56] For example, mediation is a constitutive function of the church, and it frequently is served by the institution of the priesthood. However, mediation may take place without the priesthood, for an institution is only an organizational mechanism for the function. Institutions may come and go, but the function always remains.

The first function of a church is constitution.[57] By its constitutive function a church receives and mediates the New Being. Expansion is the church function that is behind missionary activity, education, and evangelization of fallen-away members.[58] The constructive function of the churches includes both *theoria* (the aesthetic and cognitive functions) and *praxis* (the personal and communal functions).[59] The aesthetic function struggles to express the meaning of the church through the medium of religious art—pictorial, musical, and visual. Theology is the cognitive function which interprets religious symbols and relates them to the categories of rational knowledge. The personal function of the church is the development of saintliness in its members, while the communal function promotes the Holy Community in which justice and holiness flourish together. The problem in all these functions of the church is how to preserve their autonomy of form within the body of the church.[60] Must aesthetic expressiveness, cognitive truth, personal humanity, and communal justice be twisted out of shape in order to fit within the cadre of the church? Tillich feels it is possible to maintain autonomy of form in these functions by the Spiritual Presence; in other words, through theonomy.

We come now to the relating function, the function that governs the mutual interaction between the churches and other groups in society. The relating function operates in a threefold way: "the way of silent interpenetration, the way of critical judgment, and the way of political establishment."[61]

By silent interpenetration the churches radiate the Spiritual Presence into the social units with which they are contiguous. "One could call it the pouring of priestly substance into the social structure of which the churches are a part."[62] The rapid spread of secularism obscures this influence, but if the churches disappeared overnight, society would be impoverished. Interpenetration also means that the current of influence flows from society toward the churches *via* the cultural forms developed in society. "The most obvious of these influences is felt in the continuous transformation of the ways of understanding and expressing experiences in a living culture."[63] To put it another way, the churches' creative function of *theoria* and *praxis* draws upon society for the forms in which its substance is preserved and conveyed.

Critical judgment is the second mode of the relating function of the churches. By it they publicly expose and energetically protest the negativities of society. "If the silent penetration of a society by the Spiritual Presence can be called 'priestly,' the open attack on this society in the name of the Spiritual Presence can be called 'prophetic.'"[64] The success of this criticism may be modest, but even a rejected criticism has been heard. Prophetic judgment will not create the Spiritual Community, but it can advance toward it by encouraging "a state of society which approaches theonomy —the relatedness of all cultural forms to the ultimate."[65] But again, the relationship between the churches and society is mutual. By a kind of "reverse prophetism" society criticizes ecclesiastical injustice and forms of saintliness which verge on the inhuman. In the nineteenth and twentieth centuries society's criticism of the churches resulted in their loss of the laboring class, but eventually it forced them to revise their views on social justice and the nature of man.

The third mode by which the churches are related to society is political establishment.[66] Although at first sight this seems to be a non-religious arrangement, Tillich recalls that the Christ has not only a priestly and a prophetic office, but also a royal one.[67] So, too, the churches. Their royal character consists in exercising sufficient influence to safeguard the free exercise of their priestly and prophetic duties. The danger is that power politics may replace spiritual persuasion in achieving this objective. Sometimes the royal office of the churches is exercised by a political establishment in which the reciprocity of influence between church and state is clearly evidenced. The church is never totally free; inevitably there are limits imposed by its political milieu. But these restrictions are tolerable, even desirable, as long as the church remains unhindered to express itself as the Spiritual Community. A political arrangement between church and state is inimical to the interests of both, only if it permits either party to assume a totalitarian control over the other.

In general, the churches as actualizations of the Spiritual Community relate to society by belonging to it and by opposing it. But even in its opposition, "the world which is opposed by the church is not simply not-church but has in itself elements of the Spiritual Community in its latency which work toward a theonomous culture."[68]

PROTESTANTISM

Thus far, discussion had been limited to the Christian churches *in globo,* but Tillich also has much to say about the factions within Christianity, especially Protestantism. He usually refrains from the term "the Protestant church" and prefers to speak of "Protestantism" which he understands as "a special historical embodiment of a universally significant principle."[69] The principle, of course, is the Protestant principle: "The Protestant principle, in name derived from the protest of the 'protestants' against decisions of the Catholic majority, contains the divine and human protest against any absolute claim made for a relative reality, even if this claim is made by a Protestant church."[70]

Protestant Reality and Protestant Principle

Consistent with his twofold definition of religion, Tillich distinguishes between the Protestant reality—the institutionalized ecclesiastical groups originating with the Reformation—and the Protestant principle which animates them as the soul does the body.

In his book *The Protestant Era,* he unflinchingly asks the question: Is the Protestant era at an end?[71] Is Protestantism as an historical reality dying, is its soul fleeing a moribund body that failed to adjust to the demands of its times? According to Tillich's diagnosis, the social, political, economic, and spiritual disintegration of the masses can be relieved only by a tight centralization of power in all these areas. Protestantism, however, inspired by its principle of prophetic protest against hierarchical authority, ecclesiastical or political, which wraps itself in the mantle of the sacred, stands opposed to the trend toward centralization. Protestantism, out of step with the rhythm of history, leaves the field open to the three forces capable of mass reintegration of society: communism, nationalism, and Roman Catholicism. Grim as the Protestant prospect is, however, Tillich concedes to the Protestant churches the possibility of rejuvenation. But renewal will be achieved neither by a rearguard defensive action nor by a superficial borrowing from Catholicism, but by a third way—by a Protestant movement that transcends all churches, political parties and ideologies and yet impregnates them. His vision of the new Protestantism merits description in his own words:

. . . the prophetic spirit which lists where it will, without ecclesiastical conditions, organization, and traditions. Thus it will operate through Catholicism as well as through orthodoxy, through fascism as well as through communism; and in all these movements it will take the form of resistance against the distortion of humanity and divinity which necessarily is connected with the rise of the new systems of authority. But this imperative would remain a very idealistic demand if there were no living group which could be bearer of this spirit. Such a group could not be described adequately as a sect. It would approximate more closely an order or fellowship and would constitute an active group, aiming to realize, first, in itself that transformation of Protestantism which cannot be realized either by the present churches or by the movements of retreat and defense.[72]

But whether the Protestant era ends or not, the Protestant principle will never die. If the Protestant reality expires under the protesting blast of the Protestant principle, then the power and vitality of the principle is proved all the stronger. For Tillich maintains:

This principle is not a special religious or cultural idea; it is not subject to the changes of history; it is not dependent on the increase or decrease of religious experience or spiritual power. It is the ultimate criterion of all religious and all spiritual experiences; it lies at their base, whether they are aware of it or not.[73]

Grace

Tillich quite honestly faces up to the problem which results from his interpretation of Protestantism:

No church can be founded on a protest, yet Protestantism became a church. . . . The inner dilemma of Protestantism lies in this, that it must protest against every religious or cultural realization which seeks to be intrinsically valid, but that it needs such realization if it is to be able to make its protest in any meaningful way.[74]

To put the question even more radically: "By the power of what reality does the Protestant principle exercise its criticism? There must be such a reality, since the Protestant principle is not mere negation."[75] Tillich's ultimate answer is the New Being manifest in Jesus as the Christ. Before arriving at it, however, several intermediate steps must be taken.

The basis of the solution is rooted in the axiom that the negative can live only from the positive, that negation must build upon affirmation. Thus, protest can exist only within a Gestalt to which it belongs, Gestalt being understood as "the total structure of a living reality," a structure which includes both form and negation of form, a Yes and a No. "This union of protest and creation we call 'the Gestalt of grace.' "[76]

Tillich is well aware that grace as a reality, grace as embodied in a structure, goes against the Protestant grain, for it sounds perilously similar to the Roman Catholic teaching which supposedly objectifies grace.[77] And the objectification of grace opens the door to a whole legion of Catholic doctrines such as a sacred hierarchy, an infallible ecclesiastical authority, and the system of automatic sacraments. Many Protestants would consider a Gestalt of grace a betrayal of the essence of Protestantism. Tillich, however, feels

that the jargon of Reformation controversy should not be allowed
to obscure the theological facts, that the choice is not simply between the Roman Catholic objectification of grace and a completely structureless Protestant grace. There is a third possibility
which is clearly seen in the Protestant notion of faith. Faith is *in*
man, but not *from* man. Consequently, Protestantism can assert
"that grace appears *through* a living Gestalt which remains in itself what it is," while "the Protestant protest prohibits the appearance of grace through finite forms from becoming an identification of grace with finite forms."[78]

Granted that the Gestalt of grace embraces both the positive
and the negative, where is the protest voiced? Tillich answers: in
the secular world. For according to the Protestant principle, grace
cannot be tied down to any particular form, not even to a religious
form. History shows that nonreligious, even anti-religious, movements can express a religious protest more effectively than religion
itself. Consequently, Protestantism stands in a special relationship
to secularism, a relationship which is summed up as follows:

Protestantism, by its very nature, demands a secular reality. It demands
a concrete protest against the sacred sphere and against ecclesiastical
pride, a protest that is incorporated in secularism. Protestant secularism
is a necessary element of Protestant realization. The formative power
of Protestantism is always tested by its relation to the secular world. If
Protestantism surrenders to secularism, it ceases to be a Gestalt of
grace. If it retires from secularism, it ceases to be Protestant, namely, a
Gestalt that includes within it the protest against itself.[79]

The secular world not only protests against religion, but it is, in
turn, shaped by Protestant influence. Secular thought is driven to
seek its ultimate meaning; secular activity, its ultimate purpose.
In Tillichian terminology the dialectical relationship of the secular
world to the Gestalt of grace is best called theonomy, "which indicates that neither ecclesiastical heteronomy nor secular autonomy
can have the last word in human culture."[80] But if theonomy
smacks too much of heteronomous Catholicism, then Tillich sug-

gests the term "Protestant secularism" which says the same as theonomy, but highlights the intimate connection between the Gestalt of grace and the secular world.

In addition to the Gestalt of grace, Tillich also expounds grace as the experience of acceptance. One of his most eloquent sermons, "You Are Accepted," portrays the experience of grace which overcomes sin.[81] Grace is neither a magical power nor is it an accumulation of gifts. He movingly relates how grace touches us at the deepest level of our being:

Sometimes at that moment a wave of light breaks into our darkness, and it is as though a voice were saying: "You are accepted. *You are accepted,* accepted by that which is greater than you, and the name of which you do not know. . . . Do not seek for anything; do not perform anything; do not intend anything. *Simply accept the fact that you are accepted!*" If that happens to us, we experience grace. After such an experience we may not be better than before, and we may not believe more than before. But everything is transformed. In that moment, grace conquers sin, and reconciliation bridges the gulf of estrangement. And nothing is demanded of this experience, no religious or moral or intellectual presupposition, nothing but *acceptance.*[82]

Tillich supports his notion of grace as acceptance by an appeal to modern psychotherapy.[83] Psychically disturbed persons cannot be helped by telling them what to do, by holding up a norm to them. They can be helped only by accepting them in spite of their unacceptability. The therapy of acceptance is, in reality, a therapy of grace.

What is the connection between grace as acceptance and the Gestalt of grace? Faith is the common denominator, "for faith means being grasped and being transformed by grace," by the divine action which operates through a Gestalt to effect the justification which is acceptance.[84] Furthermore, to experience grace is to experience the New Being in Jesus the Christ who conquers estrangement and whose Cross is the ultimate norm of protest. To experience grace in any fashion is to receive the impact of the

Spiritual Presence. But grace is always a gift, the result of the divine initiative; it can never be produced by human efforts. Grace "qualifies all relations between God and man in such a way that they are freely inaugurated by God and in no way dependent on anything the creature does or desires."[85]

The Sacramental Element

Tillich insists upon the sacramental element in Protestantism, "for this element is the one essential element of every religion, namely, the presence of the divine before our acting and striving, in a 'structure of grace' and in the symbols expressing it."[86] His support of the sacramental principle is foreshadowed by his other theological concepts: the Gestalt of grace, the medium of the Spiritual Presence, the bearer of revelation, and religious symbolism. The experience of the holy must be mediated in a concrete and, therefore, sacramental fashion, for "the sacramental is nothing else than some reality becoming the bearer of the holy in a special way and under special circumstances."[87] Within this general definition he discerns three meanings for the term "sacramental":

The largest sense of the term denotes everything in which the Spiritual Presence has been experienced; in a narrower sense, it denotes particular objects and acts in which a Spiritual community experiences the Spiritual Presence; and in the narrowest sense, it merely refers to some "great" sacraments in the performance of which the Spiritual Community actualizes itself.[88]

It is with the sacramental principle in the broadest sense that Tillich is chiefly concerned, for neglect of it undermines all sacramental elements in the church. Protestantism has long attacked Roman Catholic demonization of the sacraments which attributes magical powers to them. However, Tillich decries Protestant indifference to the sacramental principle, and he criticizes Protestant personalism which focuses attention upon the personality of

Jesus. For, in so doing, Protestantism emphasizes the moral demand of the holy, but risks losing the sense of the presence of the holy, and consequently undercuts the basis for its own prophetic protest.[89]

Two factors are discernible in every sacrament: a relationship to nature, and a participation in salvation history.[90] Although, in principle, anything from the world of nature may convey the Spiritual Presence, certain elements are specially qualified to act as sacramental symbols. Symbols must participate in that which they symbolize, not merely by an arbitrary connection, but by their very nature. For instance, water has a special power which peculiarly fits it to become a sacramental material. Tillich is vague in explaining this unusual power, for he merely states that "water, on the one hand, is a symbol for the origin of life in the womb of the mother, which is a symbol for the creative source of all things, and that, on the other hand, it is a symbol of death—the return to the origin of things."[91] Thus, by its very character, water has a necessary relation to baptism. Whatever the explanation of individual elements such as water, the sacramental principle asserts that nature is open to and, in fact, participates in the holy.

But "natural sacraments" swiftly fall prey to the demonic, and the only way they can escape demonization is by union with the New Being in Jesus the Christ. Nature has no true sacramental power apart from the history of salvation. Hence, sacraments cannot be manufactured; they "originate when the intrinsic power of a natural object becomes for faith a bearer of sacramental power."[92] Their origin is linked to the source of all faith, to the Spiritual Presence manifest in Jesus the Christ whose Cross offers the only sure guarantee against the forces of demonization.

Since the sacramental principle embraces the whole world of nature and since faith is not restricted by time and place, the question arises: Is the Spiritual Presence bound to any definite sacramental media?[93] Tillich responds "yes" and "no." Yes, in the sense that every sacramental act must be subject to the criterion of the New Being in Jesus as the Christ, or demonization would result.

Furthermore, sacraments must somehow refer to the central historical and doctrinal symbols of Christianity which have emerged within the history of salvation. No, in the sense that the Spiritual Community may adopt new sacramental symbols, for it is entirely possible that a symbol may gradually fade and die, that is, lose its sacramental power.

Protestant Principle and Catholic Substance

The Gestalt of grace and the sacramental principle lead one to conclude that Tillich is somewhat sympathetic to the Roman Catholic church. To a very large extent, this conclusion is true. In fact, during the struggle against Hitler in 1933, Tillich seriously contemplated becoming a Catholic when it appeared that the German Protestant church might allow itself to be swallowed up by National Socialism.[94] His respect for the Roman church is based upon the theological principle of sacramental substance, namely, the concrete manifestation of the holy in cult, doctrine, and authority. Unfortunately, he finds this spiritual substance encased in a hard crust of heteronomy against which he tirelessly hurls the protest of the Protestant principle.[95] He writes:

> From earliest times I was opposed to the most potent system of religious heteronomy, Roman Catholicism, with a protest which was at once both protestant and autonomous. This protest was not directed and does not direct itself in spite of theological contrasts to the dogmatic values or the liturgical forms of the Catholic system, but is concerned with its heteronomous character, with the assertion of a dogmatic authority. . . .[96]

He feels that Catholicism identifies itself with the Spiritual Community to the exclusion of all other religions, thus elevating itself to a level above any criticism. It shields its ambiguous sociological aspect behind its theological character.[97]

However, despite his frequent and trenchant criticisms of Roman Catholicism, Tillich acknowledges its religious power and theological importance. This recognition is formulated in his phrase "Protestant principle and Catholic substance" which expresses Catholicism's need for prophetic criticism and Protestantism's need for concrete embodiment of the Spiritual Presence.[98] He clarifies the dialectical relation of Protestant principle to Catholic substance in his essay "The Permanent Significance of the Catholic Church for Protestantism."[99] The twofold experience of the holy as being and as demand gives rise to two types of religion: the sacramental, priestly type founded upon the ontological presence of the holy, and the eschatological, prophetic type stemming from its moral insistence. Both components are actually present in both types, but one of them will predominate. The significance of Catholicism for Protestantism is that the former vitally represents the priestly and sacramental elements which the latter lacks today. It is the permanent ambiguity of the Catholic Church that, although it demonically attributes holiness to finite beings, nevertheless it does provide a solid doctrine of the church according to which "the moral perfection of the community does not bring about the holiness of the church, but rather the holiness of the church sanctifies the community by preaching the forgiveness of sins and by leading it to the New Being upon which the church rests."[100]

From this basically sacramental understanding of the Catholic Church flow other useful consequences for Protestantism. First of all, in regard to the problem of church authority, "not the legal, but the sacramental side of Catholic authority must today be taken up by Protestantism and reinterpreted," for even the prophets of Israel fell back upon the sacramental covenant between Yahweh and his people for the source of their authority.[101] Secondly, Catholicism has preserved the power of symbols in its cult and doctrine, while Protestantism has sadly neglected them. Thirdly, Protestantism must tap the reservoir of Catholic mysticism, since its own mystical content has been considerably dried up by activism and moralism. Lastly, there is a Catholic rationalism that stamps its dogmatics and ethics with a clarity, consistency, and philosophical exactness that Protestant theology could well emulate. This same rational approach incites Catholics to produce an apologetics that correlates reason and revelation, and, while Protestants cannot accept the Catholic solution, they can imitate the urgency with which Catholicism presses the question. Tillich sums it all up when he says, "Neither the prophetic type of Christianity can long survive without the priestly type, nor can the eschatological, without the sacramental."[102]

It has been pointed out that Tillich's positive approach to the Protestant-Catholic relationship could be very fruitful in the ecumenical dialogue.[103] Moreover, in his book *Christianity and the Encounter of the World Religions* he provides principles by which the religions and quasi-religions of the world can honestly respect one another by a mutual recognition of the Spiritual Presence that animates them all. Yet, what he expects from the ecumenical movement is a limited, short-range success and long-range failure:

In practical terms it is able to heal divisions which have become historically obsolete, to replace confessional fanaticism by interconfessional co-operation, to conquer denominational provincialism, and to produce a new vision of the unity of all churches in their foundation. But neither the ecumenical nor any other future movement can conquer the ambiguity of unity and division in the churches' historical existence. Even if it were able to produce the United Churches of the World, and even if all latent churches were converted to this unity, new divisions would appear. The dynamics of life, the tendency to preserve the holy even when it has become obsolete, the ambiguities implied in the sociological existence of the churches, and, above all, the prophetic criticism and demand for reformation would bring about new and, in many cases, Spiritually justified divisions. The unity of the churches, similar to their holiness, has a paradoxical character. It is the divided church which is the united church.[104]

REFLECTIONS AND APPRAISAL

Now that Tillich's ecclesiology has been proposed at length, the contribution of the church toward a cultural theonomy can be better appreciated. Although the ambiguous churches are not immune to demonic distortion, nevertheless "the impact of the Spiritual Presence on the functions of cultural creativity is impossible without an inner-historical representation of the Spiritual Community in a church."[105] Culture is not vague and indeterminate; cultural creations are produced by definite individuals and social groups. The Spiritual Community must be just as specific if its force is to be felt. The Spiritual Community must be localized in a human community; the Spiritual Presence, concretized in the symbols of cult and doctrine. And yet, the Spiritual Community is broader than any church which represents it, for the Spirit cannot be fettered. The Spiritual Presence works latently to prepare for the fuller manifestation of the Spiritual Community in a church. Consequently, the role of the Spiritual Community as embodied in the churches can be described as both cause and effect. The Spiritual Presence is felt within a culture because the Spiritual Community has first opened men's hearts to it, and the free stirring of the Spirit within the cultural realm leads men to the Spiritual Community. As Tillich puts it: ". . . the free impact of the divine Spirit on a culture prepares for a religious community or is received because such a community has prepared human beings for the reception of the Spiritual impact."[106]

Due to the comparatively recent publication of the third volume of *Systematic Theology*, Tillich's ecclesiology has not received much attention up to this date. The method of correlation, symbolism, and the New Being have dominated the discussion. However, his doctrine of the church has not gone entirely unnoticed. Some theologians are impressed by the Protestant principle, especially its union with Catholic substance.[107] But others are more critical: Tillich is said to place the church in a purely vertical relationship to God,[108] the distinction between the latent and manifest church is challenged,[109] and, from a Barthian viewpoint, the criticism is levelled that the Spirit which constitutes the churches is not the Spirit of Jesus.[110] Nels Ferré is severe with Tillich because of his total rejection of the supernatural; this ontological deficiency undermines his ecclesiology with the result that "*at times* Tillich's doctrine of the church seems to evaporate into a general theory of religion as a response to the unconditional."[111]

Whatever the conflicts and obscurities in Tillich's conception of the church, it is remarkable for its attempt to unite the sacramental and the prophetic elements. The Gestalt of grace and the sacramental principle are vehicles for the holiness of the "is," the actual presence of the divine which, in turn, provides the positive base for the prophetic demand for the holiness of the "ought." Furthermore, his singling out the sociological side of the churches is quite instructive for the members of these churches, especially the clergy, for it portrays the image which the church presents to the non-believer who is incapable of seeing its theological side.

However, the most characteristic and the most theologically significant doctrine of Tillich's ecclesiology is the notion of the latent and manifest church. It is the fulcrum upon which are balanced the reciprocal influences of religion and culture. On the one hand, the latent church under the vivifying power of the Spiritual Presence is in preparation for the reception of the New Being in Jesus the Christ. But the latent church is not simply an infant awaiting baptism; it is already a mature, adult member of the Spiritual Community, and under the drive of the Spirit it voices criticism of the manifest church through non-sectarian, secular, or even anti-religious movements. Its protest appears as a cultural phenomenon, but the underlying inspiration is religious. On the other hand, the manifest church openly and consciously acknowledges the New Being in Jesus the Christ, and, united by the bonds of a common faith, it proclaims the Word of the Gospel and the sacraments of the New Law. But these acts of religion must be expressed in relevant cultural forms. In brief, by recognizing the latent church as part of the Spiritual Community, Tillich provides the manifest church with the basis for understanding and dealing constructively with both the non-Christian and the secular world.

The doctrine of the latent and manifest church is indeed an ambitious effort, and it is scarcely cause for surprise if on certain points it overreaches itself. For instance, does Tillich introduce the sweeping concept of the latent church at the expense of the manifest church, or, in other words, exactly how do they differ? We suppose that the distinction between the two is a matter of utmost importance which accords to the manifest church a certain special dignity and practical advantage, for the reception of final revelation in Jesus the Christ is somehow a progression beyond preparation for it. The latent church joins the Spiritual Community by participation in the New Being, but it does not know Jesus crucified. The manifest church's explicit acknowledgement of Jesus as the bearer of the New Being gains for it the symbol of the Cross, the Protestant principle of self-reformation which is the only antidote to demonization. Possession and non-possession of the Cross seems a clear-cut distinction. However, it is precisely in the latent church—in fact, in the secular world—that Tillich finds the strongest expression of the prophetic protest which recalls the manifest church to its pristine mission. How can the secular world voice truly prophetic criticism unless it too has the Cross, the symbol of the struggle against the demonic, at least implicitly? In that case the question returns: What does the explicit reception of the New Being in Jesus the Christ add to the manifest church?

Tillich can and does answer that in the manifest church one finds the Bible, the document of the reception of final revelation, the sacraments which deepen the experience of the New Being, and the corporate organization which rallies and sustains Christians in their effort to live the Gospel. Here is certainly a concrete difference between the latent and manifest churches. However, Tillich's strictures against the ambiguity of the churches immediately spring to mind, the demonization and profanization into which they inevitably fall—and one begins to wonder if the transition from the latent to the manifest church is worth the price. It seems that most of the latter's energy is expended in applying the Cross to correct its own ambiguities. The impression is that the latent church is dynamic, exciting, productive, and pregnant with hope, while the manifest church is tired, dull, weighed down with ambiguities, and moribund—despite the fact that it has received the New Being in Jesus the Christ. One is tempted to conclude almost blasphemously—*because* it has received the New Being in Jesus the Christ. Tillich would doubtlessly repudiate this harsh impression along with its perverse conclusion, but its persistence is perhaps indicative that he does not entirely succeed in expounding the true nature and role of the manifest church.

Basically, the same problem arises in Tillich's distinction between the Protestant reality and the Protestant principle. It is curious that he insists so strenuously upon the "protesting" sense of the word "Protestant," a critical, negative meaning which most Protestants prefer to subordinate to the more positive sense of the "profession" of the Gospel. Of course, he qualifies this interpretation with the Gestalt of grace and the sacramental principle, but his final judgment is that the Protestant principle is the essence of Protestantism. Therefore, he concludes that the Protestant churches may fade away, but Protestantism, in the sense of the Protestant principle, will always remain. One may conjecture whether on this point Tillich has moved away from the mainstream of the Protestant tradition. Surely the Protestant churches are essentially more than the bearers of protest. Their foundation is rooted in the Gospel message and, ultimately, somehow in the words and deeds of Jesus. They are charged to carry on his mission, which was not only protest, but, more fundamentally, positive religious witness. In brief, Tillich does not portray the professing role of the churches with the same appeal, drama, and insight that he brings to their mission of prophetic protest.

If Christology is intimately related to ecclesiology, so that the structure of the incarnation serves as a paradigm for the structure of the church, then Tillich's Christological problematic will determine or at least accord with his ecclesiological problematic. We have seen that, for Tillich, the Christological question is not the union of God and man in Jesus the Christ, but the appearance in him of essential manhood under the conditions of existence. Similarly, his ecclesiological question is the participation in unambiguous life bestowed by the Spiritual Presence. The Spirit elevates man's spirit to the transcendent unity of unambiguous life, that is, to an experiential realization that his humanity shares in essential manhood insofar as it is actualized. The actualization is fragmentary and the experience fleeting, but the impact of this revelation enkindles the courage to be what one should be. The distortions and ambiguities of existential life are not thereby banished, but one has glimpsed the New Being which alone is worthy of our ultimate concern. And the fact that all men participate in and are destined for the New Being—otherwise they would have given up the struggle to be—draws them together in the Spiritual Community. Through the New Being they are reunited to God, the ground of all being, and the power which flows from this reunion should permeate all their spiritual activities, so that, ideally, culture is grounded in being-itself, and being-itself shines through all cultural forms. Unambiguous life in the Spiritual Community is theonomous life.

Such seems to be what Tillich understands by the transcendent unity of unambiguous life in the Spiritual Community. For him, then, the heart of the mystery of the church is the reception of and participation in essential manhood, while the mystery of Christology is the undistorted appearance of essential manhood in Jesus the Christ under the conditions of existence. By way of contrast, Catholic theology, for example, describes the Christological problem as the union of God and man in Jesus, while the ecclesiological problem is the union of Jesus the Head with the all-too-human collectivity that is his Body. The Second Vatican Council proposes this analogy between the mystery of the incarnation and the mystery of the church.[112] It illustrates, first, the paradoxical nature of the church which is, on the one hand, a hierarchically organized society and, on the other hand, the Mystical Body, visible and yet spiritual, earthly and heavenly, possessing a human factor and a divine factor. Secondly, it emphasizes that the social whole which is the church acts as a channel for the Spirit of Christ, just as the human nature of Jesus serves as an instrument of salvation.

This difference in the orientation of problematics at least highlights, if it does not explain, the fact that Tillich is not so concerned about the life of Jesus and the social organism of the manifest church as he is about the appearance of essential manhood and its reception in the act of faith. It is not by accident that he prefers the term "Spiritual Community" to the term "church" with its more "earthy" connotations.

Theonomy demands reunion with the ground of being, which is achieved by the ecstasy of faith in which one's total, ultimate concern is directed toward the New Being. Thus is born the Spiritual Community of those who receive the New Being in Jesus the Christ, either explicitly in the manifest church or by anticipation in the latent church. Tillich's insistence upon the universality of the Spiritual Community is the most distinctive and most positive trait of his ecclesiology, although the problem of unity thereby becomes more pressing. There is no mistaking his passionate concern to keep the Spiritual Community open to all who will yield themselves to the grasp of the Spirit:

Believe me, you who are religious and Christian. It would not be worthwhile to teach Christianity, if it were for the sake of Christianity. And believe me, you who are estranged from religion and far away from Christianity, it is not our purpose to make you religious and Christian when we interpret the call of Jesus for our time. We call Jesus the Christ not because He brought a new religion, but because He is the end of religion, above religion and irreligion, above Christianity and non-Christianity. We spread His call because it is the call to every man in every period to receive the New Being, that hidden saving power in our existence, which takes from us labour and burden, and gives rest to our souls.[113]

The Spiritual Community is not aimlessly adrift on the tides of history, for it follows where the Spirit blows. Whither does it tend, and when will it arrive? We must now consider the question of history and eschatology.

Notes

1. TC, 49.
2. *Ibid.*, 50.
3. *Ibid.*, 51.
4. "Doctrine of the Incarnation," 147.
5. ST, I, 148.
6. *Ibid.*, 144.
7. *Ibid.*, 127.
8. NB, 23.
9. TC, 212–13.
10. IH, 41.
11. ST, III, 11–12.
12. *Ibid.*, 12–17. Cf. Chapter 1 above for a fuller treatment of dimension.
13. ST, III, 16.
14. *Ibid.*, 30–32.
15. *Ibid.*, 32.
16. *Ibid.*
17. *Ibid.*, 21–25.
18. *Ibid.*, 111.
19. *Ibid.*, 38, 57, 96.
20. *Ibid.*, 107–10.
21. *Ibid.*, 109.
22. *Ibid.*
23. *Ibid.*, 110.
24. *Ibid.*, 111–12.
25. *Ibid.*, 129.
26. *Ibid.*, 138.
27. *Ibid.*, 138–39.
28. *Ibid.*, 141–44.
29. *Ibid.*, 144–49.
30. *Ibid.*, 138–41.

31. *Ibid.*, 129.
32. *Ibid.*, 140.
33. *Ibid.*, 155.
34. TC, 212.
35. ST, III, 150.
36. *Ibid.*, 150–52, 155–57.
37. *Ibid.*, 152–55.
38. *Ibid.*, 154.
39. IH, 48.
40. ST, III, 155.
41. *Ibid.*, 157–61.
42. *Ibid.*, 158.
43. *Ibid.*, 161.
44. *Ibid.*, 162–65.
45. *Ibid.*, 155.
46. *Ibid.*, 165.
47. *Ibid.*
48. *Ibid.*, 172–73.
49. *Ibid.*, 173.
50. *Ibid.*, 245.
51. *Ibid.*
52. *Ibid.*, 219–20.
53. See also *Ibid.*, 155.
54. *Ibid.*, 217.
55. *Ibid.*, 221.
56. *Ibid.*, 182–83, 188.
57. *Ibid.*, 188–93.
58. *Ibid.*, 193–96.
59. *Ibid.*, 196–212.
60. *Ibid.*, 197.
61. *Ibid.*, 212.
62. *Ibid.*, 213.
63. *Ibid.*
64. *Ibid.*
65. *Ibid.*, 214.
66. *Ibid.*, 214–15.
67. Tillich's application here of the priestly, prophetic, and royal offices to the church comes as a surprise, for in his Christology he downgrades this threefold role of the Christ as having no systematic value. See ST, II, 168.
68. ST, III, 216.
69. PE, vii.
70. *Ibid.*, 163.
71. *Ibid.*, 222–33.
72. *Ibid.*, 232–33.
73. *Ibid.*, viii.

74. RS, 192.
75. PE, xviii.
76. *Ibid.*, 206–207.
77. *Ibid.*, 209–212.
78. *Ibid.*, 212.
79. *Ibid.*, 213–14.
80. *Ibid.*, 220.
81. SF, 153–163. See also ST, I, 258–59 where the Protestant and Catholic positions on grace are contrasted. For Catholics, grace is a supranatural substance, while, for Protestants, it is forgiveness received in one's personality.
82. SF, 162.
83. TC, 124–25, 142–43, 211. See also PE, 134.
84. PE, 212. See also ST, II, 177–79.
85. ST, I, 285.
86. PE, xix.
87. TC, 64.
88. ST, III, 121.
89. PE, xix, 108, 112.
90. See "Nature and Sacrament" in PE, 94–112, and ST, III, 120–24.
91. PE, 104.
92. *Ibid.*, 111.
93. ST, III, 123–24.
94. IH, 24–25.
95. PE, 194–95.
96. IH, 24–25.
97. ST, III, 166–67.
98. See TC, 169; ST, III, 245. Tillich contrasts Protestants and Catholics in three basic areas: Catholic objectivity versus Protestant subjectivity; Catholic authority versus Protestant autonomy; and Catholic analogy versus Protestant symbolism. "Afterword," O'M and W, 301.
99. Originally published in *The Protestant Digest* (New York), III, 1941. Our references are to the German translation in GW, VII, 124–32.
100. GW, VIII, 127.
101. *Ibid.*, 128.
102. *Ibid.*, 132.
103. Walter M. Horton, "Tillich's Role in Contemporary Theology," K and B, 43–44.
104. ST, III, 169–70.
105. *Ibid.*, 246.
106. *Ibid.*
107. See W. Norman Pittenger, "Paul Tillich as a Theologian: An Appreciation," *Anglican Theological Review*, XLIII, July, 1961, 283, and Bernard M. G. Reardon, "Tillich and Anglicanism," *ibid.*, 301–302.
108. Maurice B. Schepers, "Paul Tillich on the Church," O'M and W, 249.

109. J. Heywood Thomas, *Paul Tillich: An Appraisal,* 148.

110. Alexander McKelway, *The Systematic Theology of Paul Tillich,* 216–19.

111. "Tillich's View of the Church," K and B, 258. See also *ibid.,* 262–64.

112. See the Constitution on the Church "Lumen Gentium," Chapter I, section 8.

113. SF, 102–103.

7 / History and
the Kingdom of God

IN A CERTAIN SENSE the whole thrust of Tillich's thought is toward
a theology of history, as he himself remarks: "History became the
central problem of my theology and philosophy because of the
historical reality as I found it when I returned from the first
World War. . . ."[1] Many distinctively Tillichian concepts—theonomy, the demonic, *kairos,* the Gestalt of grace, the latent church,
the Protestant principle—were developed in function of a Protestant interpretation of history. He is deeply convinced that metaphysics itself must be approached *via* the problem of history:

> The meaning of history seems more important to the mind than does
> the meaning of being. The metaphysical interpretation of the meaning
> of history has become an urgent and practical concern. The necessity
> of acting historically in the true sense, that is, of acting so as to change
> history, is one of the strongest motives for the development of a meta-
> physics of history. . . . the recognition of the necessity of a meta-
> physical interpretation of history leads to the recognition of the necessity
> of metaphysics *per se.*[2]

The importance which Tillich attaches to history is a clear sign
that the symmetry of his theonomous union of religion and culture
can be appreciated only by viewing it within the historical dimension. God as the ground of being lies at the depths of theonomy.

The power of the New Being enables us to rejoin the ground from which existence severs us. And the Spiritual Community is the place where the transforming impact of the Spirit is felt. But *when* is theonomous fulfilment realized? This is the question of a Christian interpretation of history, and, since history moves forward to its term, it is also the eschatological question.

THE NOTION OF HISTORY

Tillich's notion of history does not readily lend itself to a clear and succinct definition. Even if one managed to compress it within a neat verbal package, such as "history is the movement of creative time toward fulfilment" or "history is the realization of meaning through freedom," the very density of the definition renders it opaque. Consequently, we follow his lead by discussing the various aspects of history—the historical dimension, man and history, historical time, the ambiguities of history—and hope in this way gradually to penetrate to a better understanding of it.

The Historical Dimension

Tillich defines life as the process of actualization of the potential. As different potencies are actuated, different life-dimensions appear—the inorganic, organic, psychological, spiritual, and historical dimensions. The historical dimension is the broadest of them all; it includes all the others and adds an element of its own. This additional element is best seen by contrasting the historical with the dimension which precedes it, the spiritual dimension. The realm of the spirit is characterized by the actualization of power and meaning, while the historical dimension looks to their fulfilment. The spiritual dimension describes the process of actualization; the historical dimension, the direction of this process. In the spiritual dimension man creates; in the historical dimension the newness of his creation appears. It should now be evident that there is no real distinction between the two dimensions, for an actualization is already a kind of fulfilment, and a process has a direction. The historical dimension, therefore, is a continuation of the spiritual dimension, and to this prolongation it adds the note of finality. History, because it is a form of spiritual creativity, is proper to man alone, but, due to the multidimensional unity of life, it is applied analogously to all dimensions of life.[3]

Man and History

The Greek word *historia* furnishes Tillich with a point of departure for determining the concept of history.[4] It signifies first an inquiry or report, and only secondly the events reported. Thus the subject-object structure of history is revealed: the interpreting subject singles out certain facts and imparts significance to them. A subjective mentality or view precedes events, not temporally, but in the sense that it determines which facts shall be remembered and the meaning they shall bear. This is historical consciousness. It is the awareness of the needs and desires of a social group, an awareness which molds the raw material of factual occurrences into an historical account. The conclusions from this semantic investigation of the word "history" can be summed up as follows: "There is no history without factual occurrences, and there is no history without the reception and interpretation of factual occurrences by historical consciousness."[5]

When Tillich turns to the human happenings which merit the name "historical events," he finds the same subject-object structure of fact and interpretation.[6] Historical events move in a horizontal direction, that is, they are motivated by a purpose. Moreover, man exercises freedom in the selection and execution of his purposes. Although freedom stands in polarity with destiny, the historical situation never so completely dominates man as to smother his freedom. Consequently, in human history one witnesses "the production of new and unique embodiments of meaning."[7] The forces of nature produce the new by division, by reproduction, and especially by evolution, but in human history the new is of a qualitatively different nature—it is newness of meaning or value. Finally, the novelty of an historical event must be weighted with significance if it is not to be a mere freak, a curiosity. To be significant means to represent something, to point beyond oneself. Historical events achieve significance by pointing to the actualization of essential human potentialities, and thus they represent moments in the development toward the fulfilment of history. As Tillich puts it: "A historical personality is historical because it represents larger events, which themselves represent the human situation, which itself represents the meaning of being as such."[8]

This analysis of historical events yields the four characteristics of human history: purpose, freedom, newness, and significance. In the realm of nature these qualities are only analogously verified: "The analogy appears in the spontaneity in nature, in the new produced by the progress in biological evolution, in the uniqueness of cosmic constellations."[9] But freedom is lacking in nature, and the meaning that is there is perceived only by man. Outside the human realm, history is anticipated, but not actualized.

Man, then, is the bearer of history, the reality in which history occurs. But this general statement must be further specified.[10] Since man actualizes himself only in a community according to the polarity of individualization and participation, "the direct bearers of history are groups rather than individuals, who are only indirect bearers."[11] A history-bearing group acts in a centered way; it must possess the power to maintain internal unity and to secure itself from external danger. This role has been fulfilled in the past by families, clans, tribes, cities, nations, and in present times by the modern state. Since history flows in a horizontal direction, a history-bearing group must have an aim or purpose which Tillich calls "vocational consciousness." He provides an interesting list of examples:

The vocational consciousness of Greece was expressed in the distinction between Greeks and barbarians, that of Rome was based on the super-

iority of the Roman law, that of medieval Germany on the symbol of
the Holy Roman Empire of German nationality, that of Italy on the
"rebirth" of civilization in the Renaissance, that of Spain on the idea of
the Catholic unity of the world, that of France on its leadership in intellectual culture, that of England on the task of subjecting all peoples
to a Christian humanism, that of Russia on the salvation of the West
through the traditions of the Greek church or through the Marxist
prophecy, that of the United States on the belief in a new beginning
in which the curses of the Old World are overcome and the democratic
missionary task fulfilled.[12]

These widely differing examples show that any area of life—
social, religious, economic, intellectual—may constitute the content of history, but, since it is the political realm which insures
the basic cohesion and centeredness of the group, Tillich assigns
a predominant importance to it. This is one of the reasons why
the biblical symbol for the fulfilment of history is political: the
Kingdom of God.

The question can legitimately be raised: Is not mankind, rather
than particular groups, the bearer of history? Tillich's answer is
negative because *de facto* a politically united mankind does not
exist, and *de jure* it will never exist, since the aim of history does
not lie within history.[13] By this is meant that the dynamics of
human freedom can never come to rest within history, or else freedom itself, and hence man, would be destroyed; and if they are
active, then a politically united mankind is unthinkable.

However, in other texts Tillich speaks of the possibility of a
supra-national center of power, and in 1943 he described World
War II as part of the upheaval leading to the emergence of a truly
unified world.[14] He states also that "the technical conquest of
space has produced a unity which makes a history of mankind as
a whole possible and has started to make it real."[15]

By way of reconciling these conflicting texts, we suggest that
Tillich discerns only an incipient stirring toward a united mankind, so that, for a long time to come, particular groups will be
bearers of history, not mankind as a whole. And even a united

mankind will act according to the pressure and leadership of particular groups.

Although history is borne by particular communities, these groups cannot be personified. "They are not entities alongside or above the individuals of whom they are constituted," and consequently, it is not "the community" that wills and acts, but individuals who act in and through a community.[16] Yet in avoiding the danger of personifying the group, the mistake should not be made of elevating the individual to a history-bearing role. Certain individuals have special historical significance—for example, Caesar or Napoleon—but they are significant only because they symbolically represent their community. The fact remains that "the individual is a bearer of history only in relation to a history-bearing group."[17]

Historical Time

The notion of history is inseparably linked to the concept of time. Time is one of the ontological categories, a characteristic stamped on every finite being, but it is verified differently in different dimensions of life. Thus, "time remains time in the whole realm of finitude; but the time of the amoeba and the time of historical man are different."[18] Tillich calls the common element which gives time its identity the element of "after-each-other-ness."[19] The flow of "after-each-other-ness" is one-way traffic; it cannot be reversed, for there is no such thing as an exactly identical repetition. In the spiritual dimension, "after-each-other-ness" is manifest as the creation of new meaning. Historical time supplies the added element of direction, so that he defines it as "time running toward fulfilment."[20] Historical time "does not return, nor repeat itself: it runs forward; it is always unique; it ever creates the new. There is within it a drive toward an end, unknown, never to be reached in time itself, always intended and ever fleeing. Time runs toward the 'future eternal.' "[21]

The aim of history is fulfilment and decision, that is, an unconditional, unambiguous fulfilment achieved through freedom, and free decision that ends in unconditional fulfilment.[22] The goal of history, therefore, is transcendent to the ambiguities of time. Clock time is not historical time, for "the ultimate stands equally close to and equally distant from each moment of history."[23] Certain consequences follow from this transcendent quality of history:

The meaning of history is untouched by the modes of past and future, by birth and death. Transcendence, therefore, can be defined neither as the beginning of time nor as the end of time, nor as the negation of time. It can be indicated only by the symbolic concepts of origin and ultimate, which do not mean either the first or the last moment of time, but something transcendent to which all modes of time are equally related.[24]

What this means in the concrete is that the theological symbols of creation and last judgment have nothing to do with the beginning and end of clock time. The end of history is the aim of history, not a temporal cessation. And the beginning of history is not the birth of the universe, but "the moment in which existence is experienced as unfulfilled and in which the drive toward fulfilment starts."[25]

In what sense can the march of historical time be called "progress"?[26] Since every creative act is a step beyond the potential, history is progressive in the sense that it is in motion, always seeking to approach the ultimately new. However, some interpreters of history have made of progress a symbol for the very meaning of history. According to them, progress means either an ever-lengthening line between the fixed points of a temporal beginning and end or an infinitely ascending line that constitutes progress itself the goal of history. Tillich admits progress in certain areas—for example, ethical content, education, technology, and science. But at the core of man's spiritual functions—the moral act of self-integration, the cultural act of creativity, and the religious act of self-transcendence—lies freedom, and "freedom is the leap in which history transgresses the realm of pure being and creates meaning."[27] The movement, then, of historical time is by unpredictable leaps rather than by a measured mounting of the steps of progress.

The Ambiguities of History

The historical dimension, like all dimensions subject to existence, suffers from ambiguity. The basic cause of this ambiguity is that, while history drives on toward fulfilment, it does not always attain it. Tillich expresses the root of historical ambiguity both negatively and positively. In negative terms, "history cannot be calculated; it has the character of a leap; and its leaps can be followed by a fall into a demonic, rather than by a rise into a divine fulfilment."[28] In more positive terms, "history, while running ahead toward its ultimate aim, continuously actualizes limited aims, and in so doing it both achieves and defeats its ultimate aim. All ambiguities of historical existence are forms of this basic ambiguity."[29] Negatively, ambiguity arises when the ultimate is not achieved; positively, when the attainment of a limited goal substitutes for ultimate fulfilment.

Each of the three processes of life—self-integration, self-creativity, and self-transcendence—is plagued with ambiguity under the historical dimension. The self-integrating function of an historical group gives rise to the ambiguous drive toward empire, the ever-widening circle in which power is exercised. Our history books witness to the integrating, creative role of empires, but, at the same time, to their destructive and profanizing effects. Again, the internal centralization demanded by a history-bearing group ambiguously tends to sacrifice the creative *élan* of personal freedom to rigid central control.[30]

Historical creativity in all areas—art, philosophy, politics—comprises a twofold movement of revolution and reaction, both of which are ambiguous.[31] Revolution obviously produces the new, but at the expense of destroying the old, while reaction preserves past creations, but is a stumbling block to advancement.

Religion or self-transcendence suffers from the most destructive form of historical ambiguity in the form of the demonic.[32] In general terms the demonic is defined as a "self-elevating claim to ultimacy." In the historical dimension, "the claim to ultimacy takes the form of the claim to have or to bring the ultimate toward which history runs."[33] Tillich employs the symbol of "the third stage" for the ultimate goal of history, the first stage being the innocence of creation, and the second stage being the Fall. The third stage can be considered "as given" or "as expected," but both views of it are ambiguous. The third stage "as given" absolutizes the present moment by declaring that the ultimate has already appeared. His prime example of it is the Roman Catholic Church which manifests the holy through its religious symbols, but ambiguously betrays it by demonically identifying the ultimate with its own symbols. The third stage "as expected" is utopianism. It generates creativity by the enthusiasm it arouses, but it ambiguously leads to cynicism and despair when its expectations fail to materialize.

The dynamics of the current of history, the irreversibility of historical time, and the existential anguish of the ambiguities of history force men to search for a meaningful interpretation of history. This brings us to the quest for the Kingdom of God.

THE QUEST FOR THE KINGDOM OF GOD

Every document reporting the past—legends, myths, chronicles, records, or scholarly history books—contains an interpretation of history which consciously or unconsciously wrestles with the meaning of existence and its ambiguities. Tillich poses the problem of the interpretation of history as follows: "What is the significance of history for the meaning of existence in general? In what way does history influence our ultimate concern?"[34] Because of the subject-object structure of history, a detached, objective answer is impossible: "historical activity is the key to understanding history."[35] One cannot stand back from the flood of history, the better to see whither it is rushing; only by plunging into the stream can one feel the strength and direction of the current. But what type of historical activity provides the key to history? More specifically, to which historical group should one be committed, which vocational consciousness should one adopt as the key to unlock the enigma of history as a whole? The option for a particular historical group and its vocational consciousness as the key to history supposes that one already knows that the key will fit—in other words, that one has already grasped the meaning of history or has been grasped by it. For "the key and what the key opens are experienced in one and the same act."[36] This is not a barren, circular argument, but the dialectic of the theological circle which operates on faith. For the Christian, the Kingdom of God is both the key and the answer to the problem of history.

An interpretation of history explains more than merely the direction and dynamics of man's spiritual creativity; historical time embraces all the dimensions of life. Consequently, "the answer to the meaning of history implies an answer to the universal meaning of being."[37] In terms of the Christian interpretation of history, the Kingdom of God embraces life in every dimension, everything in which the inner aim of history is operative, from sub-atomic particles of matter to the sublimest cultural creation.

Interpretations of History

Before presenting the Christian interpretation of history, Tillich sets up a contrast by examining various competing interpretations. He groups them under two general types: the non-historical and the historical interpretations.

Negative, Non-Historical Interpretations: The non-historical "presupposes that the 'running ahead' of historical time has no aim either within or above history, but that history is the 'place' in which individual beings live their lives unaware of an eternal *telos* of their personal lives."[38] This non-historical view appears in several versions: the tragic, the mystical, and the mechanistic.[39]

The tragic interpretation is best exemplified by the Greek view of history as an eternal cycle of genesis, greatness, and decay. The whole cycle is determined by fate, and there is no hope of an ultimate fulfilment.

The mystical interpretation is more common to the East. It affirms that one must live in history, but that history itself is barren, its ambiguities unconquerable, and its motion aimless. Consequently, although characterized by a deep compassion for the universality of suffering, it retreats from a reality which it feels powerless to transform. By mystical union with the ultimate it overcomes not reality, but its own involvement in reality.

The last version of non-historical interpretation is the mechanistic, a kind of "reductionistic naturalism." Physical time is more important to it than historical time, and it ambitions to control nature through science and technology. History is the story of man, but man is merely the supreme challenge to its power of control.

Positive, Historical Interpretations: The historical interpretation of history as opposed to the non-historical asserts that history is running toward an end which is fulfilled within history itself. It, too, comes in three versions: the progressivistic, the utopian, and the transcendental.[40]

Tillich admits that "the symbol of progress includes the decisive element of historical time, its running ahead toward an aim."[41] Thus it interprets history in a genuinely historical way. But progressivism as "the belief in progress as progress without a definite end" is the product of certain nineteenth-century philosophies.[42] Its inadequacy was swiftly revealed by the world tragedies of the twentieth century, by the emphasis upon existential meaninglessness, and by insights into the non-progressive nature of freedom which begins anew in every individual.

The second inadequate historical interpretation is utopianism. It is "progressivism with a definite aim: arrival at that stage of history in which the ambiguities of life are conquered."[43] Utopianism was a child of the Renaissance, but it has been adopted by

revolutionary movements up to the present day. Its fatal error is
demonization that ends in idolatry, for "it gives the quality of ultimacy to something preliminary."[44] A future historical situation,
by the very fact that it is historical, that is, within history, remains
conditioned, and hence cannot assume the dignity of the unconditional.

Tillich finds the "transcendental" type of historical interpretation in the early church up to Augustine and in orthodox Lutheranism. According to the transcendental view, once saving
revelation appears in history, nothing new can be expected until
the afterlife. The difficulty with this interpretation is that salvation
is for the individual alone, and the political aspect of the history-
bearing group is completely ignored. Moreover, it considers the
end of history as "a static supranatural order into which individuals enter after their death," thus effectively severing culture as
well as nature from the fulfilling process of history.[45]

The Symbol "Kingdom of God"

The irrelevancy of the non-historical interpretations of history
and the inadequacies of the historical types induced Tillich as a
member of the Religious Socialist movement of the 1920's to develop his own interpretation of the symbol "the Kingdom of
God."[46] He finds in the Kingdom of God a double character: "It
has an inner-historical and a transhistorical side. As inner-historical, it participates in the dynamics of history; as transhistorical,
it answers the questions implied in the ambiguities of the dynamics
of history."[47]

The Kingdom of God, thus conceived, has four connotations
which render it an apt symbol for the aim of history. First, it is
political and so corresponds to the political character of history-
bearing groups; but it is also transformed into a cosmic symbol
by the extension of the ruling power of God. Secondly, "Kingdom"
has a social connotation of peace and justice, and thus meets legitimate utopian expectations. However, it is also "of God," and

"with this addition the impossibility of an earthly fulfilment is implicitly acknowledged."[48] Thirdly, there is the personalistic connotation, for in the Kingdom of God no individual is obliterated by identity with the ultimate, but humanity is fulfilled in every human being. Lastly, the Kingdom of God is universal in that it embraces all realms of finite being according to the multidimensional unity of life.

In opposition to the non-historical interpretations of history, the Kingdom of God must be anchored in the temporal, and against other historical interpretations it must not be submerged in the temporal. Consequently, it is immanent and transcendent at the same time.[49] The Old Testament stresses the "immanent-political" aspect of the Kingdom, but the transcendent element is never absent, for it is Yahweh who brings the Kingdom to fulfilment. In the New Testament the "transcendent-universal" aspect emerges more clearly as a political vision is replaced by a cosmic vision that will be realized not by historical developments, but by divine interference. In a word, the Kingdom of God is both in history and above history.

THE KINGDOM OF GOD WITHIN HISTORY

The manifestation of the Spiritual Presence in the individual human spirit and in the Spiritual Community was discussed in the previous chapter without reference to the historical dimension. However, the revelation of the Spirit does not take place in a timeless vacuum; it has a history. In fact, it *is* history; it is *Heilsgeschichte,* the history of salvation. Although Tillich has some reservations about the term "history of salvation," he uses it to mean "a sequence of events in which saving power breaks into historical processes, prepared for by these processes so that it can be received, changing them to enable the saving power to be effective in history."[50] This appearance of the Kingdom of God within history is not like a fixed monument, but a process that partakes of the dynamism of the irreversible current of history.

The question of the rhythm of this process and the direction of its flow cannot be answered in general terms. One must build an answer upon a concrete revelatory experience, and Tillich takes his stand upon "the central Christian assertion that Jesus of Nazareth is the Christ, the final manifestation of the New Being in history."[51]

In this section we consider the fact and the manner of the manifestation of the Kingdom of God within history, and in the following section the meaning of the Kingdom of God, or the aim of history that lies outside history.

The Center of History

As early as 1929, Tillich wrote an essay, "The Interpretation of History and the Idea of the Christ," in which he showed that an interpretation of history necessarily leads to Christology and, conversely, that Christology must yield an interpretation of history.[52] The middle term that links the two is "meaning," for the interpretation of history is a search for meaning, and in Jesus the Christ is found the victory over meaninglessness.

That Jesus as the Christ is the source of the meaning of history is expressed by the metaphor "center." "The center of history is the place where the meaning-giving principle of history is seen."[53] Since, according to its subject-object structure, history is not a purely objective temporal process, the center of history is not a point between a temporal beginning and end. Nor is the center of history the culmination point of a progressivistic development.

There is, however, a progressive element in the sense that the center of history is "a moment in history for which everything before and after is both preparation and reception."[54] The manifestation of the Kingdom of God is revelation, and this revelatory moment is prepared for by a movement from immaturity to maturity, for "mankind had to mature to a point in which the center of history could appear and be received as the center."[55] The Old Testament is the record of the maturing process which led to the final revelation in Jesus the Christ. The point to note, however, is that what happened once in the process of original revelation happens again and again whenever the Christ is received as the center of history, regardless of time and place. As Tillich puts it: "The maturing or preparatory process toward the central manifestation of the Kingdom of God in history is, therefore, not restricted to the pre-Christian epoch; it continues after the center's appearance and is going on here and now."[56] And just as there is "an original history of preparation" for the central revelation, so too there is "an original history of reception" which is the history of the church. The reception of revelation by the manifest church is clearly documented, but it must be borne in mind that the church is also latent, and the latent church receives revelation only by anticipation of the center.[57]

The historical dimension of Christology demonstrates that "the appearance of Jesus as the Christ is the historical event in which history becomes aware of itself and its meaning."[58] In determining the center of history, Tillich erects the framework for his interpretation of history. All that follows is an elaboration of the content of that central meaning which not only explains, but creates history.

Kairos

After the maturing process of preparation, the Kingdom of God was manifested within history by the appearance of Jesus as the Christ. The moment of this breakthrough Tillich calls *kairos*, the New Testament word that means "the right time" or "the fulfilment of time." He is proud of the fact that it was he and his fellow Religious Socialists who introduced the term into the discussion of the interpretation of history. It not only expresses the dynamic movement of history, but also sums up "the feeling of many people in central Europe after the First World War that a moment of history had appeared which was pregnant with a new understanding of the meaning of history and life."[59]

Kairos is contrasted with *chronos* which is measured time or clock time.[60] *Chronos* is the quantitative side of time, while *kairos* stresses a quality of time which is approximated by the English word "timing." *Kairos* is the time of revelation. Divine revelation, though gratuitous, breaks through at the most propitious moment, prepared for by prophetic criticism and followed up by embodiment in the church. The original appearance of Jesus as the Christ is the "great *kairos*," but his manifestation is re-experienced again and again in moments of conversion which are "relative *kairoi*." These secondary *kairoi* depend upon the great *kairos* as their criterion and source of power. A relative *kairos* that extends to multitudes of people and significantly shapes the course of history is rare, but, on a more modest scale, "*kairoi* have occurred and are occurring in all preparatory and receiving movements in the church latent and manifest."[61] To these two senses of *kairos* can be added a third meaning, namely, *kairos* as a general category which the philosopher of history employs to describe any decisively important turn in history. Tillich neatly sums up the three senses of *kairos*:

> Kairos in its *unique* and universal sense is, for Chirstian faith, the appearing of Jesus as the Christ. Kairos in its *general* and special sense of the philosopher of history is every turning-point in history in which the eternal judges and transforms the temporal. Kairos in its *special* sense, as decisive for our present situation, is the coming of a new theonomy on the soil of a secularized and emptied autonomous culture.[62]

How does one become aware of a *kairos* which heralds the advent of a theonomous era? Tillich replies that "it is not a matter of detached observation but of involved experience."[63] A period of history, ripe for a *kairos*, is characterized by openness to the unconditional. This is not to say that such an age is necessarily more religious than a so-called irreligious age, "but an age that is turned toward, and open to, the unconditional is one in which the consciousness of the presence of the unconditional permeates and guides all cultural functions and forms. The divine, for such a state of mind, is not a problem but a presupposition."[64]

It is now possible to relate *kairos* to other key Tillichian concepts. First of all, the breakthrough of a *kairos* coincides with the establishment of a theonomous culture. In describing a period of *kairos*, Tillich says explicitly, "We shall call such a situation 'theonomous,' not in the sense that in it God lays down the laws but in the sense that such an age, in all its forms, is open to and directed toward the divine."[65] The problem, of course, is why a theonomous period does not endure, if it is founded upon the presence of the unconditioned in the totality of man's cultural life. Here he appeals to the dialectic of autonomy-heteronomy-theonomy to explain the waxing and waning of *kairoi* in the evolution of history. These three notions, originally introduced to depict cultural phenomena, now become an integral part of his interpretation of history.

Kairos, since it looms so large in Tillich's Protestant interpretation of history, must also be grounded in the Protestant principle. The Protestant principle demands the creative presence of the divine in history (the Yes) and the transcendence of the divine to all its historical manifestations (the No).[66] *Kairos* fulfills these conditions, for it includes both a prophetic protest, which prepares for and accompanies the manifestation of the center of history, and an affirmation of the presence of the Kingdom of God among us. "The idea of 'the *kairos*' unites criticism and creation."[67]

The Cross of the Christ proclaimed in the great *kairos* must be the constant criterion of lesser *kairoi*. For just as the holy and faith itself is open to demonic distortion, so too is *kairos*. The Religious Socialists of the 1920's and 1930's preached a *kairos*, but, at the same time, nazism exploited the concept to build an idolatrous nationalism and racism.[68] Besides the danger of being demonized, every *kairos*, even the great *kairos*, is liable to error about calculations of time and details. As Tillich remarks:

No date foretold in the experience of a *kairos* was ever correct; no situation envisaged as the result of a *kairos* ever came into being. But something happened to some people through the power of the Kingdom of God as it became manifest in history, and history has been changed ever since.[69]

The Kingdom and the Manifest Church

Up to now we have examined the fact of the manifestation of the Kingdom of God through the appearance of the Christ in a moment of *kairos*. Since the reception of Christian revelation constitutes the manifest churches, they are the representatives of the Kingdom of God within history and thereby play a twofold role: they actively contribute to the pursuit of the aim of history, and they struggle against the forces of profanization and demonization which seek to frustrate this purpose.[70] To accomplish this task, to create the new in history and to withstand the profane and the demonic, the churches draw upon the power of the New Being which is their foundation.

The churches as the embodiments of the Spiritual Community comprise only persons, but as representatives of the Kingdom of God they stand for all dimensions of life, including the animate and inanimate world of nature. This wider representative function is fulfilled through the sacraments: "To the degree in which a church emphasizes the sacramental presence of the divine, it draws the realm's preceding spirit and history, the inorganic and organic universe, into itself."[71] For the Kingdom of God symbolizes not only society, but also the multidimensional life of the whole universe.

The churches have a history, but instead of speaking of "the history of the churches," Tillich prefers the phrase "the history of the church" in order to emphasize that the many churches are embodiments of the one Spiritual Community, despite their paradoxical ambiguities.[72] In the light of this fact, one must admit that "church history is at no point identical with the Kingdom of God and at no point without manifestation of the Kingdom of God."[73] Although the church is the representative of the Kingdom of God, the two cannot be simply identified because of what Tillich calls "the riddle of church history," namely, the ambiguity of the church as spelled out in its historical dimension. The riddle of church history can be expressed in a series of questions. Why is the church, in principle universal, effectively restricted to a particular civilization? How account for the rise within Christianity itself of secular movements, such as humanism and communism? Why has the unity of the church been splintered? How explain so much profanization of the holy in church history both by Roman Catholic ritualization and Protestant secularization? What is the cause of the history of demonization in the church, from the early persecution of heretics, through the religious wars, through the fanatical stubbornness of fundamentalism, through the tyranny of Protestant orthodoxy, to the infallibility of the pope?[74]

In the face of this riddle, this scandal, one must ask: What does church history mean? Two statements can be made in reply. First, church history cannot be identified with the history of salvation or sacred history. "Sacred history is in church history but is not limited to it, and sacred history is not only manifest in but also hidden by church history."[75] It is the everlasting paradox of the church that it conceals the Kingdom of God as well as reveals it. Secondly, church history has one quality which shines through even its most distorted phases: ". . . it has in itself the ultimate criterion against itself—the New Being in Jesus as the Christ." Consequently, "the presence of this criterion elevates the churches above any other religious group, not because they are 'better' than others, but because they have a better criterion against themselves and, implicitly, also against other groups."[76] The struggle of the Kingdom of God within history is above all a struggle within the bosom of its own representatives, for the reformation of a profanized and demonized church is never ended.

Church history, however, judges not only itself, but also non-church history or world history. The influence of church history upon world history is seen where "it produces an uneasy conscience in those who have received the impact of the New Being but follow the ways of the old being."[77] Church history is not the

Kingdom of God, but the Christian civilization which it begets is a continual reminder of it.

ESCHATOLOGY: THE KINGDOM AS THE END OF HISTORY

Within world history the Kingdom of God is realized whenever political power is justly exercised, whenever constructive social growth occurs, whenever a healthy tension is maintained between temporal and eternal aspirations, and whenever the sacrifice of an individual leads to his own fulfilment.[78] However, the fragmentary nature of these victories raises the question of the non-fragmentary, total realization of the Kingdom of God, the question of the end of history.

The word "end" can mean both "finish" and "aim." It is the second meaning that poses the eschatological problem, not the cessation of clock time which is an event in the physical order.[79] The last inner-historical day is the *eschata* so poetically depicted in apocalyptic literature, but it is the singular *eschaton*, the transhistorical goal of history, about which theology concerns itself. The end of history thus becomes an immediate existential problem, for the eternal goal of history underlies every moment of time. The *eschaton* "symbolizes the 'transition' from the temporal to the eternal, and this is a metaphor similar to that of the transition from the eternal to the temporal in the doctrine of the fall, and from existence to essence in the doctrine of salvation."[80]

To forestall needless confusion, it should be noted that, for Tillich, the aim of history can be symbolized by any one of three symbols: the Kingdom of God, the Spiritual Presence, and Eternal Life.[81] The only distinction is by degrees of connotation. The Kingdom of God connotes equally the inner-historical and the transhistorical fulfilment of history, while the Spiritual Presence stresses the inner-historical, and Eternal Life stresses the transhistorical aspect.

From the Temporal to the Eternal

"Eschatology deals with the relation of the temporal to the eternal" in the sense of the elevation into Eternal Life of the new created by history.[82] This fulfilment of history does not take place on the last day of time, when one steps from this earthly realm into a heavenly realm that is an idealized reduplication of historical life, as popular imagination and theological supranaturalism would have us believe. Rather, the end of history is always present to us, cutting into our temporal existence and elevating it to the eternal. We live in two orders, the historical and the eternal, and, although they are not identical, they are within each other, for "the eternal order reveals itself in the historical order."[83] In opposition to a supranaturalistic eternity with eternal places and beings, Tillich holds that "the transcendent cannot be expressed in terms of being but only in terms of meaning,"[84] for "if any present has meaning it has eternity."[85] To put it another way, Eternal Life, the ever-present end of history, "includes the positive content of history, liberated from its negative distortions and fulfilled in its potentialities."[86] Eternal Life, then, has two characteristics: unification and purification.

Unification means that the dispersed embodiments of meaning in historical activities and institutions have an invisible, supra-historical unity, that they belong to an ultimate meaning of which they are radiations. And purification means that the ambiguous embodiment of meaning in historical realities, social and personal, is related to an ultimate meaning in which the ambiguity, the mixture of meaning and distortion of meaning, is overcome by an unambiguous, pure embodiment of meaning.[87]

In the more concrete words of one of Tillich's sermons, "There is something immovable, unchangeable, unshakeable, eternal, which becomes manifest in our passing and in the crumbling of our world."[88]

Judgment: Exclusion of the Negative

We first consider the negative aspect of the transition from the temporal to the eternal, the exclusion of negativities and ambiguities. The Greek word for judgment, *krinein,* indicates the separation of the negative symbolized by the ultimate judgment.[89] Tillich reminds us that this judgment is not a temporal event, for time is only the form of the finite, and eternity is its inner aim, or *telos.* To explain this continuous process, he has recourse to "a bold metaphor." Eternal life is likened to "eternal memory" in which the positive is remembered and the negative forgotten.[90] But since forgetting implies a moment of remembering, the negative is forgotten in the sense that it is acknowledged and rejected for what it is, nonbeing.

"Since Eternal Life is identical with the Kingdom of God in its fulfilment, it is the non-fragmentary, total, and complete conquest of the ambiguities of life. . . ."[91] The ambiguities that accompany the life processes of self-integration, self-creativity, and self-transcendence are overcome by the perfect balancing of the ontological polar elements: individualization-participation, dynamics-form, and freedom-destiny. Consequently, in the fulfilled Kingdom of God morality, culture, and religion disappear as special functions.[92] There is no morality because there is no ought-to-be which is not. There is no culture because the work of the human spirit becomes the work of the divine Spirit. And there is no religion because there is no estrangement, and God is everything in and to everything. Unambiguous, non-fragmentary fulfilment is the result of the purification of the last judgment.

Essentialization: Inclusion of the Positive

The exclusion of the negative does not suffice to explain the elevation of the temporal to the eternal. If Eternal Life is eternal memory, what is remembered? The core of the problem is how "the positive in the universe is the object of eternal memory."[93] Tillich's solution is a modified concept borrowed from Schelling and Plato: "essentialization," "a return to what a thing essentially is."[94] It does not mean a simple return to essence or potentiality by sloughing off everything accrued in existence, for on this supposition history produces nothing new, and life is only a futile process of falling away from and returning to a static essence.

Having repudiated this interpretation, Tillich proposes his own understanding of essentialization:

But the term "essentialization" can also mean that the new which has been actualized in time and space adds something to essential being, uniting it with the positive which is created within existence, thus producing the ultimately new, the "New Being," not fragmentarily as in temporal life, but wholly as a contribution to the Kingdom of God in its fulfilment.[95]

The return to essence is thus not a simple return after an interlude of meaningless existence, but a return that is a fulfilment through the realization of potentialities within historical existence. Essentialization is the return of a being to an enriched essence, to New Being. Consequently, "participation in the eternal life depends on a creative synthesis of a being's essential nature with what it has made of it in its temporal existence."[96] Essentialization applies to every being of the universe; all things participate in Eternal Life according to their enriched essence.[97]

Thus far, Eternal Life has been discussed in general terms, for it is the *telos* of all of creation. However, the destiny of the individual person requires special treatment, for his relation to Eternal Life is qualified by the fact that he alone is aware of his *telos* and is free to reject it. Estrangement witnesses to man's turning away from Eternal Life at the same time that he aspires to it. Essentialization, therefore, is dialectical. Thus, "the *telos* of man as an individual is determined by the decisions he makes in existence on the basis of the potentialities given to him by destiny."[98] The freedom of each man differs from the freedom of every other man due to the conditioning of their respective concrete destinies. Moreover, although man can recklessly squander his potentialities, some of them will be fulfilled, just as he will never realize all of them, even though he ambitions total fulfilment. In other words, there are "degrees of essentialization," a sliding scale of Eternal Life which contradicts the absolute interpretation of symbols such as heaven and hell, eternal death and eternal bliss.

However, despite the relativity of essentialization, the seriousness of the failure to attain Eternal Life is not diminished. For essentialization is not an automatic restitution, and what is restored can either exceed or fall short of the original created essence. Falling short of total essentialization is a waste of potentialities that brings with it a corresponding measure of despair.

On the basis of essentialization Tillich vigorously denies double predestination and, in fact, tends in the opposite direction toward "the doctrine of universal essentialization."[99] The individual is never essentialized in isolation. He always participates in a community, his spirit depends upon a physical and biological foundation, and his freedom is inextricably implicated with his temporal destiny, so that it becomes impossible to separate his individual eternal destiny from the destiny of mankind and of the whole universe. This doctrine of universal essentialization can be applied to that area of the problem of evil where men are prevented from achieving fulfilment because of premature death or destructive environments. The solution is "vicarious fulfilment," which is explained as follows:

. . . in the essence of the least actualized individual, the essences of other individuals and, indirectly, of all beings are present. Whoever condemns anyone to eternal death condemns himself, because his essence and that of the other cannot be absolutely separated. And he who is estranged from his own essential being and experiences the despair of total self-rejection must be told that his essence participates in the essences of all those who have reached a high degree of fulfilment and that through this participation his being is eternally affirmed.[100]

The essentialization of man is the end of history. It has nothing to do with the temporal duration of the world. If history were to end tomorrow, it would still have eternal significance, because "the depth of all things became manifest in *one* being, and the name of that being is *man*, and you and I are men! . . . there is one man in whom God found his image undistorted, and who stands for all mankind—the one, who for this reason, is called the Son and the Christ."[101]

Immortality and Resurrection

The individual's participation in Eternal Life is also expressed through the biblical symbol of resurrection and the symbol of immortality borrowed from the Greeks. In regard to immortality, Tillich isolates and discards the popular, superstitious view which pictures it as an indefinite prolongation of temporal life without a body. Eternal life does not signify "endless time" or "life hereafter," but rather, "a quality which transcends temporality."[102] The matter is further complicated if one speaks of "the immortality of the soul," for this introduces a dualism between soul and body and contradicts the biblical symbol "resurrection of the body." Error can be avoided only if the immortality of the soul is understood as "the power of essentialization."[103] Historically, misunderstandings about immortality have arisen because the distinction was not made between symbol and concept. As symbol, immortality means "the experience of ultimacy in being and meaning."[104] As concept, it refers to the existence and nature of the soul as a particular object, a purely philosophical and scientific question. Both Catholic and Protestant theologians imagined they were defending a religious *symbol*, but actually the attacks of Locke, Hume, and Kant were against the *concept* of a naturally immortal substance. To grasp this distinction is to liberate Eternal Life from "its dangerous connection with the concept of an immortal soul."[105]

Against the misleading symbol "immortality," Tillich prefers the symbol "resurrection of the body." Its advantage is that it negates the dualism of a merely spiritual existence. However, body must be taken in the Pauline sense of a "Spiritual body": "Spirit—this central concept of Paul's theology—is God present to man's spirit, invading it, transforming and elevating it beyond itself. A Spiritual body then is a body which expresses the Spiritually transformed total personality of man."[106] The resurrection of the body means that the whole personality participates in Eternal Life. "If we use the term 'essentialization,' we can say that man's psychological, spiritual, and social being is implied in his bodily being—and this in unity with the essences of everything else that has being."[107]

But does resurrection of the body as essentialization do justice to the uniqueness of the individual? Tillich answers affirmatively and adduces an interesting example from the visual arts—portraits: "It is not one particular moment in the life process of an individual that they reproduce but a condensation of all these moments in an image of what this individual essentially has become on the basis of his potentialities and through the experiences and decisions of his life process."[108] A portrait pictures a unique individual, but in an essentialized fashion.

Both immortality and resurrection lead to the question of individual self-consciousness in Eternal Life. Tillich maintains that the most that can be offered by way of explication is two negative statements. First, the self-conscious self cannot be excluded from Eternal Life, because selfhood is the polar condition for participation, and because consciousness is needed for spirit. Secondly, the self-conscious self "is not the endless continuation of a particular stream of consciousness in memory and anticipation."[109] Self-consciousness, as we know it, depends on temporal change, but there is no time in eternity. Anything beyond these negative statements is poetic imagination.

Eternal Life is life in God. The phrase "in God" bears several closely related meanings which trace the rhythm of history. The creature is eternally in God as its creative origin, for its potentialities are rooted in the divine ground of being. Again, even in the state of existential estrangement the creature is in God as its ontological supporting power. Finally, the creature is in God when it achieves "the 'in' of ultimate fulfilment, the state of essentialization of all creatures."[110] Tillich graphs the Greek interpretation of history as a circle, the Augustinian as a straight line, and his own as a curve that moves forward from creation, but downward toward existence, then rises upward and forward to essentialization.[111]

Creation and eschatology are but two sides of the same coin. The meaning of the "where from" is grasped only in the "where to," and the "where to" is determined by the nature of the "where from."[112] The goodness of creation makes possible an eschatology of fulfilment, and eschatalogical fulfilment imparts meaning to creation. Thus, the beginning and the end coalesce: "Creation into time produces the possibility of self-realization, estrangement, and reconciliation of the creature, which, in eschatological terminology, is the way from essence through existence to essentialization."[113] But we are not obliged to wait indefinitely for resurrection into Eternal Life:

Resurrection is not an event that might happen in some remote future, but it is the power of the New Being to create life out of death, here and now, today and tomorrow. Where there is a New Being, *there* is resurrection, namely, the creation into eternity out of every moment of time. . . . Resurrection happens *now*, or it does not happen at all. It happens in us and around us, in soul and history, in nature and universe.[114]

REFLECTIONS AND APPRAISAL

Tillich's theology of history situates theonomy, the union of religion and culture, within its historical dimensions. Theonomy does not exist in the tranquillity of a vacuum, but must be fought for in the arena of time and space. But even the partial achievement of theonomy, ambiguous and fragmentary as it may be, serves, in turn, as a point of reference for gauging the rhythm of history:

History comes from and moves toward periods of theonomy, i.e., periods in which the conditioned is open to the unconditional without claiming to be unconditioned itself. Theonomy unites the absolute and the relative element in the interpretation of history, the demand that everything relative become the vehicle of the absolute and the insight that nothing relative can ever become absolute itself.[115]

These partial victories of theonomy are the inner-historical side of the Kingdom of God. However, its transcendent side, total realization of theonomy, is beyond temporality. Theonomy is not utopia. By specifying the transcendent goal of history as essentialization, Tillich offers his most meaningful statement of the content of theonomy. Perfect theonomy is universal essentialization. In Eternal Life the potentialities of man's creative spirit are fulfilled. Man's essence, along with the essences of all creatures, becomes fully transparent to the eternal ground of being. God and man are reunited.

"Stimulating" is probably the best adjective to describe Tillich's interpretation of history. The sweep and vigor of his thought offers a richly developed theology of history to those who accept it, and a formidable challenge to those who criticize it. Perhaps his most original contribution is the concept of *kairos*. Erich Przywara sees in it the key to Tillich's thought, for the *kairos Christi* is the supreme conflict between the divine and the demonic in which the Kingdom of God overcomes and takes up into itself the Kingdom of Satan.[116] R. Allan Killen claims, "The *kairos* idea lies behind Tillich's concept of correlation in his formulation of theology. It is the idea that there is a time in which certain things are true and other times in which they do not apply."[117] This accounts for the changing norms of theology.

The implications of the *kairos* concept probably can be expanded to accommodate these viewpoints, but ambitious claims for its importance should not obscure its primary role in the interpretation of history. *Kairos* is the carefully prepared "timing" of the manifestation of the New Being either in the original great *kairos* in Jesus the Christ or in secondary *kairoi* throughout history. *Kairos* is "situational appositeness" in the words of Przywara,[118] and it lends dignity and meaning to those historical periods which are not immediately implicated, but which prepare for it. Every age takes on a *kairos* quality insofar as it creates anew the meaning of all ages.[119] Furthermore, *kairos* is the call to that personal commitment to historical activity which alone enables one to experience at first hand the currents of history, and thus to interpret their direction. Tillich's involvement in Religious Socialism was his personal response to what he was convinced was an imminent *kairos*.

Despite the unquestionable value of much of Tillich's theology of history—the *kairos* concept, the subject-object structure of history, the group as opposed to the individual or mankind as the bearer of history, the creation of the new as one of the marks of historical time, the inner-historical and transcendent nature of the Kingdom of God—there is still a certain incompleteness about it. One is more puzzled about what he does not say than about what he actually says. There are several major instances where his reticence is disappointing.

The first and foremost is the doctrine of essentialization which we highlighted in the expository part of this chapter, but which Tillich casually introduces as the answer to certain objections. In reality, essentialization is the vital link between his Christology and his theology of history. Jesus the Christ is the center of history, that is to say, the *place* where the meaning or goal of history is revealed. But *what* is the goal that is revealed? It is New Being, essentialized manhood. In Jesus the Christ the New Being appeared within history, and the New Being is also the transcendent aim toward which history progresses. Yet Tillich neglects to weld together the Christological and the eschatological aspects of the New Being. What does the appearance of the New Being in Jesus the Christ contribute to universal essentialization? Is the New Being of Jesus a model according to which men are to pattern their lives, or is there a deeper significance to the historical manifestation of the New Being? This is the question of the historical dimension of soteriology, and, although Tillich may have an implicit response, the question cries for an explicit answer which he does not provide.[120] To put it another way, he does not relate our resurrection to the resurrection of Jesus, a relationship which is fundamental to St. Paul, and thus his eschatology is left, as it were, dangling in mid-air.

Even granted the connection between Christology and eschatology, a further problem remains unsolved: the reunion of God and man through essentialization. How is essentialized man, to say nothing of the essentialized universe, restored to the ground of being? Tillich admits the legitimacy of the question:

Inasmuch as we have been pushed by the consistency of thought as well as by the religious expression in which fulfilment is anticipated to the identification of Life Eternal with the Divine Life it is appropriate to ask about the relation of the Divine Life to the life of the creature in the state of essentialization or in Eternal Life. Such a question is both unavoidable, as the history of Christian thought shows, and impossible to answer except in terms of the highest religious-poetic symbolism.[121]

But he backs away from a direct answer and is content with a mere reference to the Trinity and to the essential creativity of God. The Tillichian system is a symmetrical, carefully constructed arch, and it is precisely at this point that we expect to see inserted into place the keystone which is universal essentialization. But the arch is not joined, and so we are never quite sure that the missing keystone really does fit.

It is a recurrence of the Christological question—How are God and man united in Jesus?—and of the ecclesiological problem—How are the divine and human elements of the church united? The question now takes an eschatological form: How are God and man reunited by essentialization in Eternal Life? If man fulfills his human essence, does that suffice to gain Eternal, Divine Life? In other words, we must know more than Tillich tells us about the scope of human potentialities and the transcendent nature of the Godhead.

Another surprising omission in Tillich's eschatology is the absence of a treatment of death, the event which marks the end of an individual's temporal existence. Death is one of the "four last things" of eschatology, for its inevitability and radical decisiveness makes it loom large in the perspective of finality. He touches on death when he describes the existential conditions of estrangement, because death represents the absolute threat of nonbeing.[122] However, he has no place for it within the eschatological framework.

We surmise that behind Tillich's indifference to death is a certain indifference to time itself, a certain "ahistorical" attitude. The death of an individual is a datable, inner-historical moment which, because of its absoluteness, immediately broaches the question of its transhistorical significance. Tillich's attention is always focused upon this transhistorical aspect, and consequently, the inner-historical phenomenon of death fades into the background. The same is true in his doctrine of creation and final consummation. Creation is the state of essential potentiality, not an event in time. The last day is a symbol for the end of history, not the moment when the universe ceases to exist. To a certain extent, and a very large extent at that, this separation of time and finality is justified, especially since the goal of history is not to be attained within time. Furthermore, even if the first day and the last day are moments within time, they are completely shrouded from us in the mists of the past and the future.

But granted all this, is it completely realistic to make such a radical division between the temporal and the final? The fact is that mankind did not always exist within time, and we have no guarantee that it will always continue to exist. This basic fact of human contingency is dramatized by the birth and death of the individual. It has always been the Christian tradition that, within the time allotted to an individual, he determines the substance of his eternity.[123] Thus, death not only marks the end of the influence of time upon eternity, but it can also be considered the summation of a man's life. His death, therefore, is an awesome event. The same principle applies to the birth and death of the universe. Its birth is the beginning of time, and its end is not only the end of time, but its consummation. The death of the universe, too, is an awesome event. But all this supposes that time is terrifyingly important, for it is the inception of eternity, the stairway to Eternal Life. Death is, at the same time, both the culmination of time and the rude reminder that time runs out.

Even in statements in which Tillich attaches an existential urgency to time, he does so in an "ahistorical" fashion: "Beginning from and ending in the eternal are not matters of a determinable moment in physical time but rather a process going on in every moment, as does the divine creation. There is always creation and consummation, beginning and end."[124] Is it not precisely in a "determinable moment of physical time"—for example, the life, death, and resurrection of Jesus, our own death, the beginning and end of the world—that the uniqueness, the irreversibility, and hence the historic nature of time brings its full weight to bear? We are here faced with a curious twist in Tillich's thought: concern for the meaning of history leads him to downgrade historical moments.

Within Tillich's eschatology it is possible to show how his fascination with universal essentialization gradually results in depreciating the moment of death. In his concern to make the here-and-now eternally significant, his attention is riveted upon the goal of history which lends meaning to the historical process. He appreciates the suffering and the drama of man's struggle to attain the essentialization which is Eternal Life. Nothing which is gained in the struggle is ever lost, for there are degrees of essentialization, so that no one is completely excluded from Eternal Life. The suggestion is finally made of a transhistorical fulfilment which renders death no longer absolutely decisive for eternity.[125]

As a result of Tillich's stress upon the transhistorical aspect of creation and consummation, upon the universality—one is tempted to say the inevitability—of essentialization, a certain "ahistorical" quality of timelessness is introduced into his notion of history, which may well account for his failure to consider death as truly eschatological. The accent upon the eternally present goal of history may overshadow the seriousness and the dignity of specific moments of the historical process. There is a danger that he does not see the trees for the forest, that eternity undercuts time.[126]

The third instance of a somewhat awkward silence on Tillich's part is the problem of the afterlife which involves the symbols immortality of the soul and resurrection of the body. The question of the "when" of unambiguous, non-fragmentary participation in the Kingdom of God is a legitimate one, and it leads to the question of the "after." Tillich comes closest to the heart of the problem when he discusses individual self-consciousness in eternity, but he limits himself to two negative statements: the self-conscious self cannot be excluded from Eternal Life, and self-consciousness in Eternal Life is not the same as in temporal life. The symbol resurrection of the body sheds even less light, for again only two negative statements are permissible about the resurrected "Spiritual body": it is not purely spiritual, and it is not simply material. Tillich adds to the crescendo of silence by a severe criticism of the traditional doctrine of the immortality of the soul, by passing over non-Platonic notions of the soul, by failing to provide his own explanation of the soul, and by not bothering to treat the stock objection of individual annihilation. On the basis of such scant evidence, it is difficult either to affirm that he has a positive doctrine of individual, self-conscious persistence in being after death or to deny it. But the problem seems too important to leave unresolved, for it constitutes the substructure of any doctrine of Eternal Life.

Tillich's silence on the eschatological problems of essentialization, death, and immortality is disconcerting. On at least five major points (eternal memory, resurrection of the body, the self-conscious self, eternal life and death, and the nature of eternity) he explicitly restricts himself to purely negative statements, and holds that anything more would be poetry.[127] However, such a stand ill befits an apologetic, answering theology whose method of correlation is geared to respond to existential questions. Eschatological questions are the most existential of all, and Tillich's neglect to provide more positive answers makes his *Systematic Theology* terminate on an unresolved chord instead of with the resolution of the harmony of correlation.

These reflections, however, do not mean that Tillich's eschatology has nothing to offer. It is a striking coincidence that, shortly before his death, Tillich delivered two superb addresses upon eschatological themes: one on the possibilities of peace on earth, the inner-historical realization of the Kingdom of God; the other on man's right to hope for Eternal Life. He concludes the first with the realistic appraisal that "we cannot hope for a final stage of justice and peace within history; but we can hope for partial victories over the forces of evil in a particular moment of time."[128] The second ends by establishing hope upon the foundation of faith, the experience of the holy.

And now we ask the question of our personal participation in the eternal. Do we have a right to hope for it? The answer is: We have a right to such ultimate hope, even in view of the end of all other hopes, even in the face of death. For we experience the presence of the eternal in us and in our world here and now. . . . Where this is experienced, there is awareness of the eternal, there is already, however fragmentary, participation in the eternal. This is the basis of the hope for eternal life. It is the justification of our ultimate hope. And if as Christians we point to Good Friday and Easter, we point to the most powerful example of the same experience.[129]

We began with the search for Tillich's union of religion and culture. We found it in theonomy. Part I described its structure as the interpenetration of substance and form: religion is the substance of culture, and culture is the form of religion. Part II explicated the content of theonomy. At its base is God as the ground of being, but reunion with the ground can be had only through the power of the New Being which overcomes the estrangement of existence. Reception of the New Being in turn begets the theonomous community which is the Spiritual Community, but it is subject to the historical dimension. Theonomy is fully achieved only in the transcendent Kingdom of God where universal essentialization is realized.

Structure and content, however, are somewhat mechanical devices. We must now attempt to capture the depth, the breadth, and the vitality of Paul Tillich's theological vision which engendered the concept of theonomy.

Notes

1. PE, xiii.
2. RS, 81, 82–3.
3. Our interpretation of what Tillich means by the historical dimension is based upon ST, III, 11–28, 297–99, and IH, 272–73.
4. ST, III, 300–302.
5. *Ibid.*, 302.
6. *Ibid.*, 302–306.
7. *Ibid.*, 304.
8. *Ibid.*
9. *Ibid.*, 306.
10. *Ibid.*, 308–13. See also IH, 251–54.
11. ST, III, 308.
12. *Ibid.*, 310.
13. *Ibid.*, 311–12.
14. IH, 194–96, and PE, unabridged edition, 239.
15. ST, III, 341.
16. *Ibid.*, 312. See also ST, II, 58–59, 135–36.
17. ST, III, 312.
18. *Ibid.*, 313.
19. He attributes to space the element of "beside-each-other-ness." The reciprocal influence of time and space upon each other is one of his favorite themes. See "The Struggle Between Time and Space," TC, 30–39, and ST, III, 315–21.

20. ST, III, 319.
21. SF, 37.
22. IH, 278–79.
23. *Ibid.*, 280.
24. *Ibid.*, 276–77.
25. ST, III, 320.
26. *Ibid.*, 333–39, and IH, 272–75. See also his essay, "The Decline and the Validity of the Idea of Progress," *The Future of Religions,* Jerald C. Brauer (ed.), New York: Harper & Row, 1966, 64–79.
27. IH, 273.
28. *Ibid.*, 282.
29. ST, III, 339.
30. *Ibid.*, 339–42.
31. *Ibid.*, 343–44.
32. *Ibid.*, 344–46.
33. *Ibid.*, 344.
34. ST, III, 349.
35. *Ibid.*
36. *Ibid.*
37. *Ibid.*, 350.
38. *Ibid.*
39. *Ibid.*, 350–52.
40. *Ibid.*, 352–56.
41. *Ibid.*, 353.
42. *Ibid.*
43. *Ibid.*, 354.
44. *Ibid.*, 355.
45. *Ibid.*, 356.
46. *Ibid.*, 356–61.
47. *Ibid.*, 357.
48. *Ibid.*, 358.
49. *Ibid.*, 359–61.
50. *Ibid.*, 363.
51. *Ibid.*, 364.
52. Cf. IH, 242–65.
53. *Ibid.*, 250.
54. ST, III, 364.
55. *Ibid.*, 365.
56. *Ibid.*
57. *Ibid.*, 366.
58. *Ibid.*, 368–69.
59. *Ibid.*, 369. Tillich applies the notion of *kairos* not only to history, but also to ethics and even to the problem of knowledge. See PE, 155–56, and "Kairos and Logos," IH, 123–75.
60. ST, III, 369–70, and PE, 33.

61. ST, III, 370.
62. PE, 46–47.
63. ST, III, 370–71.
64. PE, 43.
65. *Ibid.*, 44.
66. *Ibid.*, xv–xvi.
67. *Ibid.*, xvi.
68. ST, III, 371.
69. *Ibid.*
70. *Ibid.*, 375.
71. *Ibid.*, 377.
72. *Ibid.*, 377–78.
73. *Ibid.*, 378.
74. *Ibid.*, 378–81.
75. *Ibid.*, 381.
76. *Ibid.*
77. *Ibid.*, 384.
78. *Ibid.*, 385–93.
79. *Ibid.*, 394. See also *ibid.*, 307, and ST, II, 120.
80. ST, III, 395.
81. *Ibid.*, 298.
82. *Ibid.*
83. SF, 23. See also NB, 120, and RS, 160.
84. "The Kingdom of God and History," in *The Kingdom of God and History,* Vol. III of the Church, Community, and State Series, London: George Allen and Unwin, 1938, 113. In this essay the essential lines of Tillich's interpretation of history are already well marked out.
85. RS, 35.
86. ST, III, 397.
87. "The Kingdom of God and History," 113.
88. SF, 9.
89. ST, III, 398.
90. *Ibid.*, 399–400.
91. *Ibid.*, 401.
92. *Ibid.*, 402–403.
93. *Ibid.*, 400.
94. *Ibid.*
95. *Ibid.*, 400–401.
96. *Ibid.*, 401.
97. *Ibid.*, 405.
98. *Ibid.*, 406.
99. *Ibid.*, 408.
100. *Ibid.*, 409.
101. EN, 76.
102. ST, III, 410. See also CB, 55, 169, and EN, 114–15, 124–25 where

Tillich describes what he considers to be the erroneous, commonplace notion of immortality.

103. ST, III, 410.

104. *Ibid.*

105. *Ibid.*, 411. See also SF, 137–38, 166–67.

106. ST, III, 412.

107. *Ibid.*, 413.

108. *Ibid.*

109. *Ibid.*, 414.

110. *Ibid.*, 421.

111. *Ibid.*, 419.

112. *Ibid.*, 299.

113. *Ibid.*, 422.

114. NB, 24.

115. PE, 47.

116. "Christian Root-Terms: *Kerygma, Mysterium, Kairos, Oikonomia*," O'M and W, 197, 202–204.

117. *The Ontological Theology of Paul Tillich*, 210. See also *ibid.*, 211.

118. "Christian Root-Terms: *Kerygma, Mysterium, Kairos, Oikonomia*," O'M and W, 202.

119. GW, VII, 240.

120. George Tavard observes about Tillich's Christology of history: "It is the *meaning* he assigns to history that leaves us still hungry and thirsty: we thought that we were being prepared for more." *Paul Tillich and the Christian Message*, 105. See also *ibid.*, 103–105.

121. ST, III, 421.

122. See CB, 42–45, and ST, II, 66–68.

123. We are speaking of the ordinary case of adults; one cannot build an eschatology around the death of infants, although eschatology must eventually account for them.

124. ST, III, 420. See also NB, 24.

125. ST, III, 416–18.

126. Many commentators have noticed this "ahistorical" tendency in Tillich's thought. See Nels F. S. Ferré, "Tillich's View of the Church," K and B, 263; Gustave Weigel, "Myth, Symbol, and Analogy," O'M and W, 191; J. Heywood Thomas, *Paul Tillich: An Appraisal*, 156; R. Allan Killen, *The Ontological Theology of Paul Tillich*, 230; and Gordon D. Kaufman, "Can a Man Serve Two Masters?" *Theology Today*, XV, April, 1958, 74–75.

127. All that can be said about *eternal memory* is that the positive is not forgotten, and the negative is not remembered, ST, III, 399–400; about the *resurrected Spiritual body*, that it is not purely spiritual, and not material, *ibid.*, 412; about the *self-conscious self in eternity*, that there is no temporal consciousness, *ibid.*, 414; about *eternal life and death*, that there is no threat of eternal death, but no security of return to essentialization, *ibid.*, 416; about *eternity*, that it is not timeless identity, and not permanent change, *ibid.*, 417.

128. Paul Tillich, *Pacem in Terris* (address delivered at the *Pacem in Terris* Convocation, Feb. 18, 1965, New York City), *Criterion* (University of Chicago), IV, No. 2, 1965, 18.

129. Paul Tillich, "The Right to Hope" (sermon delivered April 25, 1965), *Neue Zeitschrift für systematische Theologie und Religionsphilosophie* (Berlin), VII, No. 3, 1965, 376.

Conclusion
The Vision of Paul Tillich

THE ROOT MEANING of the word "conclude" is "to shut in" or "to enclose." We propose, therefore, to gather together the principal themes of Tillich's theology which best express the content and structure of theonomy. But at the same time, to enclose something connotes the exclusion of something else. Consequently, a number of other possible views are first considered in order to narrow down the elements essential to Tillich's own vision, just as one tries on many eyeglasses before finding the proper lens. Furthermore, since to conclude also means to come to a decision, our own appreciations of and reservations about his theology are likewise presented. Lastly, an attempt is made to assess Tillich's theological significance.

TYPES OF VISIONS: THE CHRIST-CULTURE RELATIONSHIP

The relationship of Christianity to culture is one of the enduring theological problems of the centuries. To its innate complexities must be added the nuances supplied by a long list of theologians who reflect differing spiritualities and the different demands of their periods of history. Out of this welter of solutions certain classic types emerge with more or less constant characteristics. It

282

is an immediate and understandable temptation to classify a theologian according to known types—for example, eschatological, incarnational, or a mixture of the two—but the subtlety of thought, with its overtones of emphasis and undertones of implication, usually frustrate such attempts at pigeonholing. Typology, however, if properly understood, can be used to sift the significant kernels of thought from the chaff of peripheral reflections, provided that a sufficient number of types be successively employed. Hence, by submitting Tillich's theonomy to the sifting process of comparison and contrast with recognized types, we hope to catch the residue of its basic elements.

To establish types which are not crude caricatures is, in itself, a large undertaking. We rely here upon the work of H. Richard Niebuhr, whose book *Christ and Culture* provides a very usable typology for the relationship of Christianity to civilization.[1] Niebuhr himself is the first to admit that types are partly artificial constructions, but this fact does not detract from their usefulness:

A type is always something of a construct, even when it has not been constructed prior to long study of many historic individuals and movements. When one returns from the hypothetical scheme to the rich complexity of individual events, it is evident at once that no person or group ever conforms to a type. . . . The method of typology, however, though historically inadequate, has the advantage of calling to attention the continuity and significance of the great *motifs* that appear and reappear in the long wrestling of Christians with their enduring problem.[2]

Thus we know in advance that Tillich's solution very probably does not fit any of the types proposed by Niebuhr. Yet, in the process of determining where it does and does not correspond, we gradually progress toward our objective of bringing into sharper focus Tillich's theological vision and ultimately his significance.

Niebuhr divides the views on the relationship of Christianity to civilization into three general groups: the type that opposes Christ to culture; the type that identifies Christ and culture; and the median types that unite and balance the other two.

Christ against Culture

The first type is summed up as "Christ against culture."[3] It is the radical interpretation of the declaration of Jesus: "My kingship is not from the world" (Jn 18:36, *RSV*). The lordship of Christ is supreme, and the world must be subjected to it. Consequently, in this view the gospel dominates reason, nature is suspect, culture is sinful, and one must be guided by the Spirit whose presence is guaranteed only by puritanical moral conduct. The Christ-against-culture people tend to band together in a rigidly exclusive community to shun the world. They are exemplified in history by Tertullian, St. Benedict, the Mennonites, and Tolstoy. The inadequacies of this radical type are patent, but Niebuhr points out that its necessity in some form or other cannot be denied:

The movement of withdrawal and renunciation is a necessary element in every Christian life, even though it be followed by an equally necessary movement of responsible engagement in cultural tasks. Where this is lacking, Christian faith quickly degenerates into a utilitarian device for the attainment of personal prosperity or public peace; and some imagined idol called by his name takes the place of Jesus Christ the Lord.[4]

Tillich obviously does not fit the Christ-against-culture type, but it forces the question: What is his principle of renunciation which safeguards the transcendence of the gospel message? It is the Protestant principle. George Tavard distinguishes the positive side of the Protestant principle, an immediate awareness of God that does not depend upon any one necessary intermediary, from the negative side which protests the demonic exaltation of any being over the ground of being.[5] The Protestant principle in this negative sense stands against culture whenever a cultural form usurps for itself the dignity of ultimacy. Thus, the Cross, the symbol of the

Protestant principle, never judges culture as such, but only its demonic distortions.

The Christ of Culture

The second type which Niebuhr presents is diametrically opposed to the anti-culture type. It is the camp of the pro-culture people, those who "feel no great tension between church and world, the social laws and the Gospel, the workings of divine grace and human effort, the ethics of salvation and the ethics of social conservation or progress."[6] They interpret culture through Christ and Christ through culture. They establish this harmony by selecting the best elements of civilization and matching them with the eternally true, rational principles exemplified in Christianity. The conflict in the world is not between man and God, but between nature and the human spirit, and Jesus Christ is the spearhead of the struggle to master nature and incorporate it within culture. Niebuhr cites the Christian Gnostics, Abelard, and Albrecht Ritschl as representatives of the Christ-of-culture group. Ritschl, in particular, stands for the rationalistic, liberal movement of the nineteenth century which Niebuhr prefers to call "cultural Protestantism."

The merit of the Christ-of-culture type is that "as a perennial movement the acculturation of Christ is both inevitable and profoundly significant in the extension of his reign."[7] Imitating St. Paul, it strives to make Christianity all things to all men to gain them for Christ. There are, however, several objections to the Christ-of-culture position. First, it constructs apocryphal gospels by exclusive attention to a single trait of Jesus, such as spiritual knowledge, reason, a sense for the infinite, the moral law, or brotherly love. The result is that "loyalty to contemporary culture has so far qualified the loyalty to Christ that he has been abandoned in favor of an idol called by his name."[8] Secondly, the cultural Christian dilutes the radical power of sin by explaining it as ignorance, superstition, or stupidity which is dispelled by the pure light of reason refracted through Christ. Finally, cultural Christianity is embarrassed by the doctrine of grace because it seems to demean the natural goodness of human nature.

Tillich's theonomy has deep affinities to the Christ-of-culture type in the sense of a close union between Christ and culture and the acculturation of Christ by the method of correlation. Nevertheless, his theological career began with a rejection of liberal or cultural Protestantism. He replaces its moralizing tendencies with an ontological approach that considers Jesus the Christ as the bearer of the New Being. He starts with the existential fact of universal estrangement, and so recognizes the power of sin to tear the cultural fabric asunder. And, lastly, his theonomy is based on the all-pervading influence of grace which grasps the human spirit in an ultimate concern and reveals the religious depths of cultural creations.

Tillich moves in the same direction as cultural Protestantism, but at a much deeper and more realistic level. The cultural Christians operate at the level of morality; Tillich, at the level of ontology. They are content with the essential harmony of Christ and the world, but he stresses existential estrangement. They are confident in the power of man's rational spirit, while he relies upon the grace of the divine Spirit.

Christ above Culture

The more common solution to the Christ-and-culture problem is to unite somehow the extremes of the first two types. This center position, therefore, acknowledges the goodness of creation, the radical character of sin, the necessity of human cultural activity, and the primacy of grace. But the reconciliation of these opposing principles can be achieved in several different ways.

One way is by a synthesis of the two, which Niebuhr terms the Christ-above-culture type. According to the synthetic view, there is "a gap between Christ and culture that accommodation Christianity never takes seriously enough, and that radicalism does not try to overcome."[9] Its starting point is the doctrine that Jesus did not come to abolish the law and prophets, but to fulfill them. It is exemplified in history by the theology of Clement of Alexandria and Thomas Aquinas. The synthesist holds that grace builds on and perfects nature, that the Creator and the Savior are one. Christ is above culture as its fulfilment and crown.

Tillich is in sympathy with the synthesist's drive for unity between Christ and culture and with his insistence upon grace. However, the unity is effected by a vertical structuring that is divided into layers, and this is repugnant because it resembles the natural-supernatural framework which he detests. The synthesist regards cultural efforts here below as a mere propaedeutic for the culmination of Christianity in a future afterlife. Furthermore, as Niebuhr observes, the synthesist tends to view his own culturally conditioned synthesis as absolute, so that the Christ who is above culture as its fulfilment has been first whittled down to the proportions of the prevailing culture. The result is a cultural conservatism which, to Tillich, is akin to idolatry.

Christ and Culture in Paradox

Another attempt to preserve the "both-and" of Christ and culture is a dualism which holds them together in paradox. The dualist begins with two absolute principles: grace is in God, and sin is in man, and there is no bridging the chasm. He differs from the synthesist in that he sees a deeper and more extensive corruption of man and culture, but over this human depravity is cast the cloak of divine forgiveness and reconciliation in Jesus Christ. As examples of this motif, Niebuhr refers to St. Paul, Marcion, and especially Luther. The latter distinguishes but does not divide the Kingdom of God from the kingdom of the world. The dualism is spanned by attributing to Christ the spirit or the *how* of moral action, but leaving to an autonomous culture the *what* of the content: "From Christ we receive the knowledge and the freedom to do faithfully and lovingly what culture teaches or requires us to do."[10] Although sinful culture stands under the condemnation of God, the same divine authority commands us to participate in it. Hence the paradox of Christ and culture.

Tillich would agree with Niebuhr's estimate that this dualistic paradox corresponds to the human experience in which man is forever bumping up against the prevalence of sin, and yet always receiving the gift of grace. However, this heavily negative paradox is alien to Tillich's positive paradox as evidenced in the method of correlation. The dualist's position inclines also to a cultural conservatism because it does not contribute to the content of culture, but views social and political institutions as bulwarks against sin rather than as positive agencies for good. On this score, too, Tillich does not fit the dualistic type, for his theonomy demands a positive, religious substance in culture.

Christ the Transformer of Culture

The final type considers Christ as the transformer of culture. It maintains the dualist's notion of the radical corruption of man's works, but is more optimistic in its hope that culture can be converted to Christ. The conversionist does not view creation as merely a necessary prologue to the atonement, but as a positive proof that culture has never been destitute of the directive power of Christ, even though it is shot through with sin. Culture must be converted to Christ, and this takes place within the here-and-now of history where eschatology is a present demand instead of a promise of the future. Niebuhr finds the conversionist motif exemplified in the Fourth Gospel, in St. Augustine, and in the nineteenth-century Anglican theologian F. D. Maurice.

Of all the Christ-and-culture types discussed, Tillich is closest to the conversionist type. With him, it stresses the essential goodness of creation, its existential sinfulness, and its transformation within the historical dimension by the eschatological immediacy of grace. Tillich's position, however, has certain nuances which set him off from the conversionists. In their separation of creation from the fall and in their view of history as a constantly upward movement he would probably see the taint of progressivism. By his notion of *kairos* not all moments of history are equally important, but there are certain privileged intervals of grace. Furthermore, the here-and-now realization of the Kingdom of God is always subject to the ambiguities of its inner-historical character. The transformation of culture opens the door to its demonization, and thus there is greater need for the Protestant principle.

After sifting Tillich's theonomy through the screen of typology, we are left with a residue of orientation that forms the basis of his distinctive vision of the relation of Christianity to civilization. His Protestant principle and the omnipresence of ambiguity supply the negative element demanded by the Christ-against-culture type. The shallowness of the Christ-of-culture type does not take estrangement seriously enough. Tillich fits into the center group in general, but on particular points he differs from them. The Christ-above-culture type, with its thinking in layers, is foreign to his thinking in dimensions. The dualistic type effects a paradoxical but superficial union between Christ and culture which nowhere aproaches the profundity of theonomy and correlation. And, finally, Tillich tends more toward the conversionist type, except for its optimism which smacks of progressivism.

TILLICH'S VISION: CHRIST THE DEPTH OF CULTURE

Following the pattern of the preceding types, Tillich's vision of theonomy can best be summed up as "Christ the depth of culture." What sets him off from the other types is the metaphor "depth." Christ as the depth of culture signifies a close union between the two, the union of substance with form. But religious substance lies at the depth of cultural form, a depth not always visible or attainable due to the currents of estrangement. The depths can be fathomed only in the depth-experience which is faith. It is the impact of the divine Spirit which drives man beyond the shallow surface life of autonomous secularism to the depth-dimension where he encounters the New Being. In the New Being he finds the teleological meaning of his life and the spiritual power to fulfill it.

Tillich's vision, then, comprises three elements: Christ, depth, and culture. They represent the three major themes of his theology: the New Being, ultimate concern, and man.

A Vision of New Being

Useful as Niebuhr's categories are, there is one point at which they do not quite fit Tillich's thought. It is the term "Christ." "Christ," for Niebuhr, refers to the person Jesus Christ and his message which is Christianity. Moreover, he defines Christ in strictly moralistic terms by the virtues of love, hope, obedience, faith, and humility.[11] Tillich, on the contrary, never uses "Christ" as a personal name, but always as a title or symbol. Furthermore, against an ethical interpretation, he explains the Christ in metaphysical terms. His vision, therefore, although it includes Jesus of Nazareth, penetrates through and beyond him to the New Being which he manifests. Here we have the content of Tillichian faith: "that Jesus is the Christ, the bringer of the New Being."[12]

Tillich's unabashed reliance upon ontology has made him the hope and despair of his fellow theologians. Although some of them praise his metaphysical approach,[13] most of them complain that it produces an abstract Christianity which scarcely resembles the religion of the Bible.[14] The dispute about ontology is really a dispute about method. Does the method of correlation require ontological categories? And, more fundamentally, is the method of correlation completely adequate?

Even on Tillich's supposition that theology is "apologetic" and that theological answers must be couched in the form determined by the existential questions, the application of this principle may yield different results. His analysis of the human situation convinces him that man's problems are basically ontological. There is something unassailable in this position, for ontology, by definition, deals with ultimates. Although one may flee ontology, one can never quite escape it, since everyone possesses some kind of ontology, albeit in an inchoate and disguised form. However, the fact must be faced that we live in a non-metaphysical age, and it may be unrealistic to describe man's existential situation in ontological terms when he could not care less about ontology. To do so seems even to violate the method of correlation, for the theological answers are then clothed in the ontological forms so unappealing to modern man. Tillich, of course, is aware of this problem, and he attempts to solve it by coupling traditional metaphysical terminology to moral and psychological terminology. He invigorates the dry bones of being, finitude, essence, existence, potentiality, actuality, and teleology by interpreting them in terms of courage, power, anxiety, estrangement, fulfilment, and the ambiguities of life. Whether this procedure is a happy wedding of metaphysics to psychology or a betrayal of one or the other is a problem which we leave to the philosophers to decide.[15] At any rate, it indicates Tillich's awareness that pure ontology is too strong a medicine for the modern palate.

But if the questions arising out of the human situation are not ontological, what are they? When one reflects upon man's existential condition, the mind is positively staggered by the enormity and complexity of the task. Who is competent to venture into "all areas of culture" in order to formulate man's basic problems? Yet this is what the method of correlation requires:

The analysis of the human situation employs materials made available by man's creative self-interpretation in all realms of culture. Philosophy contributes, but so do poetry, drama, the novel, therapeutic psychology, and sociology. The theologian organizes these materials in relation to the answer given by the Christian message.[16]

The only way such a project could conceivably be executed would be to suppose from the beginning that all these cultural areas are ultimately rooted in ontology. From the vantage point of his already developed ontology, Tillich then interprets the domain of culture and, at the same time, confirms his original ontological insights. The results of his existential analysis, therefore, depend upon the validity of his ontology, for he claims that the human situation is structured according to his basic metaphysical concepts. Correlation on the scale envisioned by Tillich is feasible only if it is an ontological correlation.

The other option, consequently, is to dispute his starting point, namely, the apologetic nature of theology and the method of correlation. Karl Barth feels strongly that the direction of correlation should be reversed so that the theologian proceeds from revelation to the human situation:

Should not the theological answers be considered as more fundamental than the philosophical questions and as essentially superior to them? If they were so considered, then the question and answer would proceed, not from a philosophically understood subject to a "divine" object, but rather from a theologically understood object (as the true Subject) to the human subject, and thus from Spirit to life, and the Kingdom of God to history. Such a procedure would not actually destroy the concept of correlation, but would probably apply to it the biblical sense of "covenant." This application, however, is unknown in Tillich.[17]

Barth's observation is correct insofar as Tillich's method of correlation neglects the fact that existential questions arise not only from the human situation, but also from the very presence of divine revelation. Revelation is an unmerited gift, and we can never be sure that our human questions exhaust its riches.[18] Man is not merely a questioner. He is also a hearer of the Word, and he must open himself to its full impact even when it communicates startling truths, such as the Trinity, or hard truths, such as divine punishment, things he might not ask about if the question were left to him alone to formulate. Furthermore, the question-answer dialogue is not the sole means to express the human attitude before the revelatory events. Question and answer are, after all, but figures of speech, and their limitation is seen in this, that the mystery of divine revelation can be described in other terms. It is not only an answer; it is also a fulfilment, a transformation, an elevation, and a gratuitous intervention. Man stands before revelation not simply to play the quizmaster; he stands before it as before the sun, to be cheered and warmed and inspired. In the transfiguration episode all that Peter could utter was, "Lord, it is well that we are here!" (Mt 17:4, *RSV*). Man does more than question; he also exclaims in cries of marvel, of wonder, of awe. Tillich's method of correlation directs a constant stream of question marks at the Christian revelation, but they should be balanced by a few exclamation points.

The kerygmatic aspect of theology must be given its due. As one author says of correlation, "It can still only create the impression that it succeeds, but it can never fully succeed, since the receptacle which is the question remains the old wineskin that is burst by the new wine of the answer."[19] The new wine is the kerygma, the divine good news which far surpasses human expectations. Consequently, the bad news of man's existential situation cannot be the measure of the good news of revelation. In fact, it is revelation that lays bare the roots of the human condition by revealing the true nature and extent of sin, for the bad news of the existential situation is itself a mystery that needs unveiling.

The merits and demerits of Barth's kerygmatic and Tillich's apologetic method can be argued interminably, for neither is sufficient if taken by itself. As one author points out, it is more important to see where they agree, namely, they both strive to liberate theology from a narrow outlook, Tillich by penetrating to the ontological level underlying all philosophies, and Barth by remaining on the kerygmatic plane above them all:

Tillich and Barth may be regarded as two opposite poles on the same axis of modern theological understanding. Both have written theologies in full awareness of the passing of *Weltanschauungen* in which particu-

lar theologies are always written: Tillich establishing correlation between the *kerygma* and what he believes on theological-philosophical
grounds to be implicit in every world view; and Barth trying to point
toward that in the Church proclamation which is always different from
any world view. The former has as its danger the threat of being
swamped in generalities, and the latter that of babbling in tongues.
That is to say, Tillich's formalized criteria run the risk of being made
to contain almost anything, but Barth's wholly material, concrete event
of Jesus Christ risks being so particularistically understood as to be
discontinuous with life and culture and thus irrelevant. Neither man
welcomes either risk, but each prefers his own fate to theology at the
hands of the other![20]

This discussion of theological method originated when we
attempted to assess the validity of Tillich's ontological view of
theology. His vision, however, is not primarily that of a new
method, but of the New Being in Jesus the Christ. The most
serious charge laid at his door is that he "ontologizes" the Christian mysteries, that is, he reduces them to purely philosophical
principles.[21] For example, creation means that being is essentially
good, the fall or estrangement means that man is a finite mixture
of being and nonbeing, and the New Being means that man
always participates in being enough to offset the threat of nonbeing.

Leaving aside the other examples, we consider the New Being:
Is it anything more than a philosophical principle? The New
Being is essential manhood, the complete actualization of human
potentialities, the term of the historical process of the essentialization of man, the final reunion with the ground of being. Is this
merely an ontological humanism? Otto Wolff pinpoints the problem by the parable of the prodigal son:

The lost son who returned home is not simply once again at home.
He is at home again in a way other than the fondest remembrance of
his father's house had possibly permitted him to hope, other than the
human existential question had possibly permitted him to expect. The

father had acted against expectation and beyond all expectation. The New Being that he found is other and more than mere reunion.[22]

We find it difficult simply to reject Tillich's doctrine of the New Being. It would be a loathesome chore, indeed, to set about proving that Jesus the Christ does not bring us New Being, that he does not represent the perfect essentialization toward which we strive. But, at the same time, we cannot rest satisfied with it. Tillich's Christological problematic does not show how Jesus is united to God, nor does his eschatological problematic show how man is united to God in Eternal Life. He tells us that in Jesus essential manhood appeared and that our destiny also is to realize essentialized humanity. But revelation insists that Jesus is the Son of God and promises that we shall become sons of God. Perhaps essential manhood and divine sonship are equivalent, but Tillich does not explain how. The being of man and the being of God are different, and grace is needed somehow to account for their mysterious union. If this is supernaturalism, so be it. But the problem demands a solution, and we do not think Tillich's is entirely adequate.

The charge of ontologizing is also encouraged by Tillich's tendency to slight the historical Jesus in favor of the New Being. Barthel calls attention to Tillich's ambivalent attitude toward the historicity of Jesus: on the one hand, it is of supreme importance because the New Being appeared in Jesus, but, on the other hand, the Christ would in no way be affected if no trace of the historical Jesus could be found. This ambivalence is explained by the fact that "for Paul Tillich, Jesus of Nazareth is the historical locale of a particularly striking upheaval of a creative ontological dynamism. . . ."[23] The New Being was manifest in Jesus, but not identified with him. Thus, after the resurrection the power of the New Being is just as operative as it was before the moment of the incarnation, but Jesus lies dead in the tomb. Such an interpretation tends to make Jesus expendable, once he has manifested the eternal principle that being overcomes nonbeing. If the timeless

New Being overshadows the historical Jesus, there is danger that an impersonal principle may replace the personal intervention of God.

In summary, Tillich's vision of the New Being imparts a metaphysical profundity and stability to his system. However, it is questionable if the method of correlation necessarily demands an ontological analysis of the human situation. Moreover, the very question-answer structure of the method is limited. Certainly theology must speak intelligibly to man, but revelation far outstrips the range of human questions. Finally, the separation of the New Being from Jesus runs the risk of depersonalizing the New Being and of making Jesus superfluous.

A Vision of Ultimate Concern

Tillich's vision of Christ as the depth of culture includes not only the New Being, but also the means to reach it. "The depth" signifies "the depth-experience" or "the experience of the depths" which is faith. Faith as ultimate concern is the portal through which one must pass in order to attain New Being.

There is not a single major doctrine in Tillich's systematics which is not grounded in faith as the experience of ultimate concern. In the area of theological method, it is ultimate concern which admits the theologian to the theological circle, the norm of theology is the New Being as his ultimate concern, and the experience of ultimate concern is the theological medium. The central concepts of religion and revelation are governed by faith as ultimate concern. Theonomous culture is a structure of form and substance, and the substance is the ultimate experience of the ground of being. God is the ground of being, but he is encountered only in the experience of the holy, and all religious symbols take their origin from this experience of ultimacy. Jesus is the Christ only because he is received as such by faith, and he rose from the dead only because his disciples had an ecstatic experience of the New Being. The Spiritual Community is created by the Spiritual Presence which drives man's spirit beyond itself into faith and love. The Protestant principle which constitutes the essence of Protestantism is based upon an experience of God who jealously demands that ultimacy be reserved for him alone. Finally, the Kingdom of God breaks through into history in a faith-charged moment that is the *kairos*. In a word, ultimate concern is the nervous system of the body of Tillich's theology.

But Tillich views faith as more than a foundation for the doctrines of a system; he sees faith everywhere in the world as an operative reality. The universality, or omnipresence, of faith is the common ground upon which he stands in order to conduct dialogue with both non-Christian religions and secular movements.

In trying to relate Christianity to the world, to preach it to non-Western civilizations, or to discover religious elements in secular activities, the theologian has two possible approaches. The first approach would begin with what Tillich calls "material faith," that is, the Christian faith. A study of Scripture and the history of the church is undertaken in order to isolate the minimum essentials of Christian faith. Then one turns to a particular situation—a culture, an historical period, a political or social movement—to see if and how these essential notes of faith are verified there. This approach appears to have been the one followed by theologians when a developed European Christianity started encountering non-Christian and non-Western civilizations, and it is valid enough. The difficulty is that the categories it uses may not do justice to the situation. For instance, can a tribe be said to be without faith if it lacks the notion of a supreme being? Similarly, the religious aspects of social upheavals may be missed because one looks for the wrong labels.

The other approach can be called the "formal" approach, and it is Tillich's way. He presumes that faith is active at all times and all places simply because man has such need of it. From the prehistoric caveman to the modern atheistic technocrat, man was never deserted by God's grace which brings salvific faith. To describe this omnipresent faith, including even a distorted one, Tillich uses ultimate concern, a concept simple yet profound enough to cover the incredible variations of man's religious sentiments. He does not look at a human situation and wonder if faith is there. He knows it is there, and finds it by attuning himself to the ultimate concern which throbs beneath the surface. Of course, he will have to be aware of the demonic in the guise of the divine, but his approach gets him into the heart of a strange or even hostile situation with a minimum of reserve and a maximum of sympathy.

This formal approach is, however, open to several questions. First of all, an adequate understanding of faith demands that one eventually pass from formal faith to material faith in order to put content into it. However, for Tillich the content of faith is the New Being, and this ontological orientation raises the question: Is he a philosopher of religion or a Christian theologian? It is possible to make a good case for the defense of Tillich's title of theologian as opposed to philosopher of religion. One might compare him to Thomas Aquinas or Francis Suarez who wrote extensively on philosophical subjects, but their ulterior purpose was always to gather and organize this data to elucidate the Christian mysteries. Furthermore, although Tillich theoretically distinguishes between philosophy and theology, on his own principles it is practically impossible to distinguish the philosopher from the theologian because they both deal with the ultimates of being. At times Tillich may seem to function as a philosopher of religion, as when he deals with the religions and quasi-religions of the world, but he strives to place them within the larger context of preparatory revelation and to explain their dynamics by the dialectic of heteronomy, autonomy, and theonomy. Both context and dialectic have their ultimate explanation in the grace of faith and in the New Being in Jesus the Christ. His analysis of religions and secular ideologies is always governed by the criterion of the Cross of the Christ. And the faith which he finds in them is the state of being grasped by an ultimate concern; it is produced by the Spirit, not by human activity.

These arguments demonstrate that Tillich is more than a philosopher of religion. However, they do not exculpate him from a lack of precision about the specifically Christian content of his theology. For instance, he leaves unresolved the grave problem of what George Tavard calls "the selectivity" of faith, that is to say, according to biblical evidence faith separates the believers from the non-believers. As Tavard observes, "The faith of Paul Tillich is the exact opposite. Instead of erecting the holy community out of the world, it sees the whole world as already being the holy community. Nobody escapes it. All, even unawares, belong to it. Is this still the Christian faith?"[24] Again, for example, the urgency of the missionary effort of the church stems from the fact that there is a difference between Christian and non-Christian faith, between faith and absence of faith. Yet, because of his ontologically based, universalistic approach, the content of Tillich's key doctrines, such as the New Being, faith, and the Spiritual Community, is hard to pin down. The resulting advantage is a versatility and applicability which enables him to deal with the history of religions and modern secularism with ease and assurance. But the danger is that the very fluidity of these doctrines makes them into conceptual rubber bands, shapeless forms that can be stretched to fit any content.

However, even this is not without value. One can say that Tillich brilliantly exposes the possibilities of faith, but without explaining faith itself. Perhaps two levels can be distinguished in faith: the level of search and the level of discovery. The level of search is the formal aspect of faith, its dynamics, and this is Tillich's strong suit. The level of discovery is the material aspect of faith, its content, and here he is found wanting. The Christian message must indeed become all things to all men, but it must also be itself.

Tillich's vision of faith also includes the Protestant principle, for it is born in the experience of the ultimacy of God. One can scarcely overestimate the importance of the Protestant principle in his theology. Its roots can be traced back to the experience of the holy as the *mysterium tremendum et fascinosum.* God's very presence forces the acknowledgement of the infinite gulf between him and the creature. In ontological terms, because God is the ground of being, he is also the abyss of being in that he can never be contained within the narrow confines of a finite form of being. The Protestant principle, therefore, reserves ultimacy to God, the ground of being, and denies it to beings. This is the meaning of the Cross of Jesus the Christ, for Jesus as a being sacrificed himself to the New Being. Symbols which originate in and express the experience of faith remain subject to the criterion of the Cross. Victory over religious heteronomy, over the demonization and profanization of the churches, also lies in the sign of the Cross. The very essence of Protestantism is the Protestant principle. Moreover, history is purified of progressivistic and utopian elements by its prophetic No. Eschatology must provide for both the inner-historical and the transcendent aspects of the Kingdom of God in order to reflect both the Yes and the No of the Protestant principle. In brief, the Protestant principle is a radical conception of justification by faith alone: only grace effects salvation, and anything that infringes upon this divine prerogative must be met with prophetic protest.

The Protestant principle, then, is the permanent guardian of divine transcendence which Tillich unleashes against a religion or a culture that claims ultimacy for itself. As such, it performs an indispensable negative function. However, one sometimes wonders if his praiseworthy zeal to safeguard divine prerogatives degenerates into a "watch dog" mentality that actually restricts God's saving activity and imprisons him within the ineffability of his own transcendence. To take a concrete example, the church beside the town hall is, for Tillich, a painful reminder of man's sinful estrangement. But is it not more accurate to view it with gratitude as a sign of God's saving intervention? Tillich's pessimism about ecclesiastical ambiguities completely blots out the hope which their very existence should engender. Another example is that of the sacraments. Despite his elaboration of the Gestalt of grace, the sacramental principle, and the Catholic substance, Tillich nowhere gets down to cases and develops the theology of a particular sacrament such as Baptism. What holds him back, we surmise, is the fear of objectifying grace, and so he immediately invokes the Protestant principle. Just as he accepts sacraments in general, but neglects them in particular, so he waxes enthusiastic about the Spiritual Community, but is pessimistic about the churches. Since the sacramental principle of the individual sacraments and of the church, the *Ursakrament*, eventually goes back to Christ himself as the primordial sacrament, we are not surprised that he concentrates upon the New Being, but has little to say about Jesus. In more traditional terms, he puts all the emphasis upon the *res* to the detriment of the *sacramentum*.

But emphasis or attitude can be quite important. Certainly we have need of the prophetic protest of the Protestant principle, but to employ it too often and too stridently can make us wary of moments and channels of grace. It can become a principle of hesitation that enervates the drive of our commitment. It can paralyze our religious life by the haunting fear that concrete religious symbols, institutions, and apostolates are inevitably condemned to demonization and profanization. Everyone knows that religion has its human, erroneous, even sinful side, but this awareness should never undercut our confidence that God's grace can reach us, even though conveyed in vessels of clay. Prophecy, in the sense of protest, is a delicate business indeed.

To summarize this section, Tillich's vision of the depths is a vision of an omnipresent faith as ultimate concern, and from this same experience of ultimacy is derived the Protestant principle.

A Vision of Man

A word remains to be said about the last term in the phrase "Christ the depth of culture." "Culture" is a rather general term, and what it really refers to is man, for culture is the fruit of the creative activity of man.

Commentators are quick to point out that Tillich's thought crystallizes around man. The doctrine of the microcosm is the first obvious example. One author states, "The major presupposition of Tillich's thought is the idea of the microcosm. . . . His whole thought system is founded upon this concept; to reject it is to reject the whole."[25] Another says that Tillich makes man the primary analogue for understanding the relation of God to the world: just as man is related to the different dimensions of existence by being both transcendent and immanent to them, so the unconditioned is related to the whole of existence in the same way.[26] Another lauds *Systematic Theology* for being "a magnificent essay in religious anthropology."[27]

There is no doubt that man is one of the poles around which revolves the whole of Tillich's system. He conceives the role of theology as that of mediating between the human situation and divine revelation, and the method of correlation demands that the answers of theology be clothed in the language of man's existential condition. The all-important concept of faith is defined in terms of man's experience of and need for the unconditioned. Tillich strives to establish contact with every area of culture, for it is the expression of the human spirit. In and through man he perceives the basic ontological structure of self-world upon which rests his metaphysics. Jesus the Christ is meaningful because in him appears the New Being which heals man's estrangement. The Spiritual Community is explained on the basis of man's quest for unambiguous life. And, finally, the eschatological fulfilment of the universe is accomplished in the essentialization of man, for in him is found the unity of the multiple dimensions of life.

In a certain sense any Christian theology is anthropocentric, for the Creed declares that Jesus Christ came down from heaven for us men and for our salvation. But this general orientation around human salvation can be specified in different ways. One could hold, for example, that sin is the problem of man, for man must be saved from sin; or that grace is the problem of man, for man is saved through grace; or that morality is the problem of man, for man is saved by leading a morally good life; or, finally, that faith is the problem of man, for the way to salvation is illumined by the light of faith. Tillich, however, is more radical than these other approaches. He maintains that man is the problem of man, for salvation is achieved only if man becomes what he essentially is. This fulfilled man is the New Man; he possesses New Being. Furthermore, according to the doctrine of the microcosm and the multidimensional unity of life, the universe itself is saved in the salvation of man.

Unquestionably, one of Tillich's most significant contributions is his effort to construct a theological anthropology. But he avoids an ivory-tower, progressivistic humanism by accenting the reality of estrangement, and his insistence upon the role of the divine Spirit as the origin of faith preserves him from a purely human humanism. The allegation that he is obsessed with ontology invariably overlooks the fact that he builds his ontology by reflecting upon man. The fundamental ontological structure of self-world and the ontological polarities (individualization-participation, dynamics-form, and freedom-destiny) are not only anthropocentric, but even, to a certain extent, anthropomorphic.

Christ as the depth of culture expresses Tillich's vision that inspired him to develop his concept of theonomy and so relate religion to culture. But the vision must be interpreted in the light of the whole system. When this is done, Christ the depth of culture is translated to mean that New Being is the ultimate concern of man. The New Being provides ontological breadth, ultimate concern imparts experiential depth, and the anthropological emphasis gives vitality to his vision of Christ as the depth of culture.

THE SIGNIFICANCE OF PAUL TILLICH

The significance of a contemporary theologian is never easy to assess, for the necessary historical distance is lacking. In Tillich's case, his influence has had a delayed impact due to the fact that his emigration to the United States forced him, at the age of forty-seven and in mid-career, to master a foreign language, insert himself into a different culture, and cope with an entirely new intellectual climate. It is only now, with the gradual translation of his works, that he is becoming better known on the Continent. But even in the United States, where the major part of his writings were produced, there does not seem to be any Tillichian school of thought left behind by the master. Indeed, his own principles and example militate against such a school, for, faced with any great system or thinker of the past, he invariably pronounced a Yes and a No.

However, the absence or presence of a Tillichian school is by no means a decisive criterion. The impact of a man's thought can be estimated from two different but closely related viewpoints: externally, from the way it attracts people and holds their interest; internally, from the inherent value and timeliness of its content. We conclude our study by attempting to describe Tillich's significance from these two points of view.

An Honest-to-God Theologian

Obviously, one cannot take a world-wide poll of student and professorial opinion, but the recent Honest-to-God debate in England provides a useful external measure of Tillich's influence. John A. T. Robinson, Anglican bishop of Woolwich, sparked a remarkable controversy by the publication of his little book *Honest to God* in March, 1963. His personal, urbane, and frank discussion of the problem of being a Christian in a secular age touched the minds and hearts of hundreds of thousands of his countrymen. He states the problem quite clearly:

. . . I believe we are being called, over the years ahead, to far more than a restating of traditional orthodoxy in modern terms. Indeed, if our defence of the Faith is limited to this, we shall find in all likelihood that we have lost out to all but a tiny religious remnant. A much more radical recasting, I would judge, is demanded, in the process of which the most fundamental categories of our theology—of God, of the super-natural, and of religion itself—must go into the melting.[28]

There is nothing theologically novel in *Honest to God,* and due to brevity of treatment many of its assertions are vulnerable. However, it is very pertinent to us for two reasons. First, Robinson relies very heavily upon the theology of Paul Tillich along with that of Bonhoeffer and Bultmann. Secondly, the book caused a sensation out of all proportion to its strictly theological merit— over 350,000 copies sold, translation into seven languages, intense and prolonged newspaper coverage, and a whole series of tele-vision programs. Robinson was lauded as a prophet and de-nounced as an atheist. Somehow he touched an exposed nerve.

The impact of *Honest to God* is undeniable; what interests us here is Tillich's role in it. In a later essay in which he reflects upon the causes of the Honest-to-God ferment, Robinson points out four areas in which modern secularism requires a recasting of traditional theology.[29] It is precisely in these areas that he found Tillich's thought pertinent and utilized it. The first is the possibility of metaphysics in a secularized world. Here Robinson takes no position, but only raises the question. However, if metaphysics still has a function to fulfill in the theological enter-prise, then Tillich is at hand as an experienced guide, and if it does not, then he confronts the anti-metaphysical theologian as a formidable adversary. The second area is that of the supranatural. If the supranatural is an outdated mode of thought, although the divine transcendence is still to be retained, then Tillich's doctrine of the ground of being and his concept of the multidimensional unity of life is quite apropos. The third area is the confrontation between the scientific secular mind and the mythological biblical mind. Here his theory of religious symbolism has much to con-tribute, for his "de-literalization" of myths is based upon modern biblical science, and yet retains the myth as a necessary human symbol of the divine. The last area in which secularization demands a reformation of theology is religion. Tillich's distinction between the narrow and the broad sense of religion enables him to cope with the question of worldly holiness, for he does not recognize religion as a special function of the human spirit.

In all the principal areas, then, in which secular man expects a recasting of Christianity—theological metaphysics, supranaturalism, mythology, and religion—Tillich has a great deal to say. And Robinson's astounding success in mediating Tillich's thought demonstrates that there are large numbers of people who are eager to hear it.

A Theologian of Synthesis

Tillich's vital, though indirect, role in the Honest-to-God controversy provides an external yardstick to measure the capability of his thought to generate a response. But his significance is primarily to be weighed by the inherent worth of what he attempts to do, for the immediate external success of being accepted and followed depends upon the internal success of his system.

In searching for a way to describe the over-all characteristic of the structure of his theology, we propose what Tillich himself says about the nature of Christianity:

... early Christianity did not consider itself as a radical-exclusive, but as the all-inclusive religion in the sense of the saying: "All that is true anywhere in the world belongs to us, the Christians." And it is significant that the famous words of Jesus, "You, therefore, must be perfect, as your heavenly Father is perfect" (which was always an exegetic riddle), would, according to recent research, be better translated, "You must be all-inclusive as your heavenly Father is all-inclusive."[30]

Tillich's theological endeavor is animated by the drive to be all-inclusive. In other words, he is a theologian of synthesis, not necessarily with any connotation of idealistic philosophy, but in the sense that he strives to unite many elements into a constructive, creative synthesis.[31] In terms of time, he synthesizes the nineteenth century with the twentieth, classical ontology with modern personalism, essentialism with existentialism, liberal theology's concern for culture with socialism's demand for radical reform, tradition with modernity.[32] In terms of space, he synthesizes not only the Old World with the New World, but, as Mircea Eliade so eloquently testifies, Tillich's latest interest up to the very day of his death was to bridge the gap between Western Christianity and Eastern religions.[33] In terms of content, he synthesizes religion and culture, for his basic vision is that the Christ is the depth of culture, that New Being is the ultimate concern of man.

As a theologian of synthesis, Paul Tillich is especially significant today when the pressing problem of Christianity is how to construct a synthesis which includes the secular world. In describing the task before the church, he describes his own contribution to it:

With respect to the secular world, the defense against secularism—this is now the great issue—must not be a narrowing down. The church must take the secular into itself and transform it, as the old church did when it took all the great values of both the classical Greek and the Hellenistic realm into itself, besides the basic Jewish strain. This also occurred in the Middle Ages with the Germanic-Romanic tribes; the church took them in. And I do not see any other way of reinvigorating Christianity.[34]

Finally, Tillich's qualities of all-inclusiveness and synthesis make him *par excellence* an "ecumenical" theologian.[35] This is not to say that he is a "compromise" theologian who is acceptable to widely differing Christian confessions. Writing from a Roman Catholic point of view, we have been forced to stand our distance from him on a number of points due to an occasional lack of precision in his thought, an unacceptable emphasis, or an outright disagreement. And many of his fellow Protestants react in the same way, but, of course, not always for the same reasons. Nevertheless, Paul Tillich is an ecumenical theologian, for his system is not a narrow denominationalism, but a broad Christian synthesis that has room for the Protestant principle and the Catholic substance, angry protest and ineffable mysticism, the demons of primitive religions and the technology of industrial society. One finds in Paul Tillich an intellectual stimulation and a spiritual inspiration that enlarges one's view of and love for the world and the Christ.

The only fitting way to terminate this study is to permit Paul Tillich the honor of the last word. On October 12, 1965, the day before the heart attack which was to bring about his death ten days later, he delivered a lecture entitled "The Significance of the History of Religions for the Systematic Theologian." It strikingly symbolizes the end of a distinguished career in the theological enterprise. But, more incredibly in view of his age and his own highly developed systematics, it points beyond itself in true Tillichian fashion to a future synthesis of all the religions of the world in a "Religion of the Concrete Spirit." He states:[36]

First, one must say that revelatory experiences are universally human. Religions are based on something that is given to a man wherever he lives. He is given a revelation, a particular kind of experience which always implies saving powers. One never can separate revelation and salvation. There are revealing and saving powers in all religions. God has not left himself unwitnessed.

But now my last word. What does this mean for our relationship to the religion of which one is a theologian? Such a theology remains rooted in its experiential basis. Without this, no theology at all is possible. But it tries to formulate the basic experiences which are universally valid in universally valid statements. The universality of a religious statement does not lie in an all-embracing abstraction which would destroy religion as such, but it lies in the depths of every concrete religion. Above all, it lies in the openness to spiritual freedom both from one's own foundation and for one's own foundation.

To the very end Paul Tillich is characterized by the breadth of his vision and the depth of his commitment.

Notes

1. H. Richard Niebuhr, *Christ and Culture*, New York: Harper and Row, paperback, 1956 (first published 1951).
2. *Ibid.*, 43–44.
3. *Ibid.*, 45–82.
4. *Ibid.*, 68.
5. "The Protestant Principle and the Theological System of Paul Tillich," O'M and W, 85–86.
6. *Christ and Culture*, 83.
7. *Ibid.*, 101–102.
8. *Ibid.*, 110.
9. *Ibid.*, 121.
10. *Ibid.*, 175.
11. Cf. *Christ and Culture*, 14. Niebuhr admits that his viewpoint is that of the moralist. See *ibid.*, 15–29 for the description of Christ's virtues.
12. ST, III, 174.
13. See for instance Gérard Siegwalt, "La théologie systématique de P. Tillich," *Revue d'Histoire et de Philosophie Religieuses*, XLI, 1961, 177–83. Siegwalt exclaims that *Systematic Theology* surpasses most dogmatic publications of the last one hundred and fifty years. *Ibid.*, 174.
14. Cf. for example Jean-Paul Gabus, "La théologie systématique de P. Tillich," *Revue d'Histoire et de Philosophie Religieuses*, XXXV, 1955, 473–477.
15. A serious study of William L. Rowe concludes that Tillich's ontology is not valid because it is meaningful "only when understood in quasi-psychological terms." *An Examination of the Philosophical Theology of Paul Tillich*, University of Michigan: dissertation, 1961, 211.
16. ST, I, 63.
17. "Introductory Report," Alexander J. McKelway, *The Systematic Theology of Paul Tillich*, 13.
18. See Otto Wolff, "Paul Tillichs Christologie des 'Neuen Seins,'" *Neue Zeitschrift für systematische Theologie*, III, 1961, 131.
19. *Ibid.*, 140.
20. Edward A. Dowey, Jr., "Tillich, Barth, and the Criteria of Theology," *Theology Today*, XV, April, 1958, 57.
21. See George Tavard, *Paul Tillich and the Christian Message*, 50, 79, 137, and Avery Dulles "Paul Tillich and the Bible," O'M and W, 131. Pierre Barthel shows how Tillich's correlation of human questions and revelatory symbols is achieved by reducing both to the lowest common ontological de-

nominator. *Interprétation du Langage Mythique et Théologie Biblique,* 152–98.

22. "Paul Tillichs Christologie des 'Neuen Seins,'" *Neue Zeitschrift für Systematische Theologie,* III, 1961, 137–38.

23. Pierre Barthel, *Interprétation du Langage Mythique et Théologie Biblique,* 169.

24. *Paul Tillich and the Christian Message,* 38–39.

25. David H. Hopper, "Towards Understanding the Thought of Paul Tillich," *The Princeton Seminary Bulletin,* LX, April, 1962, 42–43.

26. R. H. Daubney, "Some Structural Concepts in Tillich's Thought and the Pattern of the Liturgy," K and B, 273.

27. Kenelm Foster, "Paul Tillich and St. Thomas," O'M and W, 105.

28. John A. T. Robinson, *Honest to God,* Philadelphia: Westminster Press, 1963, 7.

29. John A. T. Robinson, "The Debate Continues," *The Honest to God Debate,* David L. Edwards (ed.), Philadelphia: Westminster Press, 1963, 232–75.

30. CEWR, 35–36.

31. The synthetic quality of his work has been remarked on by many commentators. See, for example, Robert Clyde Johnson, "A Theologian of Synthesis," *Theology Today,* XV, April, 1958, 36–42; Kenelm Foster, "Paul Tillich and St. Thomas," O'M and W, 97; Lewis Stanley Foster, *The Ontological Foundation of Paul Tillich's Theory of the Religious Symbol,* Yale University: dissertation, 1962, iii; Gustave Weigel, "Contemporaneous Protestantism and Paul Tillich," *Theological Studies,* XI, 1950, 177–202; and Gérard Siegwalt, "La théologie systématique de P. Tillich," *Revue d'Histoire et de Philosophie Religieuses,* XLI, 1961, 191–92.

32. See Noriyoski Tamaru, "Motiv und Struktur der Theologie Paul Tillichs," *Neue Zeitschrift für systematische Theologie,* III, 1961, 38.

33. See "Paul Tillich and the History of Religions," in *The Future of Religions,* Jerald C. Brauer (ed.), New York: Harper and Row, 1966, 31–36.

34. *Ultimate Concern: Tillich in Dialogue,* D. Mackenzie Brown (ed.), New York: Harper and Row, 1965, 94–95.

35. René Marlé, "Paul Tillich," *Cahiers Universitaires Catholiques* (Paris), Dec., 1965–Jan., 1966, 136–37.

36. *The Future of Religions,* Jerald C. Brauer (ed.), New York: Harper and Row, 1966, 81, 94.

Bibliography

(Only the material actually cited or referred to in this study)

TILLICH BIBLIOGRAPHIES

Albrecht, Renate (ed.), *Paul Tillich: Gesammelte Werke*, Band I, Stuttgart: Evangelisches Verlagswerk, first edition, 1959, 389–427. (Complete bibliography of Tillich's works up to 1959.)

Ford, Lewis Stanley, *The Ontological Foundation of Paul Tillich's Theory of the Religious Symbol*, Yale University: dissertation, New Haven, 1962, 251–64. (Especially useful for secondary sources, in particular the dissertations on Tillich.)

Kegley, Charles W., and Bretall, Robert W. (eds.), *The Theology of Paul Tillich*, New York: Macmillan, paperback, 1961 (first published 1952). (Selective bibliography of Tillich's works up to 1952.)

Leibrecht, Walter (ed.), *Religion and Culture: Essays in Honor of Paul Tillich*, New York: Harper and Brothers, 1959, 367–96. (Most elaborate and complete bibliography of Tillich's works up to 1959.)

BOOKS BY PAUL TILLICH

Tillich, Paul, *Biblical Religion and the Search for Ultimate Reality*, Chicago: University of Chicago Press, 1955.

———, *Christianity and the Encounter of the World Religions*, New York: Columbia University Press, 1963.

————, *The Courage to Be,* New Haven: Yale University Press, paperback, 1952.

————, *Dynamics of Faith,* New York: Harper and Brothers, paperback, 1958 (first published 1957).

————, *The Eternal Now,* New York: Charles Scribner's Sons, 1963.

————, *The Future of Religions,* Jerald C. Brauer (ed.), New York: Harper and Row, 1966.

————, *Gesammelte Werke,* Renate Albrecht (ed.), Stuttgart: Evangelisches Verlagswerk.

Band I, 1959	Band VI, 1963
Band II, 1962	Band VII, 1962
Band III, 1965	(Several volumes remain to be
Band IV, 1961	published.)
Band V, 1964	

————, *The Interpretation of History,* New York: Charles Scribner's Sons, 1936.

————, *Love, Power, and Justice,* New York: Oxford University Press, paperback, 1960 (first published 1954).

————, *Morality and Beyond,* New York: Harper and Row, 1963.

————, *The New Being,* New York: Charles Scribner's Sons, paperback, 1963 (first published 1955).

————, *The Protestant Era,* Chicago: University of Chicago Press, abridged edition, paperback, 1957 (unabridged edition first published 1948).

————, *Die religionsgeschichtliche Konstruktion in Schellings positiver Philosophie, ihre Voraussetzungen und Prinzipien,* Breslau: H. Fleischmann, 1910.

————, *The Religious Situation,* New York: Meridian Books, paperback, 1956 (originally published in Berlin, 1926 as *Die Religiöse Lage der Gegenwart;* first translated in 1932).

————, *The Shaking of the Foundations,* New York: Charles Scribner's Sons, paperback, 1962 (first published 1948).

————, *Systematic Theology,* Chicago: University of Chicago Press.
Vol. I, 1951
Vol. II, 1957
Vol. III, 1963

————, *Theology of Culture,* New York: Oxford University Press, 1959.   .

———, *Ultimate Concern: Tillich in Dialogue*, D. Mackenzie Brown (ed.), New York: Harper and Row, 1965.

ARTICLES AND ESSAYS BY PAUL TILLICH

Tillich, Paul, "An Afterword: Appreciation and Reply," in *Paul Tillich in Catholic Thought*, Thomas A. O'Meara and Celestin D. Weisser (eds.), Dubuque, Iowa: Priory Press, 1964, 301–11.

———, "Art and Ultimate Reality," *Cross Currents*, X, 1960, 1–14.

———, *Der Begriff des Übernatürlichen, sein dialektischer Charakter und das Prinzip der Identität, dargestellt an der Supernaturalistischen Theologie vor Schleiermacher* (Habilitationsschrift, Universität Halle-Wittenberg), Part One, Königsberg-Neumark: H. Madrasch, 1915. Part Two never published.

———, "Denker der Zeit: Der Religionsphilosoph Rudolf Otto," *Vossische Zeitung* (Berlin), No. 308, July 2, 1925.

———, "Existentialist Aspects of Modern Art," in *Christianity and the Existentialists*, Carl Michalson (ed.), New York: Charles Scribner's Sons, 1956, 128–147.

———, "God as Reality and Symbol," *Essays and Studies* (Tokyo Women's Christian College), XI, March, 1961, 101–109.

———, "Jewish Influences on Contemporary Christian Theology," *Cross Currents*, II, No. 3, 1952, 35–42.

———, "Die Kategorie des 'Heiligen' bei Rudolf Otto," *Theologische Blätter* (Leipzig), II, January, 1923, 11–12.

———, "The Kingdom of God and History," in *The Kingdom of God and History*, Vol. III of the Church, Community, and State Series, London: George Allen and Unwin, 1938, 103–42.

———, "Kirche und Kultur," *Sammlung gemeinverständlicher Vorträge und Schriften aus dem Gebiet der Theologie und Religionsgeschichte*, No. 111, Tübingen: J.C.B. Mohr, 1924. Translated as "Church and Culture" in *The Interpretation of History*, 219–241.

———, "Logos und Mythos der Technik," *Logos* (Tübingen), XVI, November, 1927, 356–65.

———, "*Pacem in Terris*," *Criterion* (University of Chicago), IV, No. 2, 1965, 15–18.

———, "The Problem of Theological Method," *Journal of Religion*,

XXVII, No. 1, January, 1947, 16–26. Reprinted in Will Herberg (ed.), *Four Existentialist Theologians,* 238–55.

————, "Rechtfertigung und Zweifel," *Vorträge der theologischen Konferenz zu Giessen,* N. 39, Giessen: Alfred Töpelmann, 1924.

————, "A Reinterpretation of the Doctrine of the Incarnation," *Church Quarterly Review,* CXLVII, January, 1949, 133–48.

————, "Rejoinder," *The Journal of Religion,* XLVI, January, 1966, No. 1, Part II, 184–96.

————, "Relation of Metaphysics and Theology," *The Review of Metaphysics,* X, September, 1956, 57–63.

————, "Reply" in Gustave Weigel, S.J., "The Theological Significance of Paul Tillich," *Gregorianum,* XXXVII, No. 1, 1956, 34–54. "Reply" is pp. 53–54. Whole article reprinted in O'Meara and Weisser, *Paul Tillich in Catholic Thought,* 3–24.

————, "The Right to Hope," *Neue Zeitschrift für systematische Theologie und Religionsphilosophie* (Berlin), VII, No. 3, 1965, 371–77.

————, "Theology and Architecture," *Architectural Forum,* CIII, December, 1955, 131–36.

————, "Theonomie," *Die Religion in Geschichte und Gegenwart,* second edition, Hermann Gunkel and Leopold Zscharnack (eds.), V, Tübingen: J.C.B. Mohr, 1931, 1128–29.

————, "Über die Idee einer Theologie der Kultur," *Philosophische Vorträge der Kant-Gesellschaft,* N. 24, Berlin: Reuther und Reichard, 1919, 28–52.

————, "What Is Wrong With the 'Dialectic' Theology?" *The Journal of Religion,* XV, April, 1935, 127–45.

BOOKS ON TILLICH

Hamilton, Kenneth, *The System and the Gospel,* New York: Macmillan, 1963.

Hennig, Karl (ed.), *Der Spannungsbogen: Festgabe für Paul Tillich,* Stuttgart: Evangelisches Verlagswerk, 1961.

Kegley, Charles W., and Bretall, Robert W. (eds.), *The Theology of Paul Tillich,* New York: Macmillan, paperback, 1961 (first published 1952).

Killen, R. Allan, *The Ontological Theology of Paul Tillich,* Kampen, Netherlands: J. H. Kok, 1956.

McKelway, Alexander, *The Systematic Theology of Paul Tillich*, Richmond, Va.: John Knox Press, 1964.

O'Meara, Thomas A., O.P., and Weisser, Celestin D., O.P. (eds.), *Paul Tillich in Catholic Thought*, Dubuque, Iowa: Priory Press, 1964.

Rhein, Christoph, *Paul Tillich: Philosoph und Theologe*, Stuttgart: Evangelisches Verlagswerk, 1957.

Tavard, George H., *Paul Tillich and the Christian Message*, New York: Charles Scribner's Sons, 1962.

Thomas, J. Heywood, *Paul Tillich: An Appraisal*, Philadelphia: Westminster Press, 1963.

ARTICLES AND DISSERTATIONS ON TILLICH

Adams, James Luther, *Paul Tillich's Philosophy of Culture, Science and Religion*, New York: Harper and Row, 1965.

Barth, Karl, "Introductory Report," *The Systematic Theology of Paul Tillich*, Richmond, Va.: John Knox Press, 1964.

Barthel, Pierre, *Interprétation du Langage Mythique et Théologie Biblique*, Leiden: E. J. Brill, 1963. Chapter III is: "L'interprétation *ontologique* du mythe par la théologie de la corrélation de Paul Tillich," pp. 152–98.

Bennett, John C., "A Protestant View of Authority in the Church," *Theology Digest*, XI, No. 4, 1963, 209–19.

Brauer, Jerald C., "Preface," *The Journal of Religion*, XLVI, January, 1966, No. 1, Part II, 89–91.

Clarke, Bowman L., "God and the Symbolic in Tillich," *Anglican Theological Review*, XLIII, July, 1961, 302–11.

Dowey, Jr., Edward A., "Tillich, Barth, and the Criteria of Theology," *Theology Today*, XV, April, 1958, 43–58.

Dulles, Avery R., S.J., "Paul Tillich and the Bible," *Theological Studies*, XVII, 1956, 345–67. Reprinted in O'Meara and Weisser (eds.), *Paul Tillich in Catholic Thought*, 109–32.

Ford, Lewis Stanley, *The Ontological Foundation of Paul Tillich's Theory of the Religious Symbol*, Yale University: dissertation, New Haven, 1962.

———, "The Three Strands of Tillich's Theory of Religious Symbols," *The Journal of Religion*, XLVI, January, 1966, No. 1, Part II, 104–30.

316 *Bibliography*

Foster, Kenelm, O.P., "Paul Tillich and St. Thomas," *Blackfriars*, XLI, 1960, 306–13. Reprinted in O'Meara and Weisser (eds.), *Paul Tillich in Catholic Thought*, 97–105.

Fox, Marvin, "Tillich's Ontology and God," *Anglican Theological Review*, XLIII, July, 1961, 260–67.

Gabus, Jean-Paul, "La théologie systématique de P. Tillich," *Revue d'Histoire et de Philosophie Religieuses*, XXXV, 1955, 454–77.

Hammond, Guy B., "Tillich on the Personal God," *The Journal of Religion*, XLIV, October, 1964, 289–93.

Hartshorne, Charles, "Tillich and the Other Great Tradition," *Anglican Theological Review*, XLIII, July, 1961, 245–59.

Hendry, George S., "Review of Tillich's *Systematic Theology*, Vol. II," *Theology Today*, XV, April, 1958, 78–83.

Herberg, Will (ed.), *Four Existentialist Theologians*, A Reader from the Works of Jacques Maritain, Nicolas Berdyaev, Martin Buber, and Paul Tillich, New York: Doubleday, paperback ed., 1958.

Herrigel, Hermann, "Die philosophische Theologie Tillichs," *Die Sammlung* (Göttingen), XIII, May, 1958, 234–41.

Homans, Peter, "Transference and Transcendence: Freud and Tillich on the Nature of Personal Relatedness," *The Journal of Religion*, XLVI, January, 1966, No. 1, Part II, 148–64.

Hopper, David H., "Towards Understanding the Thought of Paul Tillich," *The Princeton Seminary Bulletin*, LV, April, 1962, 36–43.

Johnson, Robert Clyde, "A Theologian of Synthesis," *Theology Today*, XV, April, 1958, 36–42.

Johnson, William Hallock, "Tillich's Science of Being," *The Princeton Seminary Bulletin*, LVI, October, 1962, 52–62.

Kaufman, Gordon D., "Can a Man Serve Two Masters?" *Theology Today*, XV, April, 1958, 59–77.

Kucheman, Clark A., "Professor Tillich: Justice and the Economic Order," *The Journal of Religion*, XLVI, January, 1966, No. 1, Part II, 165–83.

Kuhlmann, Gerhardt, *Brunstäd und Tillich: zum Problem einer Theonomie der Kultur*, Tübingen: J.C.B. Mohr, 1928.

Leibrecht, Walter (ed.), *Religion and Culture: Essays in Honor of Paul Tillich*, New York: Harper and Brothers, 1959.

McLean George F., O.M.I., *Man's Knowledge of God According to Paul Tillich*, dissertation abstract: The Catholic University of America, Washington, D.C., 1958.

———, "Paul Tillich's Existential Philosophy of Protestantism," *The Thomist*, XXVIII, 1964, 1–50. Reprinted in O'Meara and Weisser (eds.), *Paul Tillich in Catholic Thought*, 42–84.

———, "Symbol and Analogy: Tillich and Thomas," *Revue de l'Université de Ottawa*, XXVIII, 1958, 193–233. Reprinted in O'Meara and Weisser (eds.), *Paul Tillich in Catholic Thought*, 145–83.

Marlé, René, S.J., "Paul Tillich," *Cahiers Universitaires Catholiques* (Paris), Dec., 1965–Jan., 1966, 136–37.

Niebuhr, Reinhold, "The Contribution of Paul Tillich," *Religion in Life*, VI, 1937, 574–81.

O'Connor, Edward, "Paul Tillich: An Impression," *Thought*, XXX, 1955–56, 507–24. Reprinted in O'Meara and Weisser (eds.), *Paul Tillich in Catholic Thought*, 25–41.

O'Hanlon, Daniel J., S.J., *The Influence of Schelling on the Thought of Paul Tillich*, Gregorian University: dissertation, Rome, 1957.

O'Meara, Thomas A., O.P., "Paul Tillich and Ecumenism," *Reality* (Dubuque, Iowa), X, 1962, 151–80. Reprinted in O'Meara and Weisser (eds.), *Paul Tillich in Catholic Thought*, 273–99.

Peters, Eugene H., "Tillich's Doctrine of Essence, Existence, and the Christ," *The Journal of Religion*, XLIII, October, 1963, 295–302.

Pittenger, W. Norman, "Paul Tillich as a Theologian: An Appreciation," *Anglican Theological Review*, XLIII, July, 1961, 268–86.

Przywara, Erich, S.J., "Christian Root-Terms: Kerygma, Mysterium, Kairos, Oikonomia," *Religion and Culture: Essays in Honor of Paul Tillich*, Walter Leibrecht (ed.), 113–19. Reprinted in O'Meara and Weisser (eds.), *Paul Tillich in Catholic Thought*, 197–204.

Reardon, Bernard M.G., "Tillich and Anglicanism," *Anglican Theological Review*, XLIII, July, 1961, 287–302.

Robinson, John A.T., *Honest to God*, Philadelphia: Westminster Press, paperback, 1963.

Rowe, William L., *An Examination of the Philosophical Theology of Paul Tillich*, University of Michigan: dissertation, Ann Arbor, 1961.

———, "The Meaning of 'God' in Tillich's Theology," *The Journal of Religion*, XLII, 1962, 274–86.

Scharlemann, Robert P., "Tillich's Method of Correlation: Two Proposed Revisions," *The Journal of Religion*, XLVI, January, 1966, No. 1, Part II, 92–103.

Siegwalt, Gérard, "La théologie systématique de P. Tillich," *Revue d'Histoire et de Philosophie Religieuses*, XLI, 1961, 173–92.

Smith, D. Moody, "The Historical Jesus in Paul Tillich's Christology," *The Journal of Religion*, XLVI, January, 1966, No. 1, Part II, 131–47.

Sommer, Günter Friedrich, *The Significance of the Late Philosophy of Schelling for the Formation and Interpretation of the Thought of Paul Tillich*, Duke University: dissertation, Durham, North Carolina, 1960.

Tamaru, Noriyoski, "Motiv und Struktur der Theologie Paul Tillichs," *Neue Zeitschrift für systematische Theologie*, III, 1961, 1–38.

Tavard, George H., "Christ as the Answer to Existential Anguish," *Continuum* (Chicago), IV, Spring, 1966, 3–12. Reprinted in O'Meara and Weisser (eds.), *Paul Tillich in Catholic Thought*, 224–36.

——, "Le principe protestant et le système théologique de Paul Tillich," *Revue des Sciences Philosophiques et Théologiques*, XLVI, 1962, 242–53. English translation in O'Meara and Weisser (eds.), *Paul Tillich in Catholic Thought*, 85–96.

Time, "The Requirements of Peace," February 26, 1965, 32–34.

——, "To Be or Not to Be," March 16, 1959, 46–52.

Weigel, Gustave, S.J., "Contemporaneous Protestantism and Paul Tillich," *Theological Studies*, XI, 1950, 177–202.

——, "Myth, Symbol, and Analogy," *Religion and Culture: Essays in Honor of Paul Tillich*, Walter Leibrecht (ed.), 120–30. Reprinted in O'Meara and Weisser (eds.), *Paul Tillich in Catholic Thought*, 184–96.

——, "The Theological Significance of Paul Tillich," *Gregorianum*, XXXVII, 1956, 34–54. Reprinted in O'Meara and Weisser (eds.), *Paul Tillich in Catholic Thought*, 3–24.

Williams, Daniel D., "Tillich's Doctrine of God," *The Philosophical Forum* (Boston University), XVIII, 1960–61, 40–50.

Wisse, Stephan, *Das Religiöse Symbol*, Essen: Ludgerus-Verlag, 1963.

Wolff, Otto, "Paul Tillichs Christologie des 'Neuen Seins,'" *Neue Zeitschrift für systematische Theologie*, III, 1961, 129–140.

Zabala, Albert J., S.J., *Myth and Symbol: An Analysis of Myth and Symbol in Paul Tillich*, dissertation: Institut Catholique de Paris, 1959.

INDEX

(For general classifications see also the table of contents)

Abelard, 285
Absolute, the. *See* Unconditioned
Abyss, 17, 52, 62-64, 125, 138.
  See also Ground and abyss
Acceptance, 192-193. *See also*
  Grace
Actualization: in the historical
  dimension, 244-246; of essential
  manhood, 196, 237; of potentialities, 7, 69-71, 83, 147, 170-173, 200-201; of the spiritual
  community, 218; process of,
  209-211
Adam, 171-172, 174, 177
Ambiguity(ties), 25-26, 80 *n. 82*,
  84, 95, 99-101, 133, 250-251,
  263-264; and fragment, 213-214; nature of, 65; of the
  churches, 218-219, 230-231,
  235-236, 260-261; of the holy,
  65-66; of life, 7, 210-211; of
  religion, 71, 89
Analogia imaginis, 183
Analogy, 141-142, 183. *See also*
  Symbols (Symbolism)

Anselm, 135
Anxiety, 49, 56-57, 132, 134, 172-173
Architecture, 86
Art, 85-86, 92
Athanasius, 98
Atheism, 53-55, 63, 78-79 *n. 28,*
  115
Atonement, 192
Aubert, Roger, 74-75
Augustine, 98, 135, 254, 269, 288
Authority, 8, 94-97, 118 *n. 63,*
  231
Autonomy, 54, 87-89, 91, 98-99,
  167, 221

Barth, Karl, 8, 17, 22, 106-112,
  114, 120 *n. 133,* 185, 292-294
Barthel, Pierre, 295
Being, 26, 34-35, 59, 125, 127,
  131-132, 141, 177 *n. 75. See
  also* Abyss, Ground and abyss,
  Essential being
Being and nonbeing, 134, 145,
  294-295

Being-Itself, 28, 32-33, 63-64, 132, 152-153
Benedict, St., 284
Bergson, Henri, 130
Bible, 27, 29-30, 38-39, 45-46, *n. 106*, 60, 164 *n. 123*, 182
Böhme, Jacob, 19
Bonhoeffer, Dietrich, 155, 305
Boundary, xvii, 5-6, 19, 36
Brightman, Edgar, 23
Buber, Martin, 19
Bultmann, Rudolf, 16, 181, 305

Calvin, John, 19, 29
Calvinism, 64, 174
Catholic, Catholicism. *See* Roman Catholic (Catholicism)
Cause, 134, 137-138
Chalcedon, Council of, 186, 198
Christianity, 12, 53, 120-121 *n. 138*, 179-180, 194-195, 238-239, 282-283, 289, 297-299, 306-307
Christology, 18, 188, 195-199, 237, 256-257, 271-272, 295
Chronos, 257-258
Church(es), 18, 208, 231, 299; ambiguities of, 260-261; and theonomy, 115, 233; essence of, 218; functions of, 220-222; manifest and latent, 215-217, 219-220, 234-236, 238, 257, 260-261; mystery of, 237-238; paradox of, 218-219; related to society, 220-223. *See also* New being, Protestantism, Roman Catholic (Catholicism), Spiritual community
Church history, 27, 76
Civilization, 83, 282-283, 289
Clement of Alexandria, 98, 287
Communism, 10, 217, 224

Content, religious, 20. *See also* Substance, religious
Conversion, 219-220
Courage, 57-58, 134, 237
Creation, 133, 144-147, 269; and the fall, 146, 173-174, 200; and time, 249, 273
Cross, 18, 33, 59, 97, 167, 188, 190-191, 198, 215-217, 235, 259, 284-285, 300
Cult, 71, 216
Culture, 101-102, 108, 116 *n. 7*, 208, 233, 264, 282-283, 302-303; concept of, xviii, 69, 82-85; theology of, 84-86; types of, 86-87, 98-99. *See also* Civilization, Religion and culture

Death, 132, 273-275
De Lubac, Henri, 154
Demonic, the, 10-11, 16, 25, 64-66, 88-89, 93-97, 143, 156, 251
Demonization, 32, 53, 59-60, 215, 217, 228-229, 235-236, 254, 259, 261, 289
Depth, 7, 57, 72, 87, 102-104, 170, 188
Destiny. *See* Freedom, and destiny
Dilthey, Wilhelm, 19
Dimension(s), 6, 32, 69-70, 210-211, 244-245, 248, 250-251
Divine, the, 64, 89
Dogma, 39, 71, 186
Dostoievsky, F. M., 93
Doubt, 8, 18, 23, 49, 56-57, 75, 81 *n. 114*
Dreaming Innocence, 171
Dynamics, and form, 84, 129-130, 132. *See also* Form, Polarity (ties)

Ecclesiology, 233-234, 237-238

Ecstasy, 46, 49, 73-74, 212. *See also* Faith, Ultimate concern

Ecumenism, 232, 307-308

Education, 86

Einstein, Albert, 55

Eliade, Mircea, 307

Eschatology, 36, 115, 145, 214, 262, 269, 271-272, 276, 288, 295

Essence, 15, 133, 145-146, 218; and existence, 10, 71, 168-173, 209-210, 262, 265

Essential being, 132, 183-184

Essential God-Manhood, 179, 185, 197-198

Essential Manhood, 179, 185, 196-197, 237-238, 294-295

Essentialization, 265-276, 294-295

Estrangement, 16, 30, 40, 72, 169-170, 175-177, 200-201, 210. *See also* Existence, Sin

Eternal, the, 91, 262-263

Eternal life, 262-269

Eternity, 274-275

Exegesis, 38-39

Existence, 15, 30, 54, 133, 145-146, 168-169, 183-185. *See also* Essence, and existence, Estrangement, Sin

Existential, defined, 202 *n. 6*

Existential questions, 30-31, 37-38, 40

Existentialism, 12, 15-16, 169-170

Existentialist, defined, 202 *n. 6*

Experience, structure of, 127

Faith, 33, 49, 57-58, 76, 180, 227, 238; and doubt, 75, 81 *n. 114;* and the historical Jesus, 181-183, 204 *n. 78;* and love, 212-213; and the resurrection, 190, 199-200; and the spiritual community, 215, 219-220; as ultimate concern, 46; content of, 58, 77, 159, 290, 298-299; experience of, 61-62, 66, 296; formal and material, 52-53, 297-298; related to religion and revelation, 73-74; truth of, 59-60; universality of, 77, 297. *See also* Ecstasy, Revelation, Religion, Ultimate concern

Fall, 16, 146, 170-174, 200, 262

Ferré, Nels, 234

Fichte, Johann G., 15

Finite, the. *See* Infinite, the, and the finite

Finitude, 88, 131-132, 134, 150, 200

Form, 31, 52, 89, 93, 101-102, 132; and dynamics, 84, 129-130; cultural, xvii, 20, 82, 84-86, 98, 221-222

Fragmentary, 105, 177-178, 184, 192, 213-215, 217, 237, 269, 276

Freedom, 133, 146, 150, 247-249; and destiny, 130-132, 171-174, 177

Freud, Sigmund, 15-16, 42 *n. 36,* 130

Fulfilment, 52, 68, 133, 147, 184, 211, 217, 244-250, 255, 263-269, 274, 287

Geist, xviii, 68-69, 82, 86

Gestalt of Grace, 111, 225-227

God, 17, 59, 63-64, 70, 97, 103, 137-138, 144-147, 155, 228, 300; as personal, 139-140, 152-153; existence of, 31, 55, 109, 134-135; experience of, 61-62, 135-136; union with, 272, 295. *See also* Being, Being-Itself,

Ground and abyss; Infinite, the, and the finite; Power
Grace, 60, 107, 241 *n. 81*, 285-289, 295; as acceptance, 16, 225-228
Ground and abyss, 19, 55, 68, 73, 93, 140, 147; of being, 17, 52, 62-64, 67, 70, 92, 103-104, 136-137, 141, 150, 155, 161 *n. 75*
Guilt, 14, 18, 175, 203 *n. 52*
Guardini, Romano, 81 *n. 114*
Gunkel, Hermann, 16

Hamilton, Kenneth, 195
Hammond, Guy, 152
Harnack, Adolf von, 111
Hartshorne, Charles, 161 *n. 72*, 164 *n. 126*
Heaven, 266
Hegel, G. W. F., 19, 23, 68, 169
Heidegger, Martin, 16
Hell, 266
Heresy, 43 *n. 68*
Hermeneutics, 5, 39
Heteronomy, 87, 91-99, 118-119 *n. 55*, 167, 230
Historical Jesus, 17-18, 181-183, 204 *n. 76, n. 78*, 295-296
History, 14, 27, 55, 245-247, 250, 256-257, 260, 267-268; and theonomy, 115, 243-244, 269-270; end of, 184, 248-249, 251, 262-263; interpretation of, 10, 86, 92, 251-254, 269; of salvation, 229, 255, 261
Hitler, Adolf, 11, 13, 230
Holiness, 25-26, 61-64, 231, 234
Holy, The, 25-26, 32, 117 *n. 26*, 143, 229; and the secular, 60, 88, 104-106, 114-115; experience of, 17, 46, 61-67, 73, 98, 228, 231, 276

Homoousion, 186
Honest-to-God Debate, 304-306
Hope, 115, 276
Humanism, 91, 216
Hume, David, 267

Idealism, German, 15
Identity, principle of, 14
Immanence, divine, 146-147, 166 *n. 139. See also* Pantheism
Immortality, 267, 275
Incarnation, 33, 145, 179-180, 185, 237-238
Individualization, 129, 132
Infinite, the, and the finite, 12, 14, 19, 25, 63, 94, 105, 132-134, 141, 185, 300
Inspiration, 27

Jesus the Christ, 29, 40, 52-53, 96-97, 108, 178-180, 183, 186-187, 196-198, 203 *n. 66*, 205 *n. 102*, 215-216, 229, 238-239, 240 *n. 67*, 256-258, 267, 290, 295-296. *See also* Cross, Historical Jesus, New Being, Resurrection
John the Baptist, 96
Judgment, 107, 249, 264
Justification, 18, 56-57, 60, 192-193

Kähler, Martin, 18, 204 *n. 76*
Kairos, 10, 257-259, 270-271, 289
Kant, Immanuel, 19, 68, 112, 135, 174, 267
Kierkegaard, Søren, 19, 48, 78 *n. 4*, 169
Killen, R. Allan, 195, 270
Kingdom of God, 31, 247, 251-252, 254-257, 260, 262, 264, 276

Language, 84, 100-101
Law, 87, 91-92, 95, 97, 101, 117
  n. 54-55, 176
Leibrecht, Walter, 113
Levels, 6-7, 128, 210
Liberalism, Nineteenth-Century,
  9, 18, 29, 109-110, 113, 119
  n. 120, 285-286
Life, 7, 65, 69, 71, 209-214, 237,
  268-269; divine, 139, 272
Liturgy, 27
Locke, John, 267
Logos, 35, 108, 128, 179-180
Love, 194, 212-213, 215
Luther, Martin, 18, 29, 43 *n. 68*,
  49, 287
Lutheranism, 10, 12, 18-19, 254

Macrocosm, 83, 196
Man, 30, 48-49, 52, 68, 128, 247-
  248, 295, 303. *See also* Essen-
  tial Manhood, Spirit, human
Manichaeism, 66, 156
Marcion, 287
Marx, Karl, 15, 54, 169
Marxism, 86
Mary, Virgin, 33
Maurice, F. D., 288
Me on, 130-131, 145
Meaning, 15, 56, 58, 68, 82-83,
  211; meaning and history, 245-
  246, 251-252, 256-257; ulti-
  mate, 11, 54, 263; uncondi-
  tioned, 51-52, 63-64, 69, 86
Mediator, 179
Medicus, F., 15
Mennonites, 284
Metaphysics. *See* Ontology
Messiah. *See* Jesus the Christ
Method of Correlation, 30-31, 37-
  40, 124, 150, 162 *n. 90*, 200,
  270, 276, 286, 288, 290-292

Microcosm, 83, 129, 141-142,
  196, 302-303
Miracle, 72
Morality, 17, 62, 64, 69, 101-
  102, 264
*Mysterium tremendum et fasci-
  nosum*, 17, 62-64, 66, 73, 137-
  138, 300
Mystical Body, 237-238
Mysticism, 14, 231
Myth, 32, 44 *n. 79*

Nature, 14, 148-149, 163 *n. 189*,
  172-173, 229, 284-287
Nazism, 9-11, 112, 120 *n. 132*,
  259
New being, 29, 40, 52-54, 167-
  168, 177-179, 182-185, 192-
  196, 208-209, 214, 220, 227,
  234-237, 261, 265, 271, 294-
  296. *See also* Jesus the Christ
Nicholas of Cusa, 19
Nicaea, Council of, 186
Niebuhr, H. Richard, 83, 283-290
Niebuhr, Reinhold, 173-174
Nietzsche, Friedrich, 19, 130
Nonbeing, 56, 59, 73, 125, 131-
  132, 135, 156, 168-169. *See
  also* Being and nonbeing, *me
  on, ouk on*

Object. *See* Subject-object
Ontology, 33-34, 37, 45 *n. 101*,
  56, 93-94, 127-128, 174, 243,
  290-292, 303
Origen, 98, 114
Original sin, 177. *See also* Fall
Otto, Rudolf, 17-18, 62, 68, 111
Ouk on, 131, 145, 169

Pantheism, 150-151
Paradox, 107-108, 196-197, 288
Participation, 129, 132, 140, 237

Pascal, Blaise, 164 *n. 123*
Peace, 276
Pentecost, 214
Personalism, 33, 228
Philosophy, German, 9-10, 12-13, 34-38, 44 *n. 85, n. 104*, 49, 298-299. *See also* Theology, and philosophy
Pittenger, W. Norman, 158
Plato, 169-170, 174, 265
Polarity (ties), 52, 84, 87, 111, 128-133, 138, 210, 264, 303
Potential (ities), 6-7, 53, 71, 83, 130, 133, 169-173, 200-201, 209-210, 265-266
Power, 95; of being, 58, 63-64, 67, 97, 136, 155, 160 *n. 22*, 201, 211
Prayer, 152
Praxis, 85, 99, 221-222
Predestination, 266
Priesthood, 220
Profane, 87-88, 117 *n. 26. See also* Secular
Profanization, 65, 71, 89-90, 215, 261. *See also* Secularism, Secularization
Progress, 249-250, 253, 256, 289
Prophetic criticism, 231, 258, 300-301. *See also* Cross, Protestant principle, Protestantism
Protestant principle, 18-19, 59-60, 97, 108, 190-191, 219, 223-225, 230-232, 236, 259, 284-285, 289, 299-301. *See also* Cross
Protestantism, 90, 111, 119 *n. 120*, 120 *n. 132*, 182, 223-226, 228-229, 285-286; and Catholicism, 62, 231-232, 241 *n. 98*; and secularism, 105-106, 114, 226-227
Providence, 147

Przywara, Erich, 270-271
Psychology, 15-16, 86, 291
Psychotherapy, 227

Rahner, Karl, 154
Reason, 87, 97
Reformation, 6, 29, 98, 226
Regeneration, 192-193
Religion, xxi-xxii *n. 3*, 7, 17, 33, 42, 68-70, 73-74, 81 *n. 111*, 89-90, 97, 178, 231, 264; ambiguities of, 65, 218-219; and culture, xvii-xix, 27, 40, 54-55, 75-76, 82, 101-102, 105, 113, 156, 217; description of, xviii, 67, 71-72; philosophy of, 12-13, 160-161 *n. 45*, 298; two senses of, xviii, 18, 70-71, 76, 81 *n. 103, n. 111. See also* Depth, Faith, Self-transcendence, Ultimate Concern
Religions, non-Christian, 178, 216, 232, 297-299, 308
Religious Socialism, 10-11, 254, 271
Religious Socialists, 257, 259
Renaissance, 6, 98, 253
Resurrection, 188-190, 195, 198-200, 267-269, 272, 275
Revelation, 27, 30-31, 37-38, 45 *n. 104*, 46, 72-74, 81 *n. 111*, 158-159, 165, 192, 214, 255-258, 260, 292-293, 308
Rhein, Christoph, 156
Risk, 56
Ritschl, Albrecht, 285
Robinson, John A. T., 304-306
Roman Catholic (Catholicism), 29, 90, 177, 224, 228, 230-231, 251; and Protestantism, 62, 231-232, 241 *n. 98*; theology, 149, 153-154, 225-226, 237

Rondet, Henri, 154

Sacralization, 114
Sacraments, 27, 33, 64, 228-230,
    234-235, 260, 301
Sacramental element, 228, 234
Sacred, 117 *n. 26. See also* Holy,
    The
Sacrifice, 198-199
Salvation, 16, 57, 178, 191-194,
    262
Salvation-History. *See* History of
    Salvation
Sanctification, 192-193
Sartre, Jean-Paul, 54
Satan, 117 *n. 49*
Scepticism, 56-57
Schelling, F. W. J. von, xxii *n. 9*,
    12-14, 68, 148, 164 *n. 117*,
    169, 173-174, 202 *n. 6*, 265
Schleiermacher, F. E. D., 19, 68,
    111
Schopenhauer, Arthur, 169
Schweitzer, Albert, 16
Science, 86, 253
Secular, the, 87-89, 104, 117 *n.
    26. See also* Profane; Holy, the
Secularism, 120-121 *n. 138*, 226-
    227, 305-307. *See also* Auton-
    omy
Secularization, 87-91, 114-115.
    See also Profanization
Self, The, 46, 49, 128, 130-131
Self-creativity, 210-211, 250. *See
    also* Culture
Self-Integration, 210-211, 250.
    See also Morality
Self-Transcendence, 42 *n. 36*, 49,
    52-53, 69-70, 73, 89, 104-105,
    130, 150, 210-211, 250-251
Sin, 16, 105, 175-176, 285-288.
    See also Estrangement, Fall

Sinn, 15, 51-52, 63
Socialism, 86
Soteriology, 188, 197, 272
Soul, 267, 275
Space, 91, 134, 277 *n. 19*
Spinoza, Benedict, 19, 23
Spirit, Divine, 48-49, 97, 99, 211-
    213, 217-218, 237-239, 255.
    See also, Spiritual Presence
Spirit, human, xxi-xxii *n. 3*, 15,
    52-53, 68-69, 72, 83, 99, 212-
    213
Spirit Christology, 187-188
Spiritual Community, 214-215,
    218, 233-238. *See also* Church
    (es)
Spiritual Presence, The, 99-101,
    115, 212-213, 218-220, 229,
    234. *See also* Spirit, Divine
Style, Cultural, 84-86
Suarez, Francis, 298
Subject-object, 100-101, 127-128,
    245
Substance: category of, 134, 137-
    138; religious, xvii-xviii, 84-86,
    98
Supernatural. *See* Supranatural,
    the
Supranatural, the, 31, 73, 148-
    149, 153-154, 163 *n. 103*, 287
Supranaturalism, 108-109, 120 *n.
    132*, 147-150, 182, 263, 295
Symbol (Symbolism), 30-33, 37,
    56, 59, 71, 103-104, 141, 156-
    159, 162 *n. 90*, 182, 188, 211,
    229-230, 249; and history, 251,
    254-255, 262; and ontology,
    33-34, 142-144; and ultimate
    concern, 28, 55, 143-144; ele-
    ments of, 143-144, 162 *n. 90;*
    language of theology, 32, 44
    n. 80; of God, 139-140. *See also*
    Analogy

Tavard, George, 195, 198, 201, 284, 299

Technology, 20, 85-86, 90-91, 99, 253

Temporal, the, 91, 262-263

Tension, 7, 132-133, 136, 200

Tertullian, 284

Theism, 55, 59, 71

Theology, 12-13, 15-16, 21-34, 107, 109-112, 157, 182, 243, 305-306; and philosophy, xix, 34-36, 170-292; apologetic, 22, 31, 40, 45 *n. 104*, 232, 290-293; kerygmatic, 22, 45 *n. 104*, 293; norm of, 28-30, 40; sources of, 26-27, 29-30, 38-39; systematic, xxi-xxii, 26, 85

Theonomy, 82, 87, 100-106, 108, 111-115, 151, 159, 167-168, 191, 201, 226, 237, 258-259, 270, 276-277, 286, 289-290; and the Church, 208, 221, 233; and history, 243-244, 269-270; notion of, 97-99, 112-113, 120 *n. 135*

Theoria, 84-85, 99, 221-222

Thomas Aquinas, 154, 287, 298

Tillich, Paul: challenge of, 113-114; evolution of his thought, xix-xx, xxii *n. 9;* family life, 7-8; German university student, 8-9; in World War I, 9-10; influenced by English language, xx; interest in art, 20; love of the sea, 19; opposition to nazism, 10-11; preference for the city, 19-20; professor in Germany, 12-13; professor in U.S., 9, 13; religious unity of his life, 20-21; sympathy for Roman Catholicism, 230-231; synthetic nature of his theology, 306-308; vision of, xvii, 289-290, 303

Time, 91, 134, 248-249, 273-275

Tolstoy, Leo, 284

Tradition, 34 *n. 68*

Transcendence, Divine, 140, 146-148, 150

Thomas, J. Heywood, 195

Trinity, 272, 292

Troeltsch, Ernst, 19, 111

Ultimate concern, 8, 29, 35, 50-51, 54, 65-66, 72, 85-86, 102-104, 143-144, 170, 296-297; and faith, 46, 52-53, 73-74, 77; and God, 55, 136, 152-153, 164 *n. 125;* and history, 76, 251; and the holy, 17, 61-62; and religion, xviii, 18, 67, 70-74; and theology, 23-26, 28, 39-40; and theonomy, 106, 113; and the Spirit, 99, 115, 220; defined, 24-26

Unconditioned, the, 50-52, 63-64, 66, 69, 108, 157, 258

Utopianism, 251, 253-254

Vatican Council, Second, 237

Vocational consciousness, 246-247, 252

Weigel, Gustave, 195

Wellhausen, Julius, 16

Wolff, Otto, 294

World War I, 9-11, 20, 95, 243, 257

World War II, 11, 247